THE
CLASSIC
ASIAN
COOKBOOK

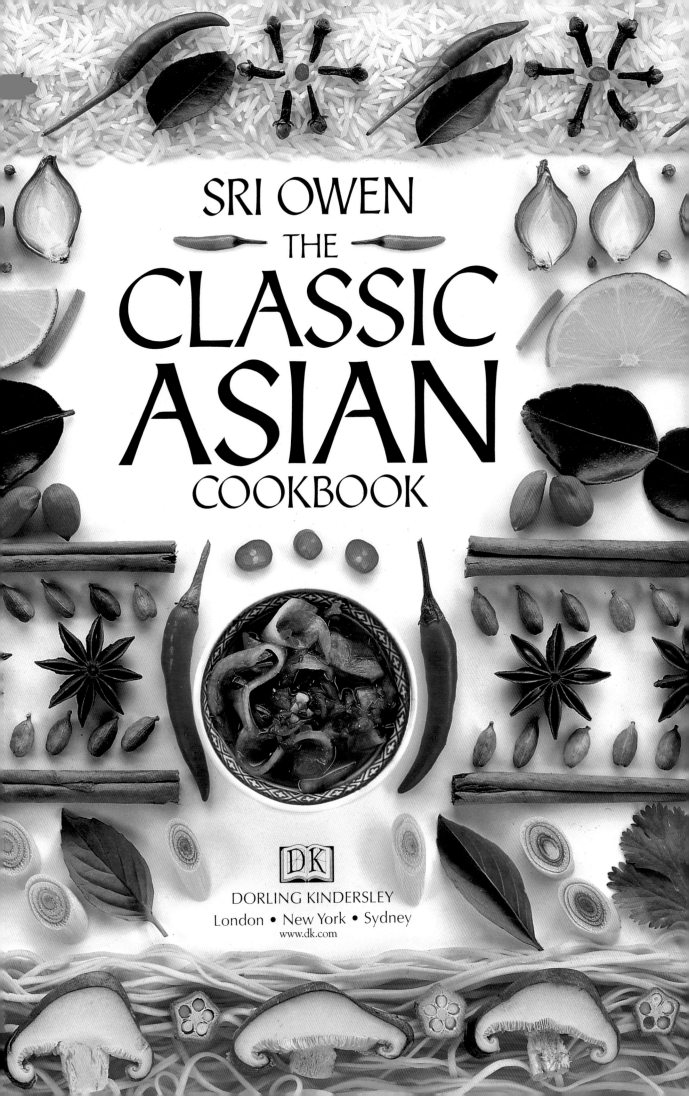

SRI OWEN
THE
CLASSIC
ASIAN
COOKBOOK

DK

DORLING KINDERSLEY

London • New York • Sydney
www.dk.com

A DORLING KINDERSLEY BOOK
www.dk.com

Project Editor
Kate Scott

Art Editor
Sue Storey
at Patrick McLeavey & Partners

Senior Editor
Nicola Graimes

Senior Art Editor
Tracey Clarke

DTP Design
Karen Ruane

Managing Editor
Susannah Marriott

Managing Art Editor
Toni Kay

Photography
Clive Streeter and Patrick McLeavey

Food Stylist
Oona van den Berg

Production Controller
Patricia Harrington

*To the memory of my mother
Dianah Poeradidjaja Djamil*

First published in Great Britain in 1998 by
Dorling Kindersley Limited,
9 Henrietta Street, London WC2E 8PS

A CIP catalogue record for this book is available
from the British Library.

ISBN 0-7513-0439-5

Reproduced by Scanner Services SRL
Printed and bound in Spain by Artes Gráficas Toledo S.A.U.
D.L. TO: 1777-1999

CONTENTS

INTRODUCTION 6
THE CUISINES OF ASIA 8

INGREDIENTS 18
*A vibrant photographic library
of essential Asian ingredients*

Vegetables **20**
Fruit, Nuts & Seeds **22**
Rice, Noodles & Wrappers **24**
Herbs & Spices **26**
The Storecupboard **28**

CLASSIC DISHES 32
*A selection of classic dishes and their
ingredients – the perfect introduction
to Asian cookery*

Snacks & Appetizers **34**

Ikan Masak Molek (Malaysia) **36**
Fish curry

Muc Don Thit (Vietnam) **38**
Stuffed squid

Oson (Korea) **40**
Steamed stuffed fish

Gaeng Keo Wan Kai (Thailand) **42**
Green curry of chicken

Satay **44**

Baak Ging Ap (China) **46**
Peking duck

Rogan Josh (India) **48**
Lamb in rich chilli sauce with yogurt

Bara-zushi (Japan) **50**
Sushi rice with julienne of omelette

Gado-gado (Indonesia) **52**
Cooked vegetable salad with peanut sauce

RECIPES 54

Over 100 inspiring recipes, including the more exotic dishes of Asia as well as familiar favourites

Soups **56**
Snacks & Appetizers **62**
Fish & Seafood **74**
Poultry **86**
Meat **98**
Vegetables & Salads **112**
Noodles & Rice **120**
Sauces & Accompaniments **128**
Desserts **136**

MENU PLANNER 142

TECHNIQUES 146

A practical guide to special equipment and preparation techniques, featuring step-by-step photography

Equipment **148**
Preparing Fish & Seafood **150**
Preparing Meat **152**
Preparing Vegetables **154**
General Techniques **156**

INDEX 157

ACKNOWLEDGMENTS 160

INTRODUCTION

I was born among the mountains of Sumatra and spent the first part of my life there. My grandmother had rice fields, a vegetable garden, a hectare or two of coffee bushes. I accompanied her on her rounds of inspection, gathered wild herbs at the edge of fields, and watched her cook. Then the whole household would eat together, sitting cross-legged on straw mats, eating with our fingers as the grown-ups exchanged the gossip of the day. It was perhaps the best possible education for a small child in the appreciation of good food and convivial good manners.

As a high-school student and undergraduate in Java, I knew every street-food vendor in town and could bargain with anyone for the freshest vegetables in the market. I took for granted my familiarity with the dishes of Central Sumatra and West and Central Java, and of West Malaysia as well. In every city there were eating houses that specialized in the food of other regions and islands, and I got to know most of them. One of my friends was a Chinese student who loved Cantonese cooking and taught me the basic techniques and recipes. As a young university lecturer I went on trips to Jakarta and was invited to some of the best Chinese restaurants in Glodok, the old commercial centre, where the food was as good as the best I have eaten since in Singapore and Hong Kong.

In 1964 I came to London, the wife of a young English teacher. Then, I broadcast topical talks for the BBC Indonesian Service, and in my spare time hunted for spices and chillies to recreate some of the flavours my cooking and my palate demanded. Shopping trips to the Netherlands kept me going in those early years, but soon all sorts of new foods were appearing in Britain. My dinner party menus became more and more adventurous, and seemed to be well received. My first book, *The Home Book of Indonesian Cookery*, was published in 1976, and I set myself to the serious enjoyment of learning and cooking everything I could, first from Indonesia, then from a widening circle of Asian countries and traditions. And not for the world would I have missed the food of Europe, the Middle East, Mexico and North America, and of course the cuisines of the countries I keep going back to, Australia and New Zealand.

With the food came the history of how ingredients and recipes have travelled the trade routes of the world. I had always known that Indonesian cooking was deeply influenced by Persian, Indian, Chinese and even Dutch cuisine, but I then found out how the classic dishes of each country can absorb all kinds of novelties and still keep their own essential character. It was a turning-point; from then on I thought of myself as a creative professional cook. For a while I ran a delicatessen in South London, cooked for Harrods, as well as for my own local customers, and gave Indonesian and Thai cookery classes and dinners. This was fun and it went

well enough, but I knew I still had to travel to many countries in Asia, and to many islands of my own country, that I had never seen. This book is one of the results of this period of travel that has taken up so much of my life and that of my husband in the past ten years.

Much as I like to write about food, frankly, I love eating and I love cooking much more; so I have only included the recipes that I have enjoyed cooking and eating several times at least during the time in which this book was researched and written. It is always hard to choose what to include, but obviously I had to strike a balance between all 14 different countries featured and the various chapter headings of the book – meat, vegetables and so on. Knowing what to leave out is even harder, but I have not selected dishes that require an unreasonably long time to prepare. With unfamiliar food we all need a little help with planning the whole meal, so I have offered four Indian menus and three menus each from China, Indonesia/Malaysia, Thailand and Japan. There are also menus suitable for entertaining, and for vegetarian meals. I hope you will enjoy all these, but do, once you are familiar with the flavours and techniques, start experimenting, especially with combinations of Eastern and Western dishes in the same meal and indeed the same course; this can be very rewarding.

Sri Owen

THE CUISINES OF ASIA

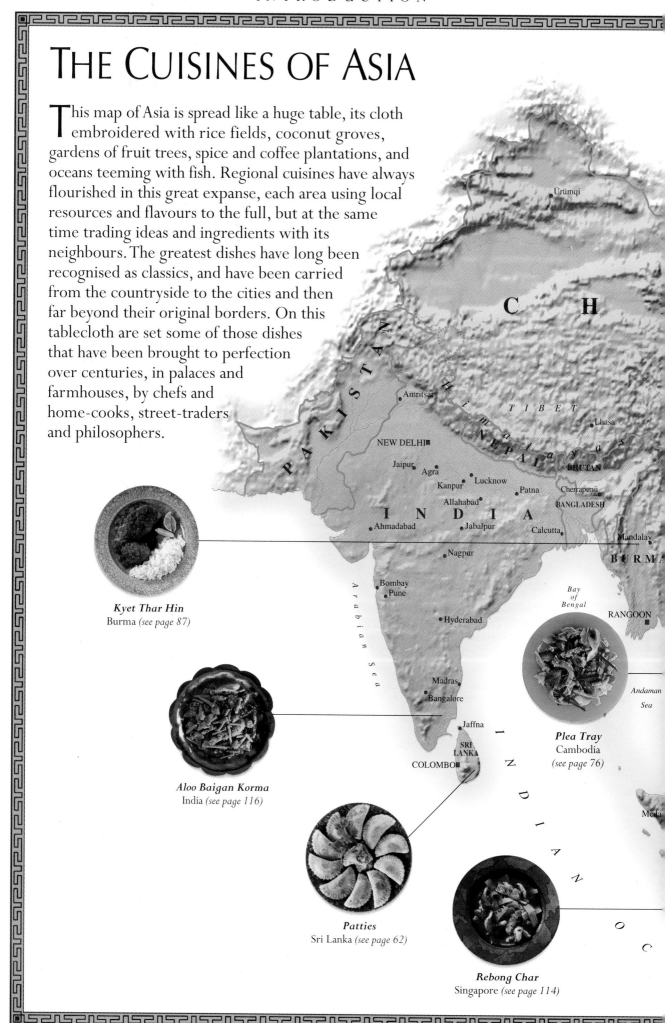

This map of Asia is spread like a huge table, its cloth
embroidered with rice fields, coconut groves,
gardens of fruit trees, spice and coffee plantations, and
oceans teeming with fish. Regional cuisines have always
flourished in this great expanse, each area using local
resources and flavours to the full, but at the same
time trading ideas and ingredients with its
neighbours. The greatest dishes have long been
recognised as classics, and have been carried
from the countryside to the cities and then
far beyond their original borders. On this
tablecloth are set some of those dishes
that have been brought to perfection
over centuries, in palaces and
farmhouses, by chefs and
home-cooks, street-traders
and philosophers.

Ürümqi

C   H

PAKISTAN

TIBET

Lhasa

Amritsar

Himalayas

NEW DELHI

NEPAL

BHUTAN

Jaipur

Agra

Lucknow

Kanpur

Patna

Cherrapunji

Allahabad

BANGLADESH

Ahmadabad

Jabalpur

Calcutta

Mandalay

I   N   D   I   A

BURMA

Nagpur

Bombay
Pune

*Bay
of
Bengal*

RANGOON

Hyderabad

Arabian Sea

Madras

Bangalore

*Andaman
Sea*

Jaffna

SRI
LANKA

COLOMBO

Indian Ocean

Mela

Kyet Thar Hin
Burma *(see page 87)*

Aloo Baigan Korma
India *(see page 116)*

Plea Tray
Cambodia
(see page 76)

Patties
Sri Lanka *(see page 62)*

Rebong Char
Singapore *(see page 114)*

Baak Ging Ap
China (see page 46)

Chapchae
Korea
(see page 122)

Sushi
Japan
(see page 71)

Pad Som Sin Moo
Laos (see page 99)

Muc Don Thit
Vietnam
(see page 38)

Gaeng Keo Wan Kai
Thailand (see page 42)

Pancit Guisado
Philippines
(see page 121)

Rempah-rempah
Malaysia
(see page 70)

Gado-gado
Indonesia (see page 52)

Sea of
Okhotsk

Hokkaido

Sapporo

Harbin

Changchun

Shenyang

NORTH
KOREA

Sea
of
Japan

Sendai

BEIJING

Tianjin

PYONGYANG

Shijiazhuang

Taiyuan

SEOUL
SOUTH
KOREA

Honshu

TOKYO

Yokohama

N   A

Lanzhou

Shandong
Peninsula

Yellow
Sea

Pusan

Kyoto

Nagoya

JAPAN

Xi'an

Zhengzhou

Nanjing

Korea Strait

Hiroshima

Kobe

Osaka

Fukuoka

Shikoku

Kyūshū

bi Desert

Chengdu

Wuhan

Shanghai

Chongqing

Nanchang

East
China
Sea

Changsha

Guiyang

Fuzhou

Kunming

TAIPEI

TAIWAN

HANOI

Hai Phong

Canton

Kowloon

Hong Kong

P A C I F I C   O C E A N

AOS

VIENTIANE

Hainan

South
China
Sea

Luzon

Dagupan

Da Nang

MANILA

LAND

GKOK

CAMBODIA

PHNOM PENH

Ho Chi
Minh City

PHILIPPINES

Iloilo

Cebu

Si
arat

Zamboanga

Mindanao

Davao

M A L A Y S I A

Kota Kinabalu

BRUNEI
BANDAR SERI BEGAWAN

Celebes
Sea

KUALA LUMPUR

Borneo

Manado

SINGAPORE

Kuching

Pontianak

I N D O N E S I A

Celebes

Moluccas

Manokwari

lembang

Jayapura

Irian Jaya

New
Guinea

JAKARTA

Java Sea

Ujung
Pandang

Banda
Sea

Semarang

Bandung

Java

Surabaya

Flores Sea

Arafura
Sea

PAPUA
NEW
GUINEA

N

INDIA

*Aloo Baigan Korma
(see page 116)*

This vast land-mass must surely be, culturally, the richest and most complex area of the world. Over the centuries every great power, friendly or not, sooner or later "discovered" India, introducing new food habits and customs and exchanging them for recipes, spices and exotic fruits. From the cook's point of view, however, India has always given more than it has received. Almost every ingredient required for an Indian meal is native to the country, and the cooking of each region has developed around its own produce. In India, Pakistan or Bangladesh, as in my own country of Indonesia, I am always aware of the differences among regional cuisines; yet these cannot hide the family likeness that all the regions share.

FAMILIAR INGREDIENTS

Many ingredients are familiar to other parts of Asia: spices, herbs and other aromatic flavours; tamarind, palm sugar or jaggery; coriander leaves and seeds; cumin, cardamom, ginger, turmeric and chilli – these, along with rice or wheaten bread and fish, are much the same as in neighbouring lands. The main difference in Indian cuisine is the use of milk and dairy products, which until recently were almost unknown in most other parts of Asia. These are made into *paneer* and other soft cheeses and ghee, or clarified butter, which is the cooking medium of the north as coconut milk is of the south. And whereas most Asians consume large amounts of fruit and vegetables, only India has a true vegetarian tradition. *Dhal,* or lentils, are a major source of protein for everyone. At a family meal, besides lentils, there are at least two vegetable dishes, and unlike a typical Thai salad, an Indian lentil or bean salad is without meat. Meat dishes, on the other hand, usually contain vegetables, and curry normally has plenty of sauce, enriched with spices and thickened with well-ground chillies and plenty of sliced onions softened in ghee or oil. In the recipes for this book I have included enough meat to satisfy Western appetites, but an Indian family might have equal satisfaction from dunking chapatis in the curry sauce, or pouring the sauce over a plateful of basmati rice.

Samosa (see page 65)

CULINARY RULES

The Indian subcontinent has nurtured two major religious faiths, Hinduism and Buddhism, and has embraced a third, Islam. Muslim food originally came from the Ottoman Empire and from Persia, and was the basis of what we now know as Moghul cooking. Hindus and Muslims observe dietary rules which prohibit the consumption of beef or pork, appoint times for feasting or fasting, and favour milk products and vegetables. There is an understanding that the soul has to be nourished as well as the body, for fasting, or abstaining from meat, feeds the spirit; milk products provide the body with the nutrients it requires. Rules bring order to the world and help us make the best use of limited resources. They do not prevent people enjoying food. Indeed, the rules have challenged Indian cooks over the centuries to greater heights of invention. It is no wonder that from these three nations – India, Pakistan and Bangladesh – have come some of the most brilliant cooks, and the most passionate foodies, that I have ever met.

SRI LANKA

Patties (see page 62)

Sri Lanka has perfect beaches, high hills in the centre, fertile plains for growing rice, and a huge variety of tropical and sub-tropical vegetables and fruit, all in an area rather smaller than Ireland. One of this island's many wonders is that the tourist business has not yet overwhelmed it. Though it has suffered political troubles in recent years, in the long term I am optimistic about the Sri Lankan people, as I am about the Balinese; their personalities and cultures are strong enough to adapt and reassert themselves. In the past, Sri Lanka, though close to southern India, has remained culturally independent, and its food reflects this. True, it bears the traces of many invaders and colonists – Tamils, Portuguese and the Dutch left their marks, and though the British left little behind in the way of cooking, their tea plantations among the hills are still productive. Cakes, sweet dishes and snacks still popular around the coastline of the Indian Ocean show Dutch and Portuguese influences. The patties on page 62, for example, are found not only here but three thousand miles away in Menado on the northern tip of Sulawesi, where they are still called by the Portuguese name, *panada*. Sri Lankan *sambol* is also very similar to the *sambal* of Malaysia and Indonesia. There is a distinctive Sri Lankan culinary style and flavour, however, which I have tried to bring out in the recipes that follow. Curries use characteristically dark-roasted spices or are coloured red with chillies. Coconut milk and ghee (clarified butter) are both used as a cooking medium. And, as in South-east Asia, a great quantity of highly flavoured, savoury, sharp-tasting, sweet or hot accompaniments allow everyone at the table to create a dish to his or her own taste.

BURMA

*Kyet Thar Hin
(see page 87)*

The recent history of Burma – or Myanmar, as its rulers now wish it to be called – has to a great extent cut it off from the outside world. Like Indonesia, Burma has never been a great place for restaurants, and the best Burmese food has always been found in family homes. Traditions of hospitality are as strong in Burma as they are anywhere else in Asia, and no guest ever goes hungry. Large families and frequent Buddhist celebrations mean big, elaborate meals, shared with the extended family and a wide circle of friends. The atmosphere of such a gathering is festive but informal, a celebration of the bounty of nature. Traditionally, the hostess and her daughters, having supervised many hours of work in the kitchen, would have their meal first before dressing in their finest clothes and coming out to greet their guests and look after them throughout the meal. The rice and curries are displayed for everyone to help themselves, flanked by what an old Burmese friend of mine used to call the "toly-molies" – sauces, relishes, pickles and chutneys, and chopped raw vegetables and herbs – for the guests to decorate and flavour their food just the way they like it. These complement fine cooking behind the scenes, where the basic flavours of Burma – onion, ginger, garlic, chilli and dried shrimp paste – are blended in curry pastes.

THAILAND

*Gaeng Keo Wan Kai
(see page 42)*

Thai food has had a big impact in the West during the last twenty years. There are several reasons for this, but the key has been Thai self-confidence and flair for opening small restaurants, where the staff are friendly and the cooking is usually good. Ingredients are flown in from Bangkok – lemongrass, kaffir limes, two sorts of basil, galangal, dried shrimps, pea aubergines, small white aubergines, green vegetables – and the dishes are cooked to more or less authentic recipes; even in the takeaways customers seem to like Thai food as it is, and there has been no compromising of flavours as there has been in too many Indian and Chinese restaurants. The basis of much Thai food is an aromatic sourness and the delicate heat of chillies, flavours that blend well with meat, vegetables and seafood. A marriage between Thai and French or other Western cooking has produced "fusion cuisine", which has passed beyond being merely trendy and is now well established – though it can only work well if the cook is equally familiar with both traditions. In Thailand itself, food commands respect and much attention, and I love to spend a morning walking through a small-town marketplace, watching street-food vendors, and then having a long lunch in an open-sided restaurant with a shady verandah. But even better is to be invited for the evening to a friend's house, especially if it is a very old friend who will first take me shopping with her and then give me the run of the kitchen as dinner is being prepared.

CAMBODIA

Plea Tray (see page 76)

Laos, Vietnam and Cambodia make up what used to be called Indo-China – a name which, for a lover of Asian food, sounds like a paradox, for you could hardly find two cultures more distinct than those of China and India. But this region has had plenty of contact with both, and still has preserved its own character. Its complex history even includes almost a century under French rule, and a few French restaurants are still in business there today, although French and local food are regarded as two quite different things. Cambodia, focused on the mouth of the Mekong River, shares in the Vietnamese "rice bowl" of the delta, with its rich soil and plentiful water for irrigation; the huge artificial lakes near the Angkor temples were probably built to control its flow. Like Laos to the north, it has (or had until recently) enough forest to provide game, particularly deer. Cambodian cooks use salty fish sauce, coconut milk, and aromatic herbs such as lemongrass and kaffir lime leaves. Chillies are added sparingly, but chilli addicts will demand raw chillies or extra-hot cooked side dishes.

LAOS

Pad Som Sin Moo
(see page 99)

I once introduced a Lao friend to the Thai chef of a famous London restaurant, and they were delighted to find that, although they were from opposite sides of the Mekong River and spoke different dialects, they could understand each other. Landlocked as it is, this country – almost as big as Vietnam but with a much smaller population – has had a stormy history that shows little sign of lapsing into calm. Its southern portion occupies the fertile valley of the Mekong, while in the north are high mountains thinly populated by a number of tribes. Its food traditions have much in common with those of its Thai and Vietnamese neighbours, but the *Montagnards,* or northern mountain-dwellers, have given it a taste for "sticky" rice (often called glutinous or sweet rice). My Lao and Thai friends found they could understand each other's cooking, too, despite differences mainly in the proportions of spices used in mixes that were otherwise basically similar. There are very few Lao cookbooks; the only one I possess is a transcript, with an English translation, of a collection of traditional recipes dictated by an old man who had been *maître chef des cuisines* in the royal palace at Luang Prabang. They were published by Alan Davidson, British Ambassador to Laos in the early 1970s. The old chef's instructions, as printed, are difficult to interpret and impossible to follow exactly, but I have tested and developed a few of them with excellent results. Naturally, there is a strong southern Chinese influence: coconut milk is often used, and many dishes are deep-fried, stir-fried or steamed.

VIETNAM

Muc Don Thit
(see page 38)

Like its neighbours, Laos and Cambodia, Vietnam uses a lot of *nuoc mam*, fish sauce, to give its food the sharp savoury tang that is one of its principal traits. The country's most popular sauce, *nuoc cham*, is based on it. There is, of course, Chinese influence, but I suspect that few Chinese would approve of the quantity of garlic that goes into an authentic Vietnamese meal, especially in the south of the country. People here are what I call "wet eaters" – many soup dishes contain enough meat, fish and vegetables to be eaten as one-dish meals, though of course with plenty of rice. They also like to cool down in hot weather with salads, and have adopted the Chinese classification of foods into *yin* and *yang*, those that cool the body and those that heat it. Vietnamese food has a special appeal to health-conscious eaters because so many dishes are cooked in water, not oil, and many vegetables are served raw or very lightly cooked. More important, however, is the balance between *yin* and *yang*, and between the different textures of the meal: wet and dry, soft and chewy, smooth and crunchy.

MALAYSIA

Rempah-rempah
(see page 70)

Malaysian food is as varied as the origins of its people, many of whose ancestors came from neighbouring countries and islands. The climate, soils and natural resources are similar to those of western Indonesia and the islands of Java and Sumatra, so it is not surprising that many favourite Malaysian dishes have an Indonesian flavour. Often, it is difficult to tell on which side of the water a recipe originated. But Malaysians also have numerous links with China, Indo-China, India and southern Thailand, and all these have contributed to the use of spices, herbs and aromatics in cooking. Pungent shrimp paste and fiery chillies are as popular here as in any part of Southeast Asia, and at the right time of year the air is full of the bewitching scent of ripe durian fruit. Over the course of two or three centuries, a great number of merchants and craftsmen left their homes in south China and settled in the towns along the Malay Peninsula and the northern coastline of Borneo. They prospered, and married local women who were thereafter addressed by the polite title of *nyonya* or *nonya*, "lady". Their cooking combined recipes and tastes from both sides of the family, so that Nonya food is now recognized and written about as a tradition in its own right, and Nonya restaurants are found not only in Malaysia and Singapore but in Europe, Australia and America.

Satay Daging
(see page 67)

SINGAPORE

Rebong Char
(see page 114)

Singapore is one of the great gastronomic centres of the world, where cooks and restaurants represent the finest cuisines from all over Asia and beyond. Food could almost be said to be modern Singapore's only link with the past, and even food has been affected by the speed of economic growth. The colourful street-food stalls that once thronged the city have long since been tidied into covered food courts. However, this has the advantage that you can eat well, at low cost, and be confident that what you are eating was prepared in hygienic conditions. In 1981 I took my two young sons to Singapore as part of their first visit to Southeast Asia. In the evenings we ate Malaysian food in the open air at Newton Circus, and hoped it would not rain, or we ate satay in a food court near the waterfront. Then we fed the younger boy at McDonald's, and the whole family ended up with ice cream at the Raffles Hotel. That, I think, is pretty typical of the Singaporean food scene today, though the city's tastes continue to develop apace in all directions. The nearest thing to a local cuisine is Nonya cooking, which has continued to develop among Singapore's predominantly Chinese community: a combination of Chinese techniques (such as stir-frying) and ingredients (soy sauce, 5-spice powder) with the tropical flavours of chilli, coconut and peanut sauce.

INDONESIA

Gado-gado (see page 52)

The classic Indonesian landscape is one of terraced ricefields mounting from the river valley to the foothills of the local volcano. Yet this is typical only of Java and Bali, parts of Sumatra and Sulawesi, and a few other islands. Millions of Indonesians depend more on sago or cassava than on rice. The real staple food of Indonesia is fish, from the sea and from lakes and rivers, as well as from the flooded rice fields. Indonesians, living among their 15,000-odd islands, have always been sailors, traders and fishermen. When fish could not be eaten fresh, they had to be dried in the sun and salted, and fish spread out to dry are still a common sight.

BALANCING TASTES

The basic diet of many Indonesians is plain boiled white rice, with fish, *lalab* (raw or plainly cooked vegetables) and a few hot chillies. Mere hotness, however, is not all that people demand of food. Most Indonesian cooking is inspired by a love of sourness delicately balanced by sweetness. The sweetness comes largely from coconut milk, often used as a cooking medium, or coconut palm sugar. Many agree that sour notes offer more subtlety and greater range, and tamarind, lemongrass, fruit and galangal are among the sources. The other contrast to sweetness, saltiness, is provided not only by salt but by fermented products, particularly soy sauce, introduced by the Chinese, and *terasi*, a pungent shrimp paste.

TYPICAL MEALS

Sate Pusut (see page 66)

The usual family meal, in a reasonably well-off household, consists of rice with one or two meat or fish dishes, vegetables, and soup to wash everything down – many people will not drink even water with a meal. Many savoury dishes are variants on a few basic ideas: there are innumerable versions of *sambal goreng*, for example, in which spices, onions, garlic, shrimp paste and chilli are fried in a little oil, then added to the main ingredient to flavour it while it cooks. There are many recipes for stuffings and marinades, and for meat or fish wrapped in leaves (usually banana leaves) or cooked in a segment of a large bamboo, or in the hard sheath of a coconut flower. These retain the juices, nutritional value and flavour. Cooking times are often very short, because much time has been spent preparing and cutting up the ingredients. Many Indonesians prefer to eat with their fingers, of the right hand only. A whole chicken may be torn in pieces and shredded by hand, but any chopping or carving must be done in the kitchen. Most dishes are boiled, steamed, fried, grilled or barbecued over charcoal. In the past, the only way to bake food was to wrap it in leaves and put it for several hours in a trench lined with hot embers. Dessert is usually fresh fruit, while sweets and cakes are eaten in the afternoon, especially when visitors call. Ninety per cent of the population is Muslim (making this the largest Islamic nation in the world), and the end of Ramadan, the fasting month, is marked by at least two days of social visiting, when junior family members (or employees) visit senior ones (or employers) to ask forgiveness for the year's trespasses, drink sweet black tea, and eat cakes of steamed glutinous rice flour and coconut.

PHILIPPINES

*Pancit Guisado
(see page 121)*

The scenery, the people, even the languages of the Philippines seem familiar to visitors who arrive from Indonesia, but culturally the nations are very different. The Filipinos were converted centuries ago to Catholicism by their Spanish overlords, whereas Indonesia is predominantly Muslim. Almost a century after the Spanish left Manila, their language, culture, and food still have great prestige. It was Spanish ships that brought new foodstuffs from Central and South America – tomatoes, potatoes, sweetcorn, and above all the ever-present chilli and its milder relatives. Some popular Spanish dishes have been adopted and have evolved over two or three hundred years into luxury feast-day dishes – for example, *paella* has become *bringhe* (cooked with coconut milk instead of olive oil) and *adobo*, originally a Spanish relish, has become a party dish of pork or chicken. Chinese influence is also strong, but Filipino food would be unimaginable without rice, fish, and the tropical fruit that grows on every patch of cultivated land.

CHINA

*Baak Ging Ap
(see page 46)*

A country as big as China, with at least a fifth of the world's people and scarcely a fifteenth of its arable land, with every climate from cool temperate to monsoon tropical, inevitably has many different regions, each with its own style of cooking. Most people outside China will be familiar with the big four, based on Beijing in the wheat-growing north, Shanghai on the coast, Canton in the south and Szechuan in the landlocked west. The last is the favourite of those who like food to be strongly flavoured and peppery. But China remains one country, and this variety is underpinned by a common philosophy of food and a general agreement on the principles of cooking and its relation to life. Every activity tries to achieve a balance between the forces of *yin* and *yang*, and in the kitchen this means between foods that cool the body and those that heat it. *Yin* foods include sugar, salt, spring onions and soy sauce, many vegetables and much seafood; *yang* include vinegar, ginger, pepper and wine, and fat, oily or fried food generally. Rice is usually regarded as *yin*. Equally important is the balance between *fan*, the basic or staple food, and *ts'ai*, the secondary but more flavoursome part of the meal. Food, in other words, is medicine as well as nourishment for the body. It is no wonder that cooking, at the highest gourmet level, has always been a highly esteemed profession in China. A restaurant culture developed in Chinese cities a thousand years ago and has never looked back. However, there is plenty of good food that can be made easily at home. My own favourite Chinese recipes are those that I learned from Chinese friends, some of them professional chefs, others housewives or students. The dishes I most enjoy eating are the ones I remember from my own youth in Indonesia and Singapore. They may not be classics of the high Imperial past, but the cooking methods (stir-frying, deep-frying, steaming or slow-cooking) combined with fresh ingredients and spices give them the zest and appeal of real food.

KOREA

Chapchae (see page 122)

My recollections of a train journey across Korea are of low cloud and cool air among the hills, something like the north of England but with rice farmers. The people we met were warmly hospitable but tough and outspoken. For many centuries Korea was like the nut caught in the nutcracker between China and Japan; its people suffered greatly, but they have retained many good things gleaned from so much foreign contact. Korean food shows plenty of Chinese and Japanese influence but has kept its own delicate but unpretentious character. At first sight, Korean cooking may seem rather fiddly. The elaborate presentation, however, is achieved by simple methods, such as the precise arrangement of different-coloured vegetables, or the use of one ingredient to stuff another. Koreans, more perhaps than any of their neighbours, like to steam their food: soups and steamed fish and vegetable dishes with tofu are plentiful. Seasonings and spices are positive but discreet, based on the "five flavours" considered essential in Asian cooking – sour, sweet, salty, bitter and hot. Sourness comes from vinegar and from preserves such as *kimchee*, sweetness from rice wine, *mirin*, or strawberry or cherry wine. Saltiness is from soy sauce, bitter flavours mostly from roots such as ginseng, and hotness from pepper and chillies.

JAPAN

Sushi (see page 71)

Japanese cooking has been called "a simple art", but its simplicity, the result of centuries of refinement, is exquisite, breathtaking and not easily combined with other styles and traditions. Japanese food is more appreciated in the world at large as it becomes better known, and its savouriness and freshness are particularly appealing. Though I cook many Japanese dishes with confidence, I admit I am not yet sufficiently sure of myself to serve a complete Japanese meal in traditional style. To do this, you need to have your roots in Japanese life, to sense the importance of the sequence of dishes throughout the meal. Eating becomes a kind of theatre, and the play must have a beginning, a middle and an end. That sounds simple enough: starter, main course, dessert. But the first course usually consists of three items: an appetizer, perhaps a morsel of beautifully cut fish or shrimp with one or two ginkgo nuts or chestnuts, then a small bowl of clear soup, followed by *sashimi*, a delicacy of raw seafood. An elaborate main course will be a sequence of dishes: grilled, steamed, simmered and deep-fried, and one either cooked or dressed in vinegar. For a family meal, all these may be replaced by a one-pot dish, the equivalent of a stew or casserole. The meal ends not with a sweet, but with a small bowl of gleaming white boiled rice, a bowl of miso soup and some pickles, then green tea served with fresh fruit, beautifully sliced. At the end everyone, guests and host, feels satisfied but never over-full; the meal has been a feast for the eyes, the mind and the spirit, as well as for the palate.

INGREDIENTS

Obtaining exotic ingredients can be a challenge, but they are now usually available in cities, and most large towns have at least one ethnic food shop or supplier. As far as Chinese and Indian ingredients are concerned, only the most specialist items may still be hard to find. The same is becoming increasingly true of Thai, Indonesian, Malaysian and Vietnamese ingredients, too. In the following section and in the recipes, I have suggested alternatives when appropriate. For recipe ingredients listed as "optional", it is better to leave them out than to seek substitutes.

VEGETABLES

Asians have always had a high regard for vegetables; for hundreds of years they have recognised the therapeutic properties of many cultivated and wild plants and their importance to a healthy diet. Much of tropical Asia is very fertile and can produce several crops a year. Vegetables are often inter-cropped with rice, and even the tiniest patch of land can support a few bean plants or squash, or a banana tree. So almost everyone has a supply of fresh, healthy food.

AUBERGINES
Purple aubergines are readily available. Choose ones that are firm and shiny; those with wrinkled skins are no longer fresh. Most recipes in this book use medium-sized aubergines, though a few specify baby purple aubergines, which can usually be found in Indian greengrocers. Round, greenish aubergines, also called "apple" aubergines, and very small pea aubergines can be bought in Thai shops — they are commonly used in Thai curries.

Baby purple aubergine

Banana leaf

Plantain

Apple aubergines

Pea aubergines

Banana flower

MOOLI
This giant white radish, also known as daikon, has a peppery and slightly bitter flavour. Most Asian food shops and some supermarkets sell mooli. It can grow longer than 30cm (12in), but smaller ones are available. For salads, peel the mooli, then cut into tiny strips and soak in cold water for 30 minutes to make it crisper. It is also good added to soups or stir-fried.

BANANA LEAF
Wash before use, then cut into shapes to line serving plates or use to wrap food for cooking. If frozen, use within a few hours of defrosting.

PLANTAIN
Ripe yellow plantains make the best fried bananas. Use unripe green ones for chips or crisps.

BANANA FLOWER
Discard the hard outer petals and slice the tender centre. Boil for several minutes, and add to soups or salads.

Sliced okra

Okra

OKRA
These are called
bandakka *in Sri Lanka*
and bindhi *in India.*
The texture is rather
slimy, but they are
delicious when sliced
and fried until crisp.

YARD-LONG BEANS
Available from Thai and Indian
food shops, these should be fresh
and firm. They are excellent
eaten raw, though they are
usually lightly cooked until
tender but crisp.

ASIAN RED ONIONS
I use these for making Crisp-fried Onions
(see page 132 for recipe) because of their
low water content. Buy them from Chinese
and Thai food shops.

Fresh shiitake

Dried shiitake

SHIITAKE MUSHROOMS
Fresh shiitake have a delicate texture and are
excellent added to stir-fries. Dried ones must
be rehydrated in hot water (see page 155).
The hard stalks and soaking-water are
ideal for making stock. Fresh and dried
varieties are available from Asian food
shops and some supermarkets.

WATER SPINACH
In Southeast Asia this grows as abundantly
as watercress and is also known as "swamp
cabbage". The flavour is between that
of watercress and spinach, and the
stalk remains crunchy even when
cooked. Buy it from Asian food
shops or, if unobtainable, use
watercress or spinach
as a substitute.

WOOD EARS
Also called "cloud ears" or
"tree-ears", there are in fact
several varieties of this
mushroom – the smallest ones
have the most delicate flavour.
When rehydrated in hot water
(see page 155), they have a
pleasant crunchy texture.

WATER CHESTNUTS
You can buy these in cans from
most supermarkets, or fresh
from Chinese food shops. If
using fresh, however, choose
firm, unblemished ones, rinse
off the mud, then carefully
peel with a sharp knife.

BAMBOO SHOOTS
Use ready-prepared shoots in
cans or glass jars; fresh ones are
not worth the trouble. Leftover
shoots can be stored in a glass
bowl, covered with water; they
will keep refrigerated for up
to one week.

STRAW MUSHROOMS
These are popular in many
Asian countries, where they are
cultivated on rice straw. In the
West they are only available in
cans and have lost much of their
flavour, so I usually suggest fresh
mushrooms as an alternative.

FRUIT, NUTS & SEEDS

With the exception of marigolds perhaps, the following ingredients are not usually found growing wild, even in their countries of origin. Most have been propagated and cultivated for centuries; many have travelled and have been introduced to new homes. Even the humble peanut has become a highly sophisticated commercial product. The reason is simple – raw or cooked, these are some of the world's best-tasting and most versatile plant foods.

KAFFIR LIME
The juice of this fruit adds piquancy to chilli sauce. The peel, which is rather knobbly, is usually sliced and added to curries and similar dishes to make them more fragrant. Dried peel can be bought in packets.

QUINCE
Usually available in autumn, these fragrant fruit may be the size of an eating apple, or larger. In Asia they are used as vegetables and either filled with meat, or diced and added to stuffing mixtures for poultry and seafood.

POMELO
Larger than grapefruit, with a thick yellow-green skin, pomelo is good eaten by itself or added to almost any salad.

MARIGOLD
Fresh marigold petals from the garden give colour and flavour to Moo Wan (see page 98 for recipe) and to salads. Some Asian food shops sell the dried petals.

CANDLE NUTS
These come from Indonesia and Malaysia. Always cook them; raw ones are mildly toxic. Use almonds or macadamias as substitutes.

GINKGO NUTS
These small, pale nuts are used in Japanese and Chinese cooking. They are only available canned in the West from Chinese food stores.

CASHEW NUTS
In Asian cookery these are used whole, roughly chopped, or made into a paste. Frying them first imparts extra flavour.

ALMONDS
In this book almonds are used in several Indian recipes; they are also a suitable alternative to candle nuts.

MANGOES

The finest mangoes are Indian, Thai, and the "Manila" mangoes of the Philippines. Ripe ones are firm but not hard, and should have a sweet, orange-coloured, fragrant flesh, without any trace of fibres. Small green mangoes, available from Indian food shops, are refreshingly sour and good for pickles and chutneys.

Ripe mango

Green mango

GUAVA

This fruit varies in size and is usually pear-shaped with pink or cream-coloured flesh. It can be eaten like an apple, or peeled and thinly sliced. The seeds are edible, if you like them. For cooking, only the flesh is used; the skin and seeds are discarded.

COCONUT

Before buying a fresh coconut, shake it — you should hear the water inside. Dried and grated, or desiccated, coconut flesh is the most convenient for making coconut milk, the white liquid extracted from soaking grated coconut flesh in hot water. Coconut cream is the thick white "top" that separates from the milk when refrigerated.

Fresh coconut

Desiccated coconut

Whole coconut

MACADAMIA NUTS

Asian food shops and many supermarkets sell these roasted or fried. They make a good substitute for candle nuts.

PEANUTS

Used widely in Asian cooking, peanuts are also called groundnuts. Buy shelled raw nuts and roast them yourself for the best flavour.

Coconut milk

POPPY SEEDS

The grey-blue seeds are used mostly in bread; the cream-coloured ones are added to curry sauces as a thickening agent.

SESAME SEEDS

Important in all Far Eastern cooking, these seeds are rich in aromatic oil, and are used whole or crushed into a paste.

Coconut cream

RICE, NOODLES & WRAPPERS

Beans and grains – basically starches – are the most versatile foods available, and these pages are a tribute to the ingenuity of farmers, cooks and food manufacturers. Most natural starches can be ground to a flour, then formed into a dough to make noodles, bread or pastry. Rice too, depends on starch for its stickiness. Soya beans are amazingly nourishing and adaptable, forming the basis of tofu, as well as flavouring ingredients such as soy sauce, essential in authentic Asian cuisine.

JAPANESE RICE
Japan does not export rice, and almost all the Japanese-style rice available in the West is grown in California. There are many varieties, all short-grained "japonica" rices.

BASMATI RICE
The world's longest-grained rice, basmati is grown in the foothills of the Himalayas. The best is exported to Europe. Basmati-type varieties are also grown in Australia and the US.

JASMINE RICE
The finest rice from the world's largest rice-exporting country, Thailand, is widely available, and often called Thai fragrant rice. The grains are long, softer than basmati and slightly sticky.

GLUTINOUS RICE
When cooked the grains are soft and sticky, hence the name. White glutinous rice is grown all over Southeast Asia, but black varieties are rare and are more difficult to find in shops.

Japanese silken tofu

Chinese tofu

Fried tofu

TOFU
Japanese soya bean curd, "silken" tofu, is very soft, while Chinese tofu is firmer. They are sold in sealed plastic boxes filled with water in Asian food stores and healthfood shops. Fried beancurd absorbs sauce during cooking, and can also be stuffed.

YIFU OR YI NOODLES
These are deep-fried egg noodles that have been dried and are available from Chinese food shops. Soak in hot water for 3–4 minutes before using. If unobtainable, use fresh or dried egg noodles instead.

UDON NOODLES
Available from Japanese food shops, these round or flat noodles are made of wheat flour. They are usually served in broth, hot or cold, with chopped spring onions, flavoured with 7-spice.

SHIRATAKI
These thin strands are made from a plant known as "elephant's foot" or "devil's tongue". They are added to sukiyaki, a Japanese hot-pot, and are also sold as a gelatinous paste called konnyaku, used in soups.

SPRING ROLL WRAPPERS

These can be bought in three sizes from most Asian supermarkets. The smallest, about 12cm (5in) square, are used to make mini spring rolls. For standard-sized spring rolls (see page 64 for recipe), use the wrappers that are 24cm (9in) square. The largest, 30cm (12in) square, can be cut into strips and used to make samosa (see page 65 for recipe).

WONTON WRAPPERS

Made from a flour and egg dough, these are available fresh or frozen from Chinese food shops, sold in two thicknesses – very thin for stuffing and frying, and thick for steaming.

Spring roll wrappers

Wonton wrappers

Beancurd sheet

BEANCURD SHEET

Also sold as beancurd skins, these sheets are quite large and very brittle. Buy them from Chinese food shops wrapped in waxed paper and packed in clear plastic bags. To use, soak in cold water until pliable, and then cut with scissors. In this book, they are used for Vegetarian Goose (see page 118 for recipe).

MANDARIN PANCAKES

Essential for serving Peking Duck (see page 46 for recipe), these pancakes are made with plain flour, water and a little sesame oil. They are available, usually frozen, from Chinese food shops. Defrost completely, then steam for 8–10 minutes. Keep the steamed pancakes in a covered dish or wrapped in a tea towel or napkin as they dry out very quickly.

Mandarin pancakes

RICE NOODLES

Manufactured from rice flour, then dried, these are sold as very thin strands (rice vermicelli) or ribbons of various widths (also called rice sticks). Rice sticks are popular in Vietnam, Singapore and Malaysia, while Thais and Indonesians prefer the thinner rice vermicelli.

Rice vermicelli   *Ribbon rice noodles*

CELLOPHANE NOODLES

These are also sold as mung bean-flour noodles and bean threads (they are made from mung bean starch), and as glass vermicelli, because they look like spun glass. Cellophane noodles do not need to be boiled, merely soaked in hot water for 10–15 minutes.

Cellophane noodles   *Cellophane vermicelli*

HERBS & SPICES

Herbs and spices are at the heart of Asian cooking. Many of them were once luxuries in Asia, just as they were in Europe, while those that were cheaper were often under-valued. One flavouring that is almost universally used in Asia is the chilli – and this did not arrive from Central America until the sixteenth century.

THAI BASIL
In Thailand there are at least three kinds of basil: Anise basil (illustrated), Thai basil and holy basil all taste different, so buy the one specified in the recipe if you can.

CHINESE CHIVES
This herb is more pungent than the European chive. Chop the chives, flowers and all, and use in spring rolls and stir-fries. The opened flowers make an attractive edible garnish.

TURMERIC
This adds a warm yellow colour and distinctive flavour to Asian festival dishes. It is definitely not a substitute for saffron.

CLOVES
Used in most parts of Asia in both savoury and sweet dishes. Remember to remove whole cloves before serving.

FENUGREEK SEEDS
Very popular in Southern India, where they are always an essential ingredient in curry pastes.

FENUGREEK
Fresh fenugreek leaves, used extensively in India, can be bought from Indian food shops. Dried leaves, often called methi, *are also available.*

CORIANDER
Dry-roast the seeds before using; this gives a more aromatic result. Ground coriander loses its fragrance if stored for too long.

FRESH CORIANDER
Fresh coriander growing in pots is now sold in many supermarkets. Stronger-flavoured, mature plants with roots suitable for cooking are available from Asian food shops. Clean the roots well in cold water; they can be frozen for up to a month. (Leaves and stalks cannot be frozen.) The roots, leaves and stalks are important ingredients in Thai green curry paste; and the leaves are widely used in Indian and Chinese cooking.

KAFFIR LIME LEAVES
Found in Thai food shops, these fragrant leaves are used whole, shredded, or mixed into a paste.

CURRY LEAVES
Can be bought, fresh or dried, from Indian food shops; there is no substitute for their flavour.

Large chillies

GOLDEN NEEDLES
These are the dried buds of the tiger lily. Available from Chinese food shops, they need to be soaked in hot water before use.

STAR ANISE
The dried star-shaped fruit of a member of the magnolia family is native to China and has a marked aniseed flavour. Use whole or ground.

Medium chillies

CHILLIES
What is pleasantly warm in one person's mouth may be searingly hot in another's. The hotness is mainly in the placental tissue, so by cutting out the seeds you remove most of the heat but retain the flavour. Generally, small chillies are hotter than large, dried hotter than fresh. If a mild dish is preferred, reduce the number of chillies specified in the recipe.

NIGELLA (CENTRE) & CUMIN
Seeds are usually roasted, ground and mixed in a curry paste. White cumin is used in Southeast Asia; Indian cooks usually prefer Nigella or black cumin.

Bird's eye chillies

7-SPICE
Japanese shichimi is a blend of fragrant spices, including tangerine peel, sesame seeds, poppy seeds and seaweed flakes. Hot blends usually include sansho pepper and ginger.

Dried bird's eye chillies

GINGER
This rhizome scarcely needs an introduction, it has become so familiar. Do cook with fresh ginger rather than dried — the flavour is well worth a little extra trouble. Break or cut off a piece, then peel before slicing, chopping or crushing.

CINNAMON
Buy rolled-up quills rather than ground cinnamon — they have more flavour and keep fresh for a lot longer.

5-SPICE
The usual ingredients of this aromatic rather than hot mix are cassia, fennel seeds, star anise, cloves and anise pepper — better known as Szechuan pepper.

GREEN CARDAMOMS
Native to Southern India, these are now grown throughout the tropics. They give a more subtle flavour to a dish if the pods are removed before serving.

GALANGAL
A rhizome that gives an aromatic bitterness to savoury dishes, fresh galangal is sold in most Thai shops (the Thai name is ka), but dried or powdered galangal will do. Use ¼ teaspoon of powder for 1cm (½in) of fresh. Do not put dried pieces into a blender — they are hard enough to damage the blades.

CASSIA BARK
This is related to cinnamon, but the bark is thicker. It is used in large pieces to flavour pilaffs and similar savoury dishes. The pieces can be picked out easily and discarded before serving. For sweet dishes, cinnamon is preferred.

LEMONGRASS
Unknown in the West a few years ago, this has shot to favour as the essential ingredient in Thai cooking and is now sold in supermarkets. As the name suggests, it adds a pleasant citrus-like sourness to a dish.

THE STORECUPBOARD

These distinctive-tasting products have long shelf lives while they remain unopened (take note of any best-before dates). Once opened, soy sauce and fish sauce, wines and vinegars will keep almost indefinitely, but oils should be used within a few months. Bean sauces last for up to a month, refrigerated in a screw-top jar, but other ingredients should be used within a month or so. They may not go off but they will gradually lose flavour – and flavour, after all, is what you buy them for.

HOISIN SAUCE
The classic sauce for Peking Duck (see page 46 for recipe), made from soya beans, wheat flour, vinegar, garlic and sesame oil.

YELLOW BEAN SAUCE
Also known as "fermented yellow beans", these processed puréed soya beans are sold in jars or cans – with the addition of chillies it is called chilli bean sauce.

BLACK BEAN SAUCE
This is made from black soya beans, usually dried after fermentation. The sauce is more widely available than the dried beans, and is especially good with fish and shellfish.

CHILLI SAUCE
Buy a plain sauce, containing only chillies, salt and a little vinegar. One teaspoon is the equivalent of one fresh red chilli.

SOY SAUCE
Light soy sauce is salty and does not alter the colour of food, unlike the sweeter dark version. Tamari is a dark, mild Japanese soy.

OYSTER SAUCE
Make sure you buy real oyster sauce made with oyster juice – many brands are simply "oyster-flavoured" sauce.

FISH SAUCE
Pungent fish sauces are popular all over Southeast Asia. Nam pla is the Thai version, while nuoc mam is Vietnamese. Use the one specified in the recipe.

Rice wine · Shaohsing wine · Mirin · Sake · Chinese red vinegar · White distilled malt vinegar · Rice vinegar

WINES

Cooks all over Asia use wine made from glutinous rice. In China, the most famous is Shaohsing wine, made with mineral water. It can be bought in Chinese food stores, and the only substitute is a good dry sherry. Mirin is a sweet rice wine from Japan; when combined with soy sauce, it adds flavour to simmered dishes and gives a gloss to teriyaki. Sake, Japan's national drink, is also used in cooking, in a tenderizing marinade for meat, for example.

VINEGARS

White distilled malt vinegar is used in small quantities in Asia, but most Asian vinegars are brewed from rice. These have a low acid content and are mostly used as flavourings. Ordinary Japanese rice vinegar (e.g. Mitsukan) is pale and mild. The brown rice vinegar (togazu), made by traditional methods, is best, but is not always available. Chinese "red" vinegar (usually brown or black in colour) is made from millet or sorghum.

CHILLI OIL

Although widely available ready-made, chilli oil can be made at home by steeping chillies in groundnut oil. Add to salad dressings or dishes needing a mild chilli flavour.

SESAME OIL

Use sparingly in Chinese, Japanese and Korean cooking to add flavour. Not suitable for frying.

GHEE

The Indian cooking medium is similar to clarified butter but with a stronger flavour. Buy from Indian shops in cans or tubs.

GROUNDNUT OIL

Ideal for frying as it can be heated to high temperatures and does not flavour the food.

Sesame oil

Chilli oil

Groundnut oil

Ghee

BONITO STOCK

Bonito stock, called dashi, is made from kelp (kombu) and dried bonito flakes (katsuobushi). It is used as a soup and a stock in Japanese cooking. Instant dashi is available from Japanese stores but it is better to make your own (see page 156).

Bonito flakes

Kelp

Dashi

White miso

Red miso

Yellow miso

MISO

A Japanese flavouring made by fermenting soya bean paste with rice, salt and water. White miso (shiromiso) is used mostly in sweet dishes. Red miso (akamiso) is high in protein and salt. All-purpose miso, called yellow miso (shinshu-miso), is non-sweet and has a higher salt content.

TAMARIND

The pulp and seeds of the tamarind fruit are compressed and sold in blocks. A piece is soaked in warm water to give a sour-tasting paste or liquid (see page 101).

ASAFOETIDA

This is sold in Indian shops as a powder called hing. Store in an airtight container and use sparingly. Its powerful odour disappears during cooking and you will find that it enhances the flavour of the cooked food.

SUGARS & TREACLE

Palm sugar is often called by its Anglo-Burmese name, jaggery. It is a brown sugar, made from the sap of the coconut palm flower. If unavailable, use soft brown or demerara sugar. Kitul treacle is available from Sri Lankan food shops, but a substitute can be made at home (see page 156).

Tamarind

Grated palm sugar

DRIED ANCHOVIES

Called ikan bilis in Malaysia and ikan teri in Indonesia, these are sold in packets — with or without their heads. Before using, the heads should be broken off and discarded, then the dried fish should be fried in oil or baked in the oven until crisp and crunchy.

Palm sugar

Kitul treacle

RICE POWDER
Some of the best brands of rice powder are Chinese. (Do not confuse rice powder with glutinous rice powder.) Rice flour cannot be used as a substitute as it is not fine enough.

RICE FLOUR
This is often obtainable in supermarkets, as is glutinous rice flour. Read the label carefully when buying — they are quite different when cooked.

AGAR AGAR
A vegetarian gelatine, made from seaweed, that gels without the need for refrigeration. It is sold in strips or sticks in Asian supermarkets.

Red split lentils   *Green lentils*

LENTILS
Lentils are usually sold split. Red ones are used in soups and to thicken sauces. Green lentils, which look brown when you buy them, are used mainly in Indian dishes.

Whole mung beans   *Split mung beans*

MUNG BEANS
Whole mung beans are good for sprouting (commercial beansprouts are grown from mung beans), while the split beans are cooked and eaten like lentils.

CRISP-FRIED ONIONS
Made from small Asian red onions or shallots, these are available in supermarkets and food shops everywhere, packed in sealed containers. To make your own see page 132.

PICKLED GINGER
Only young root ginger is pickled, because it is soft and not at all fibrous. Japanese pickled ginger is often pink, because the pickling vinegar contains red shiso leaves.

PICKLED CHILLIES
Buy a good brand as some can taste too much of vinegar. Add a small quantity to spice mixtures or curry pastes.

WASABI PASTE
Fresh wasabi (*Wasabi japonica*) is rarely available outside Japan, but wasabi paste is available in tubes. Wasabi powder, sold in small tins, is made from horseradish with a little green colouring. The flavour is not as good.

PRAWN CRACKERS
Chinese prawn crackers are sold, dried, in packets; but Indonesian krupuk are tastier.

Uncooked prawn crackers

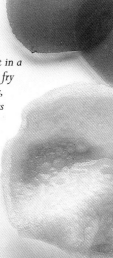

DRIED SHRIMP PASTE
This is called terasi or trassie *in Indonesia*, kapi *in Thailand and* balachan *in Malaysia.* Before using it in a spice paste or sambal, grill, fry or roast it for 5—10 minutes, until dry and crumbly (unless the paste itself is sautéed as the first stage of cooking).

DRIED SHRIMPS
Use as a condiment, crushed with chilli or garlic.

Wasabi paste

Dried shrimp paste

Dried shrimps

Cooked prawn crackers

CLASSIC DISHES

Here is a selection of 18 dishes that most people will have heard of and perhaps tasted, either in restaurants or during travels. They are quite simple to cook, and are just as much at home on the family dinner table as they are at a smart dinner party or an informal buffet. Two or three dishes can be combined successfully to create an exotic and original, but well-balanced meal.

All dishes serve 4, unless otherwise indicated.

SNACKS & APPETIZERS

Today we call it "grazing" – the habit of snacking at any time of the day. In Asia it is a long-established art, brought to perfection in the towns where street-food vendors supply refreshment to passers-by. In large modern cities, where traffic makes pavement-life less attractive, trading has now transferred to big food centres, but the cooking should be just as good.

REMPAH-REMPAH

Prawn and beansprout fritters (Malaysia)

Popular throughout most of Southeast Asia, wherever prawns are plentiful and cheap, these fritters combine beansprouts with whole and chopped prawns. They are equally delicious hot or cold, at a dinner party or for a picnic.
See page 70 for recipe.

SHUEN GUEN

Spring rolls (China)

These are said to date from the days of the Tang dynasty (6th–9th centuries AD). Then, they were stuffed with the first green vegetables of spring, which must have been welcome after the preserved foods of winter. The name and the concept have not changed, but fillings have evolved to suit the resources and tastes of different countries.
See page 64 for recipe.

PERGEDEL JAGUNG

Sweetcorn fritters (Indonesia)

Sweetcorn, or maize, was brought to Asia by Portuguese and Spanish settlers in the 16th century and is now grown almost everywhere. Equally popular at that time was another newcomer, the chilli – these fritters have just enough to give them a kick.
See page 64 for recipe.

PATTIES

Small filled pies (Sri Lanka)

*The Sri Lankan equivalent of a
spring roll – or a miniature
Cornish pasty – these little
pies are loved by children as
much as adults. You can use
shortcrust pastry or make
real Sri Lankan pastry
with coconut milk.
See page 62
for recipe.*

SUSHI

Rice rolls (Japan)

*This sophisticated snack
comes from one Asian
country where you hardly
ever see anyone eating in the
street. Instead, Japan has developed
the sushi bar, the equivalent to the
European cafe. There is a vast range of
sushi, but this kind is easy to make and
will appeal to everyone's taste.
See page 71 for recipe.*

IKAN MASAK MOLEK

Fish curry (Malaysia)

Malaysians consider fish heads a great delicacy, and fish-head curry is a popular classic. This milder version is made with whole fish so that, as is tradition, the fish head can be offered to an honoured guest, a compliment to be gracefully accepted. Serve with Bandakka Curry (see page 115 for recipe) and plain boiled rice.

INGREDIENTS

1.25 litres (2 pints) thick coconut milk (see page 141)
salt and freshly ground black pepper, to taste
2 medium red snapper or tilapia, cleaned and scaled,
or 4 medium trout, cleaned
2 tbsp Crisp-fried Onions (see page 132
for recipe), to garnish
2 tbsp chopped fresh flat-leaf parsley, to garnish

For the curry paste

3 large fresh red chillies, deseeded and chopped
4 shallots, chopped
2.5cm (1in) piece of fresh ginger root, peeled and chopped
2.5cm (1in) piece of fresh galangal (see page 27),
peeled and chopped
4 candle nuts (see page 22), or 8 blanched
almonds, chopped
5cm (2in) piece of fresh lemongrass, outer leaves
removed, centre chopped
1 tsp ground turmeric
2 tbsp tamarind water (see page 101)
1 tsp salt

PREPARATION

1 Put all the paste ingredients, plus 4 tablespoons of the coconut milk, into a blender and blend until as smooth as possible.

2 Transfer the paste mixture to a wok or a large shallow pan. Cook for about 5 minutes, until the oil separates from the coconut milk. Stir for a few seconds, then add the remaining coconut milk.

3 Cook, stirring frequently, for 30 minutes or until reduced by half. Season to taste, then place the fish, head-to-tail, in the sauce. Simmer for about 7 minutes on each side for snapper and tilapia, or about 5 minutes for trout.

4 Transfer the curry to a warm platter and sprinkle with the Crisp-fried Onions and parsley, to garnish.

5 Alternatively, the fish can be served off the bone. Remove the fish from the sauce and keep the sauce warm over a low heat. Carefully peel off the skin, separate the fillets from the backbone and remove any remaining bones. Place each fillet on a dinner plate, pour the sauce over and garnish as above.

Flat-leaf parsley

Crisp-fried onions

Black pepper

Salt

Coconut milk

Red snapper

Fresh ginger

Galangal

Candle
nuts

Lemongrass

Turmeric

Shallots

Tamarind water

Red chillies

MUC DON THIT

Stuffed squid (Vietnam)

You will find similar recipes for stuffed squid in other Asian countries, but this particular combination of pork, shiitake mushrooms and golden needles (dried lily buds) is the most successful. Garnish with chilli flowers (see page 155) and strips of spring onion, if desired. Serves 8 as an appetizer with shredded lettuce, or 4 as a main course with noodles.

Golden needles

Shiitake mushrooms

INGREDIENTS

8 small squid, about 7cm (3in) long, cleaned (see page 150), tentacles reserved and chopped
groundnut oil for frying
For the stuffing
60g (2oz) cellophane vermicelli (see page 25), soaked in hot water for 5 minutes, drained
8–10 dried shiitake mushrooms, rehydrated (see page 155), stalks removed and caps finely chopped
15g (½oz) golden needles (see page 27), soaked in hot water for 10 minutes, drained and finely chopped, optional
250g (8oz) minced lean pork
2 cloves garlic, finely chopped
4 spring onions, cut into thin rounds
3 tsp fish sauce (nuoc mam), (see page 28)
¼ tsp salt
1 small egg, lightly beaten

Cellophane vermicelli

PREPARATION

1 For the stuffing, snip the vermicelli with scissors several times in different directions, to cut them into short lengths. Pat the vermicelli dry with kitchen paper and place them in a large bowl.
2 Add all the remaining stuffing ingredients, plus the chopped squid tentacles, adding the egg last. Mix well, until thoroughly combined.
3 To fill the squid, spoon some of the stuffing into each one, pressing it down, until the squid is about three-quarters full. Close the opening of each body with a wooden cocktail stick.
4 Heat some oil for shallow frying in a wok or frying pan. Add the squid and fry, turning them frequently, for 5 minutes. While the squid are cooking, pierce each one in several places with a needle or a fine skewer. Fry the squid for another 6–8 minutes, or until they are golden brown.
5 Remove the squid from the wok with a slotted spoon and transfer to a plate lined with kitchen paper, to drain. Discard the cocktail sticks and slice each squid diagonally into 2 or 3 pieces. Serve hot or warm.

Groundnut oil

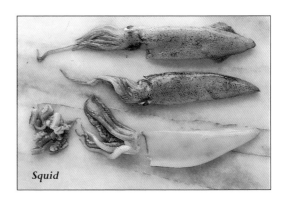

Squid

Minced pork

Garlic

Spring onions

Fish sauce

Salt

Egg

OSON

Steamed stuffed fish (Korea)

This method of stuffing fish with different coloured vegetables that have been sautéed and seasoned with soy sauce and sesame oil is typically Korean. Serves 8 as an appetizer or 4 as a main course with a dipping sauce and green salad.

INGREDIENTS

4 fillets of lemon sole, skinned, each 150–175g (5–6oz),
each sliced into 4 on the diagonal (see page 150)
¼ tsp salt, plus extra to taste
¼ tsp freshly ground black pepper, plus extra to taste
2 tbsp groundnut oil
125g (4oz) watercress
3 medium carrots, cut into julienne strips (see page 154)
6 dried shiitake mushrooms, rehydrated (see page 155),
stalks removed and caps thinly sliced
125g (4oz) chestnut mushrooms, thinly sliced
175g (6oz) French beans, halved on the diagonal
1 tsp sesame oil
2 tsp light soy sauce
2 tsp cornflour
2 eggs, separated and beaten, made into 1 thin white
omelette and 1 thin yellow omelette, cut into fine strips
For the dipping sauce
1 tsp sesame oil
2 tbsp light soy sauce
2 tbsp rice vinegar (see page 29)
2 tbsp pine nuts, roasted (see page 155), finely chopped
1–2 small dried red chillies, finely chopped

PREPARATION

1 Rub the slices of fish with the salt and pepper and set aside. Coat a non-stick frying pan with a little of the oil, add the watercress and sauté for 2 minutes. Remove from the pan, then sauté the remaining vegetables, each type separately, in a little more oil, for 2 minutes. Transfer to a plate and sprinkle with the sesame oil and soy sauce.
2 Season the cornflour with salt and pepper, then rub it over one side of each slice of fish. Arrange a few strips of each vegetable and omelette across the coated side of each slice. Roll up, lengthways, with the vegetables inside.
3 Line a bamboo steamer (see page 149) with a piece of muslin. Arrange the fish rolls side by side on it, the joins underneath. Cover and steam over boiling water for 5 minutes.
4 Remove the rolls from the steamer and transfer to a warm serving platter. Stand the rolls upright, trimming the ends a little, if necessary.

Shiitake
mushrooms

Carrots

Watercress

Groundnut oil

Black pepper

Salt

Lemon sole

5 For the dipping sauce, mix all the ingredients in a very small bowl. Serve the fish, hot or warm, with the dipping sauce.

Chestnut
mushrooms

French beans

Light soy
sauce

Sesame oil

Cornflour

Omelette

Rice vinegar

Pine nuts

Red chillies

GAENG KEO WAN KAI

Green curry of chicken (Thailand)

Thai cooks share their Southeast Asian neighbours' passion for cooking in coconut milk, as well as for sharp- and sour-tasting herbs, pungent garlic, savoury shrimp paste and hot chillies. Here, these ingredients come together in a green curry. Pea aubergines add to the unique flavour, but you can use baby new potatoes, which are also popular in Thailand. Serve with plain boiled rice and garnish with chillies.

INGREDIENTS

2 tbsp vegetable oil
750g (1½ lb) boned and skinned chicken breasts and thighs, cut into 2cm (¾in) cubes
1.25 litres (2 pints) coconut milk (see page 141)
250g (8oz) pea aubergines (see page 20), or baby new potatoes
1 tbsp chopped fresh coriander leaves, to garnish
For the paste
2 tbsp chopped fresh coriander leaves
1 tbsp chopped fresh coriander roots or stems
3 garlic cloves, finely chopped
2 shallots, finely chopped
5cm (2in) piece of fresh lemongrass, outer leaves removed, centre chopped
2cm (¾in) piece of fresh galangal (see page 27), finely chopped
1 tsp grated kaffir lime rind (see page 22)
1 tsp ground black pepper
1 tbsp each of coriander seeds and cumin seeds, roasted (see page 155), roughly crushed
½ tsp each of ground nutmeg and mace
5 fresh green chillies, deseeded and chopped
1 green pepper, deseeded and chopped, optional
2 tsp salt
½ tsp dried shrimp paste (see page 31)
4 tbsp water

PREPARATION

1 Put all the paste ingredients into a blender and blend until as smooth as possible.
2 Heat the oil in a pan over a medium heat. Add the paste mixture and fry for 4 minutes, stirring continuously. Add the chicken to the pan and stir until the pieces are well coated.
3 Lower the heat, then cover and simmer for 4 minutes. Stir in the coconut milk and simmer, stirring frequently, for 30 minutes.
4 Add the pea aubergines or potatoes to the pan and cook for 10–15 minutes, stirring frequently, until they are tender. Sprinkle with the chopped coriander, to garnish, and serve immediately.

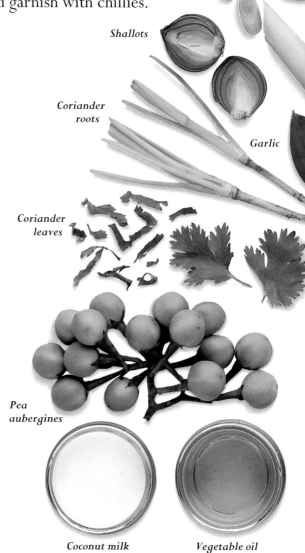

Shallots

Coriander roots

Garlic

Coriander leaves

Pea aubergines

Coconut milk

Vegetable oil

Chicken breast

GAENG KEO WAN KAI

Cumin seeds

Mace

Black
pepper

Coriander
seeds

Nutmeg

Green
chilli

Green
pepper

Salt

Kaffir lime

Galangal

Dried
shrimp paste

mongrass

SATAY

Satay, in one form or another, has spread in popularity across Asia. It is the perfect fast food, offering an infinite variety of flavours thanks to the accompanying marinades and sauces. It is equally at home served at a wedding reception or barbecue, and the skewers range from elegant metal designer pieces to disposable bamboo.

SATAY DAGING

Skewered beef (Malaysia)

These succulent chunks of meat marinated in soy sauce and spices are usually served with the classic peanut sauce.
See page 67 for recipe.

YAKITORI

Skewered chicken (Japan)

Traditionally, each part of the chicken would be prepared and cooked separately, though here only breast and thigh meat are used.
See page 67 for recipe.

*Yakitori Sauce.
See page 67
for recipe.*

*Peanut Sauce.
See page 130
for recipe.*

CHAO TOM

Skewered prawn balls and prawns (Vietnam)

These are usually made from prawn paste shaped around slivers of sugar cane. Here, I use prawn paste balls and whole prawns on decorative metal skewers.
See page 66 for recipe.

Lemongrass brush
Cut the end off a stem of fresh lemongrass and beat it until it frays — you have the ideal disposable tool to brush marinade or sauce onto your satay as it cooks.

PORK SATAY

Skewered pork (Singapore)

This street-food satay is built up from thin slices of pork interlaced with pieces of pork fat which are not meant to be eaten but make the meat wonderfully moist and savoury.
See page 67 for recipe.

SATE PUSUT

Minced fish on skewers (Indonesia)

As usual, the Balinese have taken a new idea and adapted it to be their own. A paste of minced, spiced fish is formed around a flat bamboo blade or the thin upper stem of fresh lemongrass.
See page 66 for recipe.

Nuoc Cham
See page 128 for recipe.

BAAK GING AP

Peking duck with pancakes and hoisin sauce (China)

This is not a difficult dish to make, as shown by my friend Simon Yung, chef at the Oriental Restaurant at the Dorchester Hotel, London. However, you can buy a fully prepared frozen Peking Duck (from Chinese supermarkets), then simply roast it and serve with the accompaniments below. Serves 4–6 as a main course.

INGREDIENTS

1 duck, 1½–2kg (3–4lb)
3 tbsp clear honey
2 tbsp Chinese red vinegar (see page 29)
3 tbsp Shaohsing wine (see page 29), optional
250ml (8fl oz) hot water
salt
5cm (2in) piece of fresh ginger root, peeled and chopped
10 spring onions, the white and green parts separated

To serve
1 cucumber, cut into thin sticks
hoisin sauce or yellow bean sauce
2–3 packets mandarin pancakes (see page 25)

PREPARATION

1 Scald the duck with boiling water (see page 152), then place it on a large tray.
2 Mix together the honey, vinegar, Shaohsing wine, if using, and hot water. Pour the mixture all over the top of the duck, turning it to coat the underside, then brush the excess from the tray on to the less accessible parts, such as under the wings.
3 Secure the duck on a duck hook (see page 152), placing the hooks under the wings. Hang the duck, undisturbed, in a cool, airy place for 12–24 hours, until the skin is dry.
4 Sprinkle a little salt into the body cavity of the duck, then add the ginger and the green part of the spring onions.
5 Place the duck, breast up, on a rack set over a roasting tin. Cook in an oven preheated to 160°C/ 325°F/Gas 3 for 20–25 minutes, then turn the duck over and roast for 30 minutes, until golden. Turn the duck over again, raise the temperature to 180°C/350°F/Gas 4 and roast for 15 minutes more. Transfer the duck to a carving dish and leave to rest for 5–10 minutes.
6 Cut the white part of the spring onions into thin strips and arrange with the cucumber on a plate. Put the hoisin sauce in a bowl. Place the pancakes in a steamer and steam over boiling water for 10 minutes. Separate each one carefully, then fold in half and arrange on a warm serving dish.

Salt

Shaohsing wine

Chinese red vinegar   *Honey*

Duck

7 Cut off the crisp duck skin, slice into small pieces and arrange on a warm platter. Slice the meat into similar size pieces and add to the platter
8 To eat, place a pancake flat on a plate, spoon a little hoisin sauce on to the middle and spread with the spoon. Top this with one or two pieces of duck skin and meat. Add a few slices of spring onion and cucumber, and roll up the pancake.

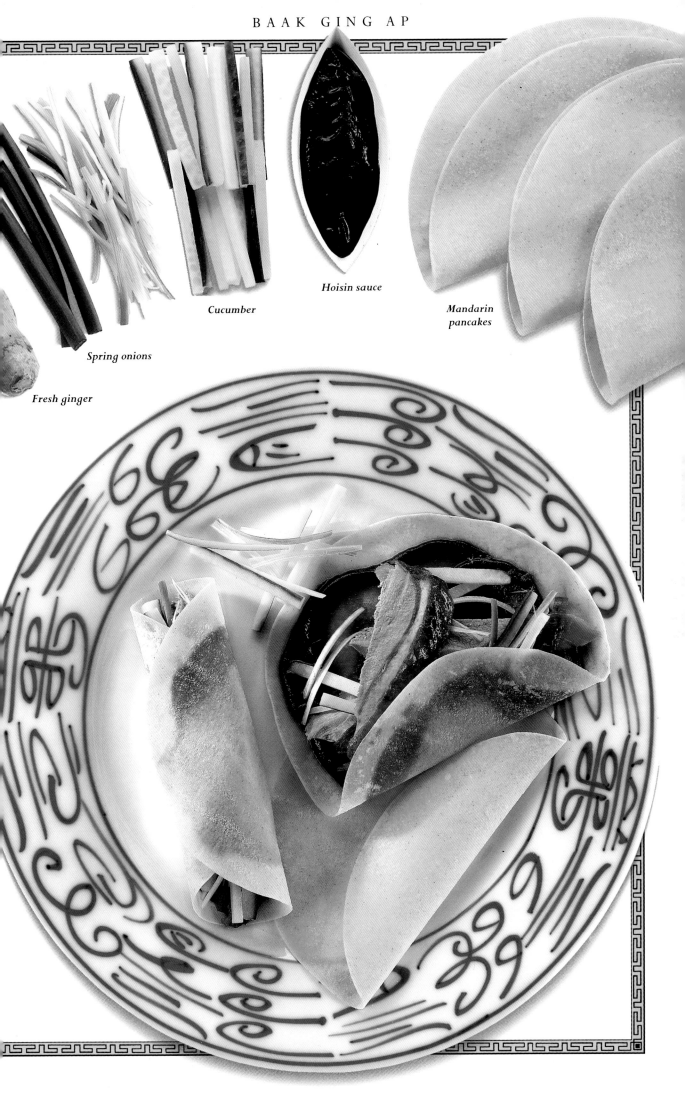

Fresh ginger

Spring onions

Cucumber

Hoisin sauce

Mandarin
pancakes

ROGAN JOSH

Lamb in rich chilli sauce with yogurt (India)

This is one of the greatest of all stews – you can make it with lamb, goat or beef. Traditionally, the fat is left on the meat to give the dish succulence, and the rich flavour is enhanced by cooking in ghee (clarified butter). My version uses lean meat and groundnut oil, but by all means use ghee if you prefer. Serves 6–8 with basmati rice.

INGREDIENTS

2kg (4lb) lean lamb from the leg or shoulder,
cut into 2cm (¾in) cubes
½ tsp chilli powder or cayenne pepper
1 tsp salt, plus extra to taste
4 tbsp groundnut oil or vegetable oil
500g (1lb) onions, finely sliced
6 green cardamom pods
2 bay leaves
120ml (8 tbsp) natural yogurt or 75ml (5 tbsp) yogurt
mixed with 3 tbsp tamarind water (see page 101)
1.25 litres (2 pints) hot water
freshly ground black pepper, to taste
½ tsp garam masala (see page 156)

For the paste
4 cloves garlic, chopped
2.5cm (1in) piece of fresh ginger root,
peeled and chopped
3–6 large fresh red chillies, deseeded and chopped
10 black peppercorns, roughly crushed
1cm (½in) piece of cinnamon stick, roughly crushed
2 tsp coriander seeds, roughly crushed
2 tsp cumin seeds, roughly crushed
3 tsp paprika
3 cloves, roughly crushed
1 tsp salt
125ml (4fl oz) water

PREPARATION

1 Put the cubed meat into a bowl, rub all over with the chilli powder and salt and set aside. Put all the paste ingredients into a blender and blend until as smooth as possible.

2 Heat the oil in a large pan, add the onions and fry until lightly golden. Add the cardamom pods and bay leaves, and stir once or twice.

3 Add the meat, increase the heat and cook, stirring continuously, for 2 minutes. Cover the pan, lower the heat and simmer for 3–4 minutes.

4 Uncover the pan, increase the heat and stir in the paste. Cover and cook for 5 minutes. Add the yogurt, stir and add the hot water. Cover the pan again and simmer for about 1 hour.

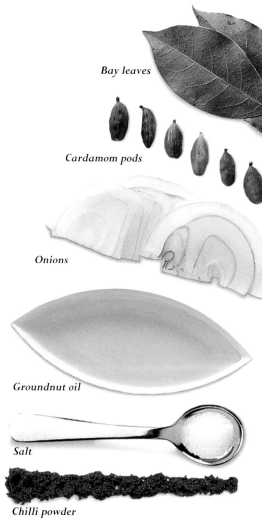

Bay leaves

Cardamom pods

Onions

Groundnut oil

Salt

Chilli powder

Lean lamb

5 Uncover the pan and cook until the sauce is reduced, and thick and creamy. Stir and season to taste. Add the garam masala and discard the cardamom pods and bay leaves before serving.

Natural yogurt

Black pepper

Garam masala

Garlic

Fresh ginger

Red chillies

Black peppercorns

Cinnamon

Coriander seeds

Cumin seeds

Paprika

Cloves

BARA-ZUSHI

Sushi rice with julienne of omelette (Japan)

This recipe is very easy to make and in Japan is regarded as an everyday dish. Here, I use a stock made by cooking mushroom stalks for 10 minutes in the soaking water from dried mushrooms. Alternatively, you can use a homemade fish stock or bonito stock (see page 30).

King prawn

Dried shrimps

Fried tofu

Light soy sauce

Mirin

Mushroom stock

Japanese rice

INGREDIENTS

750ml (1¼ pints) water
500g (1lb) short-grain Japanese rice (see page 24), washed in several changes of water, drained for 30 minutes
250ml (8fl oz) mushroom stock (see introduction, above), or fish stock or bonito stock (see page 30)
1 tbsp mirin (see page 29)
1 tbsp light soy sauce
125g (4oz) fried tofu (see page 24), quartered
30g (1oz) dried shrimps (see page 31)
8 raw king prawns, peeled and deveined (see page 82), halved crossways
60g (2oz) dried shiitake mushrooms, rehydrated (see page 155), stalks removed and caps sliced
125g (4oz) fresh shiitake mushrooms, stalks removed and caps sliced
125g (4oz) baby button mushrooms, stalks removed
125g (4oz) mangetout or sugar-snap peas, halved
2 tsp groundnut oil or vegetable oil
1 egg plus 2 egg yolks, beaten, made into 2 thin, flat omelettes, cut into fine strips
For the dressing
2 tbsp caster sugar
90ml (3fl oz) rice vinegar (see page 29)
1 tsp salt
2 tbsp hot water

PREPARATION

1 Boil the water in a pan. Add the rice and cook, uncovered, for about 10 minutes, until all the water is absorbed. Stir once, then cover, reduce the heat to minimum and cook for 10–12 minutes.
2 Remove the pan from the heat and place it, still covered, on a wet tea towel. Leave for 5 minutes, then transfer the rice to a glass bowl.
3 Mix the dressing ingredients together in a bowl, and pour, a little at a time, into the rice. Mix well, but lightly, then set aside in a cool place.
4 Heat the stock in a pan for 2 minutes. Add the mirin and soy sauce, and bring to the boil. Add the fried tofu and dried shrimps, and simmer for 3 minutes. Strain the liquid into a frying pan, reserving the tofu and shrimps. Reduce the heat, add the king prawns and stir for 1 minute.

5 Add all the mushrooms and the mangetout, and cook for 2 minutes, shaking the pan frequently as the liquid evaporates. Add the oil, stir again and remove from the heat.
6 Spoon the rice on to a serving platter. Mix in the tofu and dried shrimps and most of the mushrooms, mangetout and prawns, keeping aside a few to garnish. Arrange the omelette strips over the rice and garnish with the reserved ingredients.

Dried shiitake
mushrooms

Fresh shiitake
mushrooms

Button
mushrooms

Mangetout

Groundnut
oil

Omelette

Caster
sugar

Rice
vinegar

Salt

GADO-GADO

Cooked vegetable salad with peanut sauce (Indonesia)

Indonesians consider this their national dish, but recently the Malaysians have been claiming it as theirs also. For me, it is simply classic Javanese vegetarian food, which I have known all my life and have eaten hundreds of times since I was a little girl. For this dish, the vegetables are usually well cooked but not overcooked. However, a good Gado-gado should also have something crisp and crunchy. Here, the crispness comes from the cucumber, while the garnish of prawn crackers and fried onions provides the crunch. Serves 4–6.

INGREDIENTS

125g (4oz) cabbage or spring greens, shredded
250g (8oz) yard-long beans (see page 21), or French beans, cut into 1cm (½ in) lengths
125g (4oz) carrots, cut into flower shapes (see page 154)
125g (4oz) cauliflower, cut into small florets
125g (4oz) fresh beansprouts, rinsed and trimmed
300ml (½ pint) Peanut Sauce (see page 130 for recipe)
salt and freshly ground black pepper, to taste
For the garnish
watercress
1–2 eggs, hard-boiled, peeled and quartered
1 medium potato, boiled in its skin, then peeled and sliced
¼ cucumber, thinly sliced into half-moons
6–8 prawn crackers (see page 31), fried
1–2 tbsp Crisp-fried Onions (see page 132 for recipe)

PREPARATION

1 For the salad, boil the prepared cabbage, beans, carrots and cauliflower separately in lightly salted water for 4–5 minutes each. Drain the vegetables in a colander and keep warm. Boil the beansprouts for 2 minutes, then drain and keep warm with the other vegetables.

2 Heat the Peanut Sauce in a small pan until hot, stirring in a little hot water if it is too thick. Season to taste, then pour the sauce into a small bowl.

3 Arrange the garnish of watercress around the edge of a large serving dish and pile the cooked vegetables in the centre of the dish. Arrange the hard-boiled eggs, potatoes and cucumber on top.

4 Accompany with the prawn crackers, to crumble over the vegetables, and sprinkle with the Crisp-fried Onions. Serve immediately, while still warm, with the sauce, or leave the salad until cold and sprinkle with the onions just before serving.

5 Alternatively, the salad can be served with the sauce poured over, and the garnishes arranged separately, allowing everyone to help themselves.

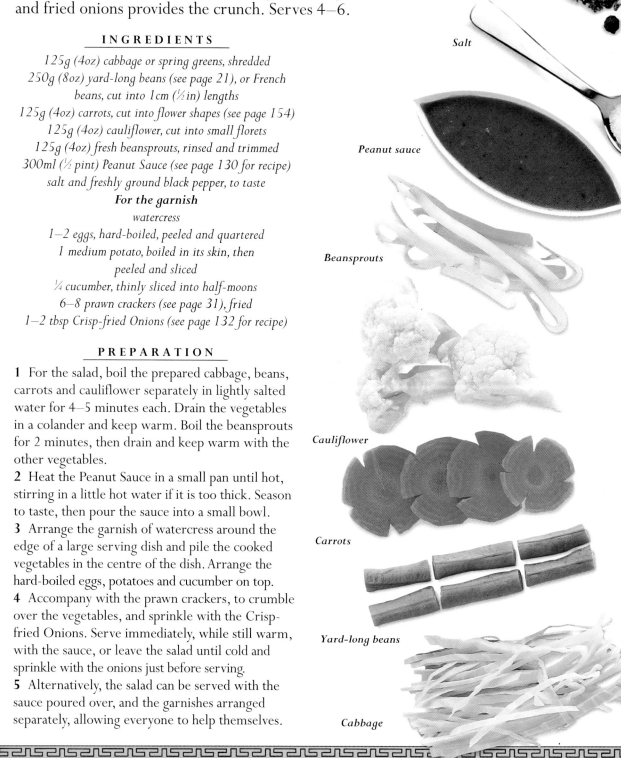

Black pepper

Salt

Peanut sauce

Beansprouts

Cauliflower

Carrots

Yard-long beans

Cabbage

GADO-GADO

Watercress

Eggs

Potato

Cucumber

Prawn
crackers

Crisp-fried
onions

RECIPES

The 14 countries covered in this book fall into
two distinct groups. India, Sri Lanka, Burma, Laos,
Thailand, Malaysia, the Philippines and Indonesia
all cook with spices and chillies, and enrich their dishes
with yogurt or coconut milk and pungent fish sauces or
shrimp pastes. The others – China, Japan, Korea,
Vietnam, Cambodia and Singapore – base the flavour
of their cooking on soy sauce and other fermented
soya bean products, and use much less chilli.

SOUPS

Some of these soups are almost unofficial national dishes in their countries of origin, probably because they are warm, nourishing and very comforting if you have grown up with them from childhood. For people in the West, they also have the attraction of being exotic. Soup is an essential part of almost every Asian meal, and often becomes a meal in itself. But whatever may be put into it in the way of fish, meat and vegetables, the basis is always a good clear stock.

MOHINGA

Fish soup with rice noodles (Burma)

This is the national dish of Burma, and is usually served with lentil fritters as part of a large dinner party or as a family meal. Serves 6–8, or more if part of a buffet.

INGREDIENTS

For the stock
750g (1½ lb) whole brill, cleaned
1.25 litres (2 pints) water
3 fresh or dried red chillies, halved
¼ tsp ground turmeric
2 stems of fresh lemongrass
1 tbsp fish sauce (nam pla), (see page 28)
For the accompaniments
1 banana flower (see page 20), optional
250g (8oz) can sliced bamboo shoots, drained and rinsed
500g (1lb) rice vermicelli (see page 25),
or fine egg noodles
2 tbsp Crisp-fried Onions (see page 132 for recipe)
4 duck or hens' eggs, hard-boiled, peeled and quartered,
or 12 quail eggs, hard-boiled and peeled
2–3 tbsp chopped fresh flat-leaf parsley
8 slices of lemon or lime
chilli sauce (see page 28), to serve
To finish the soup
2 tbsp groundnut oil or vegetable oil
1 tsp sesame oil
3 shallots, finely sliced
3 cloves garlic, finely sliced
1 large fresh red chilli, deseeded and finely sliced
1 tsp finely chopped fresh ginger root
5cm (2in) piece of fresh lemongrass, outer leaves
removed, centre finely chopped
900ml (1½ pints) coconut milk (see page 141)
500g (1lb) monkfish, filleted and cut into bite-sized
pieces, bones reserved for the stock
salt and freshly ground black pepper, to taste

PREPARATION

1 Put all the stock ingredients, along with the monkfish bones, into a large pan. Bring to the boil, then reduce the heat and simmer for 5 minutes. Remove the brill from the pan, transfer to a plate and leave to cool.

2 Peel the skin off the brill, then separate the flesh from the bones and set aside. Return the skin and bones to the stock and simmer for 30 minutes more. Strain the stock through a fine sieve into a bowl and discard the solids.

3 For the accompaniments, discard the two outer layers of the banana flower, if using. Cook the flower in lightly salted boiling water for 6–8 minutes. Drain and quarter the flower, then cut it into fairly thick slices.

4 Cook the bamboo shoots in lightly salted boiling water for 3 minutes, then drain. Arrange them with the sliced banana flower on one side of a large serving dish.

5 Put the rice vermicelli or egg noodles in a large bowl and pour over plenty of boiling water. Cover and leave to stand for 3–4 minutes. Drain the noodles in a colander and arrange on the serving dish. Arrange the remaining accompaniments on the dish, placing the chilli sauce in a small bowl in the centre.

6 To finish the soup, heat the groundnut oil with the sesame oil in a large pan. Add the shallots, garlic, chilli, ginger and lemongrass, and stir-fry for 2 minutes.

7 Stir in the coconut milk and bring to the boil. Add the cooked brill and raw monkfish, then simmer for 2 minutes. Add the reserved fish stock, season to taste and cook for another 2–3 minutes, until heated through.

8 Transfer some of the noodles and the other accompaniments to each serving bowl, ladle over the hot soup and serve immediately.

SATSUMAJIRU

Miso soup with mixed vegetables (Japan)

Traditionally, a fish-based stock (dashi) is added to this soup. This recipe, however, is completely vegetarian and extremely quick to make.

INGREDIENTS

1 litre (1¾ pints) cold water
90g (6 tbsp) unsweetened white miso,
or 4 tbsp red miso (see page 30)
60g (2oz) canned sliced bamboo shoots (drained weight),
rinsed and sliced into julienne strips (see page 154)
1 small carrot, sliced into julienne strips (see page 154)
8 fresh shiitake mushrooms or chestnut mushrooms, stalks
removed and caps thinly sliced
4 asparagus spears or 10 mangetout, very thinly sliced
on the diagonal
3 spring onions, very thinly sliced on the diagonal
large pinch of seven-spice (see page 27),
or freshly ground black pepper
salt, to taste

PREPARATION

1 Bring the water to the boil in a pan, then pour 125ml (4fl oz) of it over the miso in a bowl, stirring until the miso is dissolved. Return the liquid to the boiling water and reduce the heat to a simmer.

2 Add the bamboo shoots to the pan and simmer for 2 minutes. Add the carrot strips, mushrooms and asparagus or mangetout, and simmer for a further 2 minutes.

3 Bring the soup to the boil and add the spring onions and the seven-spice or black pepper. Add salt to taste and serve immediately.

BUN BO HUE

Noodle soup with beef and lemongrass
(Vietnam)

Like most Asian noodle- or rice-based soups, this dish is very
substantial and makes a delicious one-dish lunch. It is
equally good with or without chilli sauce. Serves 6–8.

INGREDIENTS

2 tbsp vegetable oil
1 tbsp tomato purée
1 tsp dried shrimp paste (see page 31)
1 tsp chilli sauce (see page 28), optional
2 shallots, finely sliced
250g (8oz) narrow ribbon rice noodles (see page 25)
2 tbsp fish sauce (nuoc mam), (see page 28)
salt and freshly ground black pepper, to taste
2 tbsp chopped fresh coriander leaves
2 tbsp finely sliced spring onions
½ cucumber, peeled, halved lengthways, deseeded
and sliced into half moons, to garnish
3 cos lettuce leaves, shredded, to garnish

For the stock

500g (1lb) chuck steak or brisket, cut into 2 pieces,
some of the fat removed
2 large pork chops, some of the fat removed
2 stems of fresh lemongrass, each cut into 3 pieces
1 tsp salt
1 tbsp fish sauce (nuoc mam), (see page 28)
2 litres (3 pints) cold water

PREPARATION

1 Put all the ingredients for the stock in a large pan.
Bring to the boil, then simmer for 1–1¼ hours,
skimming the froth frequently. Remove the meat
and leave to cool. Strain the stock into a large bowl.
2 Slice the beef and pork thinly, discarding the
bones of the chops. Set the meat aside.
3 Blend the oil, tomato purée, shrimp paste and
chilli sauce, if using, in a bowl. Transfer to a large
pan and place over a medium heat for 2 minutes.
Add the shallots, stir for a few seconds, then add a
ladleful of the stock and simmer for 3 minutes. Add
the remaining stock and simmer for 20 minutes.
4 Put the rice noodles in a large pan of boiling
water. Remove from the heat, cover the pan and
leave to stand for 3–4 minutes. Transfer the
noodles to a colander, rinse under cold running
water until cold, then leave to drain.
5 To serve, add the fish sauce to the stock, season
to taste and reheat. Divide the noodles among the
soup bowls, then add the beef and pork slices.
Sprinkle the coriander and spring onions over the
meat and ladle some stock into each bowl. Place the
cucumber and lettuce on top and serve immediately.

Fish sauce

Narrow ribbon
rice noodles

Shallots

Chilli
sauce

Dried
shrimp paste

Tomato purée

Vegetable
oil

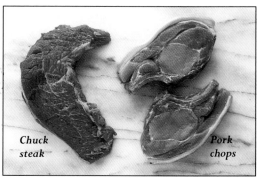

Chuck
steak

Pork
chops

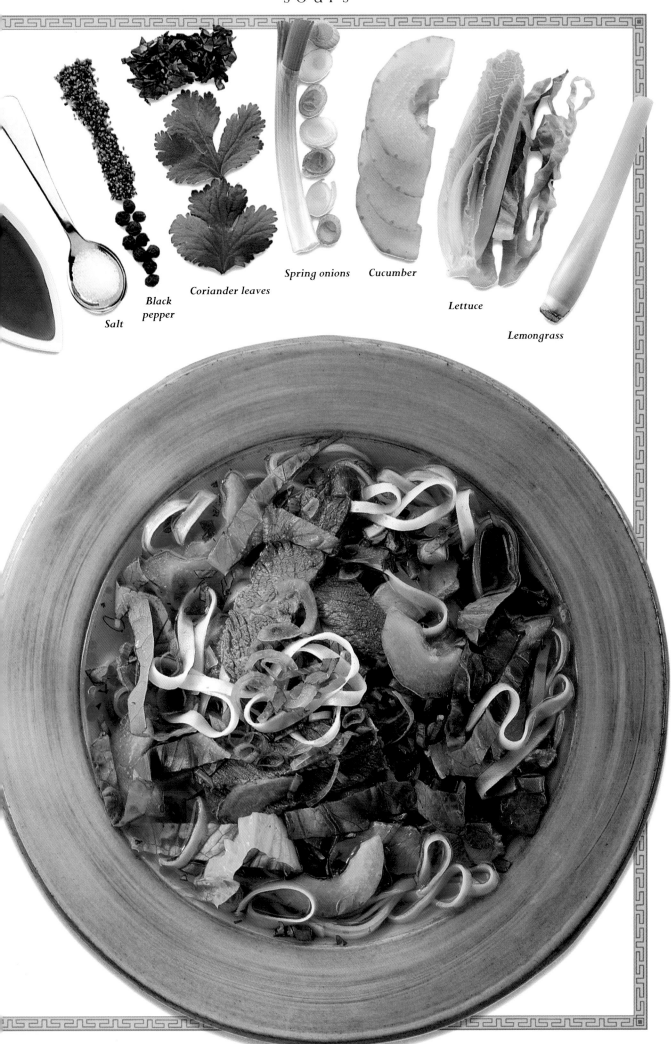

Salt

Black
pepper

Coriander leaves

Spring onions

Cucumber

Lettuce

Lemongrass

Daan Far Tong

DAAN FAR TONG

Egg drop soup (China)

*This is a classic Chinese dish that is popular throughout
Southeast Asia. It is a basic soup that depends on the
quality of the broth and the freshness of the eggs. If
you have heard that adding egg to soup is tricky, do
not worry; the eggs will scramble naturally in the boiling
broth, whichever way you combine them, so here is
the easy method. For serving the soup, bowls with lids
are useful, but not essential.*

INGREDIENTS

1.25 litres (2 pints) good clear meat or vegetable stock
1 tbsp soy sauce
salt and freshly ground black pepper, to taste
4 small eggs
2 spring onions, cut into thin rounds
4 drops of sesame oil, optional

PREPARATION

1 Heat the stock in a pan. Season well with the
soy sauce and salt and pepper, to taste, then simmer
for 5 minutes.
2 To serve, break one egg into each of the four
soup bowls and beat lightly with a fork or
chopsticks. Bring the stock to the boil, then pour
it on to the egg in each bowl, dividing it equally.
3 Divide the spring onions among the bowls; by
this time the egg will have floated to the surface of
the soup. Add 1 drop of sesame oil to each serving,
if using. If the soup bowls have lids, cover and leave
to stand for 1–2 minutes before serving.

RASAM

Vegetarian soup (India)

*In southern India, Rasam is served with some cooked rice
added at the end of cooking. However, it also makes a
one-dish vegetarian meal, with the rice served separately.
Everyone can help themselves to as much rice as they
want, and then ladle the soup over it. Serves 4–6.*

INGREDIENTS

250g (8oz) carrots, cut into thin rounds
250g (8oz) mooli (see page 20), peeled, cut into thin rounds
125g (4oz) water spinach (see page 21), or watercress
salt and freshly ground black pepper, to taste
125g (4oz) cooked long-grain rice (see page 156)
For the broth
2.5 litres (4 pints) water
30g (1oz) tamarind pulp (see page 30)
90g (3oz) red lentils, rinsed and drained
1 large tomato, quartered
1–2 large fresh green chillies, chopped
¼ tsp asafoetida (see page 30), optional
1 tsp salt

PREPARATION

1 Put all the ingredients for the broth in a large
pan. Bring to the boil, then simmer for about
1 hour. Remove from the heat and leave to cool a
little. Strain the broth through a sieve into another
pan and discard the solids.
2 Return the broth to the boil. Add the vegetables,
season to taste and simmer for 5 minutes. Add the
rice, simmer for 2 minutes, then serve immediately.

LAKSA LEMAK

Hot noodle soup with coconut milk (Malaysia)

The original Laksa Lemak is made with rice noodles or rice sticks, but in Europe, Australia and America, many Asian restaurants make it with Chinese-style egg noodles. Serves 8 as a soup or 4 as a one-dish meal. See page 72 for illustration.

INGREDIENTS

1 chicken, 1.5–1.75 kg (3–3½ lb), quartered
1.25 litres (2 pints) water
500g (1lb) raw king prawns, peeled and deveined (see page 82), shells rinsed and reserved
1 tsp salt, plus extra to taste
175–250g (6–8oz) rice vermicelli, or narrow ribbon rice noodles (see page 25), or egg noodles
600ml (1 pint) very thick coconut milk (see page 141)
freshly ground black pepper, to taste
For the paste
2–4 large fresh red chillies, deseeded and chopped
3 candle nuts (see page 22), or 5 blanched almonds, chopped
1cm (½in) piece of fresh ginger root, peeled and chopped
1cm (½in) piece of fresh galangal (see page 27), peeled and chopped
3 shallots, chopped
2 cloves garlic, chopped
1 tbsp coriander seeds, roughly crushed
2 tbsp tamarind water (see page 101)
2 tbsp groundnut oil or vegetable oil
For the garnish
125g (4oz) fresh beansprouts, rinsed and trimmed
3 tbsp diagonally sliced spring onions
125–175g (4–6oz) fried tofu (see page 24), thickly sliced, optional
Crisp-fried Onions (see page 132 for recipe), optional
1 red chilli, deseeded and finely chopped, optional

PREPARATION

1 Put all the paste ingredients into a blender and blend until as smooth as possible. Put the chicken and water in a pan, bring to the boil and boil gently for 20 minutes. Sprinkle the peeled prawns with half the salt, then cover and refrigerate.
2 Remove the chicken from the pan and transfer to a plate to cool. Take the meat off the bones, then return the bones and skin to the stock and simmer for 20 minutes more. Add the remaining salt. Cut the meat into bite-sized pieces and refrigerate.
3 Add the prawn shells to the stock and simmer for 10 minutes. Put the paste mixture into a large pan and cook, stirring frequently, for 4 minutes. Strain in the stock and simmer for 10 minutes.
4 Add the noodles to a large pan of boiling water.

Cover and leave to stand for 3–4 minutes. If using egg noodles, cook in boiling water for 3 minutes.
5 Transfer the noodles to a colander. Drain, rinse well under cold running water and drain again.
6 Bring the stock to the boil. Add the coconut milk and simmer for 8 minutes. Add the chicken, return to the boil and boil for 3 minutes. Add the prawns, then simmer for 3 minutes. Remove the pan from the heat and season to taste.
7 Divide the noodles and the first 3 garnishes between the serving bowls and ladle in the soup. Top with the Crisp-fried Onions and chilli, to serve.

KAI TOM KA

Chicken and galangal soup (Thailand)

Most Thai soups are hot and sour. This one, however, is different in that it is quite sweet and contains coconut milk. Serves 4–6.

INGREDIENTS

250g (8oz) baby button mushrooms, halved or whole
3 tbsp lime juice
1 tbsp fish sauce (nam pla), (see page 28)
1 tsp chilli oil, optional
salt and freshly ground black pepper, to taste
125ml (4fl oz) very thick coconut milk (see page 141)
handful of fresh Thai basil leaves (see page 26)
For the stock
2–3 large chicken breasts on the bone
2 litres (3 pints) cold water
2 stems of fresh lemongrass, each cut into 3 pieces
5cm (2in) piece of fresh galangal (see page 27), halved
3 fresh kaffir lime leaves (see page 26)
1 medium onion, sliced
1–2 large fresh red chillies, halved
1 tsp salt

PREPARATION

1 Put all the ingredients for the stock in a large pan and bring to the boil. Boil gently for 15 minutes, skimming off the froth as necessary.
2 Remove the chicken from the pan and transfer to a plate to cool. Take the meat off the bones, then return the skin and bones to the stock and simmer for 35–40 minutes more. Cut the meat into small bite-sized pieces and set aside.
3 Strain the stock through a fine sieve into another pan and discard the solids. Return the stock to the boil. Add the mushrooms, lime juice, fish sauce and the chilli oil, if using, and simmer for 3 minutes. Add the chicken pieces.
4 Season the soup, to taste, then stir in the coconut milk. Simmer for 3 minutes, stirring several times. Add the fresh basil leaves and serve immediately.

SNACKS & APPETIZERS

Throughout Asia there is almost no distinction between snacks, appetizers, starters and regular meals. Asians developed the art of "grazing" long ago, and they practise it at every culinary level from the simplest snack to the most elaborate and refined delicacy. Spring rolls and dim sum, for example, are some of the most exquisite mouthfuls ever invented. However, I have noticed that the Japanese differ from the rest of us in one respect – they never eat in the street.

PATTIES

Small filled pies (Sri Lanka)

These patties can be frozen successfully. Makes 25–30 patties. See page 35 for illustration.

INGREDIENTS

about 450ml (¾ pint) groundnut oil for deep-frying
For the pastry
375g (12oz) shortcrust pastry
or
375g (12oz) plain flour, plus extra for rolling pastry
large pinch of salt
1 egg yolk, lightly beaten
4 tbsp melted butter
90ml (6 tbsp) thick coconut milk (see page 141)
For the filling
125–175g (4–6oz) boned and skinned chicken breast
125g (4oz) lamb fillet, in one piece
125g (4oz) pork fillet, in one piece
½ tsp salt, plus extra to taste
1 tbsp vegetable oil
1 medium red onion, finely sliced
4 rashers of rindless streaky bacon, finely diced
1 tsp ground coriander
½ tsp ground cumin
½ tsp ground turmeric
¼ tsp chilli powder
large pinch each of ground cloves and cinnamon
seeds of 1 green cardamom pod
3cm (1½in) piece of fresh lemongrass, bruised
3 fresh or dried curry leaves (see page 26), optional
125ml (4fl oz) thick coconut milk (see page 141)
freshly ground black pepper, to taste
3 eggs, hard-boiled, peeled and roughly chopped

PREPARATION

1 If making the pastry, put the flour, salt, egg, butter and coconut milk in a food processor and process until well combined into a soft dough.

Wrap the dough in clingfilm and refrigerate for 30 minutes while preparing the filling.
2 For the filling, put the chicken, lamb and pork in a pan. Cover with water and add the salt. Bring to the boil and boil gently for 30 minutes. Remove the meat from the pan and leave to cool. (The stock can be used for another dish.)
3 When the meat is cold, put it through the fine disc of a mincer, or chop finely by hand with a cleaver or cook's knife. Set aside in a cool place.
4 Heat the vegetable oil in a wok or pan. Add the onion and fry for 2 minutes, stirring continuously. Add the bacon and cook, stirring, for 1 minute. Add the minced meat, all the ground spices, the cardamom seeds, lemongrass and curry leaves, if using. Cook, stirring, for 1 minute.
5 Add the coconut milk and cook for 10 minutes, or until all the milk is absorbed. Season to taste, then transfer the filling to a bowl to cool. Discard the lemongrass and curry leaves and add the eggs.
6 Remove the pastry from the refrigerator and leave to stand for few minutes, to soften slightly. Roll out the pastry on a floured board until it is very thin. Cut the pastry into about 20 rounds using an 8cm (3½in) pastry cutter. Re-roll the trimmings and cut out a further 5–10 rounds. Discard the leftovers.
7 To fill the patties, take one round of pastry and put a heaped teaspoonful of filling in the centre. Fold the pastry over into a half-moon shape, to enclose the filling, and seal the edges with your fingers, and then with a dampened fork. Fill the remaining patties in the same way.
8 Heat the groundnut oil in a deep-fat fryer or wok to 180°C (350°F). Add 4 or 5 patties to the hot oil and fry for 4–5 minutes, rocking them frequently with a slotted spoon, until golden brown.
9 Remove the patties from the pan and drain on kitchen paper. Cook the remaining patties in batches, then serve hot, warm or cold.

KUNG THORD

Marinated and fried prawns (Thailand)

Serve these prawns the moment you finish frying them.
They are equally good served as an appetizer or with
drinks, but they must be piping hot.

INGREDIENTS

16 raw king prawns, peeled and deveined (see page 82)
about 450ml (¾ pint) groundnut oil for deep-frying
For the marinade
60g (2oz) creamed coconut, chopped
175ml (6fl oz) hot water
2.5cm (1in) piece of fresh galangal (see page 27),
peeled and chopped
5cm (2in) piece of fresh lemongrass, outer leaves
removed, centre chopped
4 fresh coriander roots or stems, chopped
2 shallots, chopped
3 cloves garlic, chopped
2–4 small dried chillies, chopped
1 tbsp lime juice
1 tsp salt or 1 tbsp fish sauce (nam pla), (see page 28)
2 tsp rice powder (see page 31), or plain flour

PREPARATION

1 Put all the marinade ingredients, except the rice
powder or plain flour, in a blender and blend until
as smooth as possible. Transfer the mixture to a
glass bowl and leave to cool. Stir in the rice
powder or plain flour.
2 Add the king prawns to the marinade and stir
until they are thoroughly coated. Cover and
refrigerate for 1–2 hours, to marinate.
3 Heat the oil in a deep-fat fryer or a wok to
180°C (350°F). Drain the marinated prawns in a
colander, discarding the marinade. Add half the
prawns to the hot oil and fry for 2–3 minutes.
4 Remove the prawns from the pan with a slotted
spoon and drain on kitchen paper. Keep the prawns
hot in a warm oven while the second batch is fried,
then serve immediately.

SHUEN GUEN
Spring rolls (China)

The spring roll has been a popular Chinese snack for centuries. Today, almost every Asian country has its own version. This recipe uses a vegetarian filling. Makes 20 rolls. See page 34 for illustration.

INGREDIENTS

20 medium frozen spring roll wrappers (see page 25), 21–24cm (8–9in) square, defrosted
1 egg white, lightly beaten
about 450ml (¾ pint) vegetable oil for deep-frying
For the filling
3 tbsp groundnut oil or vegetable oil
500g (1lb) carrots, cut into thin strips
125g (4oz) white cabbage, finely shredded
200g (7oz) canned sliced bamboo shoots (drained weight), rinsed and cut into thin sticks
375g (12oz) mangetout or French beans, thinly sliced on the diagonal
8–10 dried shiitake mushrooms, rehydrated (see page 155), stalks removed and caps thinly sliced
250g (8oz) button mushrooms, thinly sliced
2 tsp finely chopped fresh ginger root
3 tbsp light soy sauce
175g (6oz) cellophane noodles (see page 25), soaked in hot water for 5 minutes, drained and cut into short lengths with scissors
6–8 spring onions, cut into thin rounds
salt and freshly ground black pepper, to taste

PREPARATION

1 For the filling, heat the oil in a wok. Add the carrots, cabbage and bamboo shoots and stir-fry for 2 minutes. Add the mangetout or French beans, both types of mushroom, the ginger and soy sauce, and stir-fry for 3 minutes.
2 Add the noodles and spring onions and stir-fry rapidly for 2 minutes, until the liquid evaporates but the vegetables are still moist. Season to taste, then remove from the wok and leave to cool.
3 Place one spring roll wrapper on a flat surface. Put 2 tablespoons of the cold filling on the corner nearest you. Flatten the filling a little, then roll the corner of the wrapper over it, towards the centre.
4 Fold in the two side flaps. Brush the far corner of the wrapper with a little of the egg white and continue rolling to make a well-sealed parcel. Repeat with the remaining filling and wrappers.
5 Heat the oil in a deep-fat fryer or wok to 180°C (350°F). Add 4 spring rolls, lower the heat a little, and deep-fry for 6–8 minutes, turning them several times, until golden. Remove from the wok with a slotted spoon and drain on kitchen paper.

6 Keep the spring rolls hot in a warm oven while the remaining batches are fried, then serve at once. Alternatively, leave the cooked rolls until cold, then briefly re-fry in hot oil just before serving.
7 The cooked spring rolls can be frozen for up to 4 weeks. To serve, heat the oil to 150°C (300°F) and deep-fry the frozen rolls for 6–8 minutes until the filling is heated through and the wrapper is crisp. If the oil is too hot, the outside will blister and bubble before the filling is hot.

PERGEDEL JAGUNG
Sweetcorn fritters (Indonesia)

These fritters can be refrigerated for 2 days or frozen for up to 4 weeks. Defrost them completely, then reheat gently in a non-stick frying pan for 1–2 minutes. Makes 20–25 fritters. See page 34 for illustration.

INGREDIENTS

4 fresh corn cobs, or 475g (15oz) canned sweetcorn (drained weight)
4 tbsp groundnut oil
5 shallots, finely sliced
2 tbsp chopped spring onions
1 tsp ground coriander
½ tsp chilli powder
1 tsp baking powder
3 tbsp rice powder (see page 31), or plain flour
1 tsp salt, plus extra to taste
1 large egg, lightly beaten
about 150ml (¼ pint) vegetable oil for frying

PREPARATION

1 To prepare the fresh corn on the cob, use a sharp knife to slice away the kernels close to the woody cob. Crush the fresh corn kernels or canned sweetcorn using a pestle and mortar.
2 Heat half the groundnut oil in a pan, add the shallots and fry for 4 minutes, stirring frequently, until softened but not browned. Remove from the heat and leave to cool.
3 Transfer the corn to a bowl. Stir in the shallots and all the remaining ingredients, except the oil for frying, and mix well. Add extra salt, if necessary.
4 Heat 75–90ml (5–6 tablespoons) of the vegetable oil in a frying pan. Drop a tablespoonful of the fritter mixture into the hot oil and flatten it with a fork. Continue until there are 5 or 6 fritters in the pan. Fry for about 3 minutes on each side, turning them only once.
5 Repeat the process until all the mixture is used, adding more oil to the pan after 2 or 3 batches. Serve the fritters hot or cold.

SAMOSA

Pastries with vegetable filling (India)

This classic Indian snack is now familiar almost everywhere. Samosa are very easy to make, especially when, as in this recipe, ready-made spring roll wrappers are used. The filling can be made of meat, either lamb or beef, or vegetables. Makes about 30 samosa.

INGREDIENTS

10 large frozen spring roll wrappers (see page 25), 28–30cm (11–12in) square, defrosted
1 egg, beaten
about 450ml (¾ pint) vegetable oil for deep-frying
For the filling
2 tbsp ghee (see page 29), or vegetable oil
6 shallots or 1 large onion, finely chopped
2 cloves garlic, finely chopped, optional
1cm (½in) piece of fresh ginger root, peeled and chopped
1 tbsp ground coriander
1 tsp ground cumin
½ tsp ground turmeric
¼ tsp chilli powder or freshly ground black pepper
pinch of grated nutmeg
pinch of ground cloves
4 medium potatoes, cut into medium dice
8 medium carrots, cut into medium dice
60–90ml (2–3fl oz) water
1 tsp salt, plus extra to taste
freshly ground black pepper, to taste
3 tbsp chopped spring onions
2 tbsp chopped fresh mint leaves

PREPARATION

1 Cut each spring roll wrapper into 3 equal strips with a pair of scissors. Pile the strips on top of each other, then wrap in a damp tea towel to prevent them from drying out. Refrigerate the wrappers while preparing the filling.

2 For the filling, heat the ghee or vegetable oil in a wok or pan. Add the shallots or onion, garlic and ginger and fry, stirring continuously, for 2 minutes. Add all the ground spices and cook, stirring, for a few seconds. Add the diced potatoes and carrots and cook, stirring frequently, for 2 minutes.

3 Add the water and salt to the pan, cover, and simmer, stirring occasionally, for 8–10 minutes. Season to taste, add the spring onions and mint, and cook, stirring, for 1 minute. The filling should still be moist. Transfer the mixture to a bowl and leave to cool.

4 Using one strip of spring roll wrapper at a time, make up the samosa, stuffing each one with a dessertspoon of filling (see steps below). It is important to seal the edges of the parcels well so that when the samosa are fried, oil cannot seep into the filling.

5 When all the filling is used up, heat the vegetable oil in a deep-fat fryer or a wok to 180°C (350°F). Add 3 or 4 samosa at a time and fry for 5–6 minutes, rocking them frequently with a slotted spoon, until they are golden brown.

6 Remove the samosa from the pan with the slotted spoon. Drain well on kitchen paper and keep warm in a hot oven while the remaining batches are fried. Serve hot or warm.

FOLDING & FILLING A SAMOSA

1 Take one strip of spring roll wrapper at a time and wrap the rest in a damp tea towel. Fold over one corner of the wrapper at a 30° angle and brush it with a little of the beaten egg.

2 Turn the folded edge over again to line up with one side of the strip. Press the edge that has been brushed with egg to seal the wrapper at the side so that it forms a pocket.

3 Put a dessertspoon of filling into the pocket. Place the wrapper on the work surface and fold the pocket over the remaining dough, brushing the edge with egg to seal.

SATE PUSUT

Minced fish on skewers (Indonesia)

These satay need no extra sauce – they are spicy enough already. Makes 16 satay. See page 45 for illustration.

INGREDIENTS

salt and freshly ground black pepper, to taste
750g (1½ lb) cod fillet or filleted monkfish tail
3 tbsp chopped spring onions or chives
1 egg white, lightly beaten
For the marinade
4 shallots, chopped
2 cloves garlic, chopped
2 candle nuts (see page 22), or 4 blanched almonds, roughly chopped
2 cloves
1cm (½in) piece of cinnamon stick
¼ tsp grated nutmeg
1 tsp dried shrimp paste (see page 31)
1 tsp sugar
¼ tsp ground turmeric
5cm (2in) piece of fresh lemongrass, outer leaves removed, centre chopped
1 fresh kaffir lime leaf (see page 26), shredded
2 tbsp water
2 tbsp lemon or lime juice
2 tbsp groundnut oil or vegetable oil

PREPARATION

1 Put all the ingredients for the marinade into a blender and blend until as smooth as possible. Transfer the mixture to a pan and simmer, stirring frequently, for 4–5 minutes. Season to taste, then remove from the heat and leave to cool.
2 Chop the cod or monkfish finely with a sharp knife. Transfer to a glass bowl and add the spring onions or chives, the egg white and cold marinade mixture. Mix together well, then refrigerate for at least 2 hours or, if possible, overnight.
3 Shape the fish mixture into balls, each the size of a walnut. To thread on to skewers, hold a fishball in the palm of your hand, then push 2 bamboo skewers or a lemongrass stalk through the middle of the fishball. Form the fishball into a sausage shape around the skewers. Repeat with the remaining fishballs.
4 Grill the satay over charcoal, or under a preheated hot grill, for 2 minutes on each side, then serve immediately.

CHAO TOM

Skewered prawnballs and prawns (Vietnam)

Traditionally prawn paste is skewered on to a sugar cane stick, but this is my adaptation. Serve with Nuoc Cham or Peanut Sauce (see pages 128 and 130 for recipes). Makes 8 skewers. See page 45 for illustration.

INGREDIENTS

32 raw medium prawns, peeled and deveined (see page 82), tails left whole
salt and freshly ground black pepper, to taste
2 tbsp sesame seeds
2 tbsp white breadcrumbs
½ tsp each of chilli oil and sesame oil
1 tbsp groundnut oil
For the prawn paste
500g (1lb) raw prawns, peeled and deveined (see page 82)
1 egg white
½ tsp salt
½ tsp sugar
¼ tsp ground black pepper
60g (2oz) pork fat, chopped, optional
2 tsp rice powder (see page 31), or potato flour
2 cloves garlic, finely chopped
1 tsp finely chopped fresh ginger root
1 tsp fish sauce (nuoc mam), (see page 28)

PREPARATION

1 Rub the medium prawns with some salt and pepper and set aside.
2 To make the paste, process the raw prawns, egg white, salt, sugar and pepper in a food processor until smooth. Add the remaining paste ingredients and process until well mixed. Transfer the mixture to a bowl, cover, and refrigerate for 1 hour.
3 Combine the sesame seeds and breadcrumbs on a flat plate. Divide the prawn paste into 24 portions. Roll each portion in the sesame and breadcrumb mixture, shaping it into a ball.
4 Thread the whole prawns and the prawnballs alternately on to 8 skewers, allowing 4 prawns and 3 prawnballs per skewer. Arrange the skewers on a well-oiled baking tray and cook in an oven preheated to 200°C/400°F/Gas 6 for 10 minutes.
5 Mix the chilli oil and sesame oil with the groundnut oil. Transfer the skewers to a grill pan and cook under a preheated grill for 2 minutes on each side, brushing with the oil mixture as you turn them. Serve the Chao Tom immediately.

SATAY DAGING
Skewered beef (Malaysia)

Serve Satay Daging with Peanut Sauce or Nuoc Cham (see pages 130 and 128 for recipes). Makes 18 satay. See page 44 for illustration.

INGREDIENTS

1kg (2lb) rump steak or topside, cut into 2.5cm (1in) cubes
For the marinade
3 shallots, finely sliced
2 cloves garlic, crushed
5cm (2in) piece of fresh ginger root, peeled and finely chopped
1 tbsp coriander seeds, roasted (see page 155), and roughly crushed
1 tsp ground cumin
½ tsp chilli powder
½ tsp coarsely ground black pepper
2 tbsp light soy sauce
1 tbsp groundnut oil
1 tbsp distilled white vinegar or lemon juice
½ tsp salt
1 tsp grated palm sugar (see page 30), or demerara sugar

PREPARATION

1 Mix all the ingredients for the marinade in a glass bowl. Add the cubes of beef and stir well to coat. Cover and refrigerate for at least 2 hours or, if possible, overnight.
2 Thread the meat on to 18 skewers, allowing 3 or 4 pieces per skewer. Cook the satay over charcoal, or under a preheated hot grill, for 8 minutes, turning them several times. Serve immediately.

PORK SATAY
Skewered pork (Singapore)

Here, a piece of pork fat is placed between the cubed meat on each skewer to give additional flavour. Serve with Peanut Sauce (see page 130 for recipe). Makes 18 satay. See page 45 for illustration.

INGREDIENTS

1kg (2lb) pork fillet or leg meat, cut into pieces not more than 1cm (½in) long and 2.5cm (1in) wide
125g (4oz) thick pork fat, cut into pieces not more than 1cm (½in) long and 2.5cm (1in) wide
For the marinade
4 cloves garlic, crushed
1 tsp ground black pepper
1 tsp ground Szechuan pepper
2 tsp five-spice powder (see page 27)
2 tbsp each of light soy sauce and clear honey
¼ tsp salt

PREPARATION

1 Mix all the ingredients for the marinade in a glass bowl. Add the pieces of meat and stir well to coat. Cover and refrigerate overnight.
2 Thread the meat and fat on to 18 bamboo or metal skewers, allowing about 5 pieces of meat and 1 or 2 pieces of fat per skewer. Place the fat between the meat and pack them tightly together.
3 Arrange the satay on a rack set over a roasting pan. Cook in an oven preheated to 180°C/350°F/ Gas 4 for 30 minutes, then turn the satay over and cook for 20 minutes. Brown under a hot grill for 3–4 minutes, if necessary, then serve immediately.

YAKITORI
Skewered chicken (Japan)

The glaze for the chicken doubles as a dipping sauce. Makes 8 skewers. See page 44 for illustration.

INGREDIENTS

2 boned and skinned chicken breasts and 4 boned and skinned thighs, cut into 2cm (¾in) cubes
4 spring onions, stems only, cut into 2cm (¾in) pieces
For the glaze/sauce
4 tbsp dark soy sauce
2 tbsp mirin (see page 29)
2 tbsp sake (see page 29)
1 tbsp sugar
1 tbsp tamari soy sauce (see page 28)
¼ tsp salt
400ml (14fl oz) water

PREPARATION

1 For the glaze, mix half the dark soy sauce with half the mirin, sake, sugar, tamari soy sauce and salt in a glass bowl. Blend in 120ml (4fl oz) of the water.
2 Thread the cubes of chicken and pieces of spring onion on to 8 short bamboo or wooden skewers, allowing about 3 or 4 pieces of meat and 2 pieces of spring onion per skewer.
3 For the sauce, mix the remaining dark soy sauce, mirin, sake, sugar, tamari soy sauce, salt and water together in a pan. Simmer for 10 minutes, then remove from the heat and transfer the sauce to a serving bowl.
4 Pour the glaze on to a flat plate, and turn the skewered chicken in it, to coat well. Cook the Yakitori over charcoal, or under a preheated grill, for 5–6 minutes, turning them several times. Serve immediately with the sauce.

TEMPURA
Mixed seafood and vegetables deep-fried in batter (Japan)

Deep-frying in batter is a traditional method of cooking in many countries. Although this recipe is Japanese, some Japanese cookery experts believe that it originally came from the West.

INGREDIENTS

1 small purple aubergine, halved across, each half cut into 8 segments lengthways
1 medium red onion, cut into 8 rings
1 red or yellow pepper, deseeded and cut into 10 pieces
8 raw medium prawns, peeled and deveined (see page 82)
2 medium squid, cleaned and each cut into 8 rings (see page 150), tentacles discarded
125g (4oz) skinned lemon sole fillet, cut into 8 pieces
about 450ml (¾ pint) sunflower oil for deep-frying
For the batter
2 egg yolks
475ml (16fl oz) ice-cold water
500g (1lb) plain flour
pinch of salt
For the dipping sauce
4 tbsp light soy sauce
4 tbsp mirin (see page 29)
125ml (4fl oz) bonito stock (see page 30)
2 tsp finely chopped fresh ginger root

PREPARATION

1 Dry the pieces of vegetables and seafood thoroughly with kitchen paper.

2 Prepare the batter a half quantity at a time. Put one egg yolk into a bowl and beat it lightly with a fork. Pour in half the ice-cold water and whisk lightly. Sift in half the flour and salt and stir lightly with a fork or a pair of chopsticks. Do not beat the batter – it is supposed to be lumpy.

3 Heat the oil in a deep-fat fryer or wok to 180°C (350°F). Dip the vegetables, one piece at a time, into the batter, then plunge into the hot oil until 4 or 5 pieces are frying together. Cook for 2–3 minutes, then remove with a slotted spoon and drain on kitchen paper. Keep warm while the remaining vegetables are battered and fried.

4 In a clean bowl, make the second batch of batter with the remaining ingredients. Dip half the prawns into the batter and fry for 2–3 minutes, turning them with the slotted spoon as they cook.

5 Drain the prawns on kitchen paper and keep warm with the vegetables. Repeat with the remaining prawns. Coat and fry the squid and fish in two batches each, then drain and keep warm.

Red pepper

Red onion

Aubergine

Prawns   *Squid*   *Lemon sole*

6 Put all the ingredients for the dipping sauce, except the ginger, in a small pan. Bring to the boil, then simmer for 2 minutes. Add the ginger, stir once, then transfer to a small bowl. Serve immediately with the Tempura.

Mirin

Egg yolks

Plain
flour

Salt

Light soy sauce

Bonito
stock

Fresh ginger

Sunflower oil

SIU MAI

Steamed wonton with prawns and pork
(Singapore)

When making these dim sum it is essential to buy wonton wrappers that are made for steaming – they are slightly thicker than those for deep-frying. Serve as an appetizer or as part of a dim sum lunch. Makes 20–24.

INGREDIENTS

175–250g (6–8oz) wonton wrappers for steaming (see page 25), defrosted if frozen
For the filling
375g (12oz) raw prawns, peeled and deveined (see page 82), chopped
250g (8oz) minced pork
1 tsp salt
90g (3oz) fresh shiitake mushrooms or button mushrooms, chopped
6 canned water chestnuts, chopped
2 tsp light soy sauce
1 tsp sugar
2 tbsp finely chopped spring onions
¼ tsp freshly ground black or white pepper
1 egg white, lightly beaten

PREPARATION

1 For the filling, put the chopped prawns, minced pork and salt in a bowl and knead together with your hands until well mixed.
2 Add the remaining filling ingredients and mix well with a wooden spoon. Cover and refrigerate for 30 minutes, or longer, if possible.
3 To fill the wonton wrappers, using scissors snip off a little from the corners of each wrapper.
4 Put 1 tablespoon of the filling in the centre of each wrapper and gather up the edges to make a bag. Lift it on to your hand, then squeeze gently in the middle as if to form the neck of a bag.
5 Open the bag at the top and press the filling down with a dampened teaspoon, to flatten the top. Continue until all the wrappers are filled.
6 To cook the Siu Mai, steam them in batches in a bamboo steamer (see page 149), or in an ordinary steamer, for 8–10 minutes per batch.
7 Alternatively, if you do not have a steamer, arrange some of the Siu Mai on an oiled plate. Set a trivet or a soup plate upside down in the bottom of a large pan and add enough hot water to reach the top of it. Stand the plate of Siu Mai on top. Bring the water to the boil, cover the pan and cook for 12–15 minutes.
8 Serve the Siu Mai hot or warm, accompanied by a spicy dipping sauce such as chilli sauce (see page 28), if desired.

REMPAH-REMPAH

Prawn and beansprout fritters (Malaysia)

Serve these fritters as a snack with drinks. Makes about 20 fritters. See page 34 for illustration.

INGREDIENTS

about 450ml (¾ pint) vegetable oil for deep-frying
20 small raw prawns, peeled and deveined (see page 82)
For the fritters
250g (8oz) raw prawns, peeled and deveined (see page 82), chopped
250g (8oz) fresh beansprouts, rinsed and trimmed
125g (4oz) rice powder (see page 31), or plain flour
2 tsp baking powder
1 tsp ground coriander
pinch of ground turmeric
2 fresh red chillies, deseeded and finely chopped
4 spring onions, finely sliced
1 tsp light soy sauce
1 tsp salt
2 eggs, beaten

PREPARATION

1 Put all the ingredients for the fritters in a glass bowl and mix together well with a spoon.
2 Heat the oil in a deep-fat fryer or wok to 180°C (350°F). Take a tablespoonful of the fritter mixture, place a whole prawn on top of it, then flatten it in your hands so that the whole prawn is set into the top of the fritter. Repeat the process with the remaining mixture and prawns.
3 Put 4 or 5 fritters into the hot oil and deep-fry for 3 minutes. Remove from the pan with a slotted spoon and drain on kitchen paper. Keep warm while the remaining batches are fried. Serve the fritters warm or cold.

SUSHI

Rice rolls (Japan)

The Japanese use a bamboo rolling mat (see page 149) to make rolled sushi, but a double thickness of foil will work equally well. Make the sushi as close to serving time as possible since they only keep fresh for 1–2 hours. Makes 16–24 sushi and serves 4–6. See page 35 for illustration.

INGREDIENTS

For the rice

500g (1lb) short-grain Japanese rice (see page 24), washed in several changes of water and left to drain for 30 minutes
500ml (16fl oz) cold water
300–375g (10–12oz) sliced smoked salmon
1 thin cucumber, halved lengthways and deseeded, each half cut lengthways into 4 strips

For the dressing

4 tbsp rice vinegar (see page 29)
2 tbsp caster sugar
1 tbsp hot water
½–1 tsp salt

PREPARATION

1 Put the rice and water in a heavy-based pan. Bring to the boil and boil, uncovered, for about 10 minutes, until all the water is absorbed. Stir once with a wooden spoon, then reduce the heat to minimum. Cover the pan and leave the rice to cook undisturbed for 10–12 minutes.

2 Remove the pan from the heat and leave to stand, still covered, on a wet tea towel for 5 minutes. Transfer the rice to a wooden, ceramic or glass bowl and leave to cool for a few minutes.

3 Mix the dressing ingredients together in a small glass bowl, then pour over the rice, a little at a time, and mix in gently. Do not stir the rice vigorously; the action should be like gently tossing a salad. Taste the rice as you add the dressing – you may not need all of it. Cover the bowl with a damp tea towel and set aside in a cool place.

4 Line a bamboo rolling mat, or a double thickness of foil, about 24cm (10in) square, with clingfilm. Divide the rice and smoked salmon slices into 4 equal portions.

5 Arrange a quarter of the smoked salmon on the rolling mat or foil, top with a quarter of the rice, then arrange 2 strips of cucumber on top and roll up (see steps below).

6 Remove the rolled sushi from the mat or foil and keep wrapped in the clingfilm. Repeat the rolling process with the remaining rice portions and smoked salmon. Refrigerate the rolls for 10 minutes before serving.

7 To serve, remove the clingfilm from the sushi and cut each roll across into 4–6 slices. Arrange on a plate and serve immediately.

ROLLING SUSHI

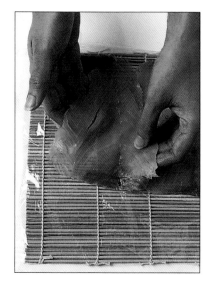

1 Arrange a quarter of the smoked salmon slices, with the long sides running top-to-bottom, to cover about half the length of the mat, but almost its full width. Leave about a 1cm (½in) margin on either side.

2 Spread one portion of the seasoned rice over the smoked salmon to cover all but a narrow strip along the furthest edge. Level the rice by pressing it lightly with the back of a fork to give an even layer.

3 Place 2 strips of cucumber across the rice. Using the mat or foil as a guide, roll up the sushi away from you into a compact sausage, making sure the clingfilm and the mat or foil are not rolled into the centre of the rice.

INDONESIA & MALAYSIA

Strong flavours, delicately balanced and blended; textures that range from crunchy to chewy, crisp to soft; the subtle use of sourness and the tang of hot chillies – all these bring to life the cooking of Indonesia and Malaysia.

LAKSA LEMAK
Malaysian hot noodle soup with coconut milk. (See page 61 for recipe.)

RUJAK
Indonesian hot,
spicy fruit salad.
(See page 137
for recipe.)

**OSENG OSENG AYAM
DENGAN SAYURAN**
Indonesian stir-fried chicken
with vegetables. (See page
86 for recipe.)

NASI KUNING
Malaysian savoury
yellow rice. (See
page 126 for
recipe.)

FISH & SEAFOOD

F ish is a staple food of almost all Asian countries, whether from the deep ocean or the village pond. To the cook it offers opportunities and a challenge. Luckily, most fish recipes can be made with a variety of different species; the important thing is to buy the freshest available, particularly if the dish is to be eaten raw or lightly cooked. Short cooking times are typical of these recipes – prawns and scallops, for example, become very tough if overdone. The flavours of Asian fish cookery are clear and emphatic, and the balance of herbs, spices and seasoning is vital.

PEPES IKAN

Marinated fish baked with coconut (Indonesia)

A classic Javanese dish, Pepes Ikan is now an acknowledged Indonesian speciality, cooked everywhere with regional variations. Needless to say, in Indonesia we prefer to cook it wrapped in banana leaves. A good alternative is to use a circle of greaseproof paper as the wrapper and cook "en papillote".

INGREDIENTS

4 tbsp tamarind water (see page 101)
½ tsp salt, plus extra to taste
2 cloves garlic, finely chopped
¼ tsp chilli powder
4 double fillets of trout, 175–200g (6–7oz) each, or 4 boned and skinned fish steaks
3 tbsp groundnut oil
4 shallots, finely sliced
2–4 large fresh red chillies, deseeded and finely sliced
1 tsp ground coriander
2 tsp chopped fresh ginger root
½ stem of fresh lemongrass, outer leaves removed, centre chopped
handful of fresh mint leaves
125–175g (4–6oz) grated fresh coconut (see page 133), or 125g (4oz) desiccated coconut soaked in 125ml (4fl oz) warm water for 5 minutes
freshly ground black pepper, to taste
fresh banana leaves (see page 20), or greaseproof paper

PREPARATION

1 Combine the tamarind water, salt, garlic and chilli powder in a bowl. Add the fish fillets or steaks and turn until well coated. Cover and leave to marinate in a cool place for 1 hour.
2 Remove the fish from the marinade and transfer to a plate. Reserve the marinade.
3 Heat the oil in a large shallow pan. Add the shallots and chillies, and stir-fry for 2–3 minutes. Stir in the coriander, ginger, lemongrass and mint leaves. Simmer for 1 minute.
4 Add the grated fresh coconut, or the soaked desiccated coconut with the soaking water, and simmer, stirring frequently, for 6–8 minutes. Add the marinade and cook, stirring frequently, for 1 minute. Season to taste, then add the fish. Stir, cover the pan and remove from the heat.
5 Cut the banana leaf into four 30cm (12in) squares, or cut greaseproof paper into four 30cm (12in) circles. Place one piece of fish in the centre of each square or circle and divide the coconut mixture between them, spreading it over the fish.
6 Fold the banana leaf over to make a parcel and secure with bamboo skewers at either end. Alternatively, fold the paper in half and tightly fold the edges together, to seal.
7 Place the parcels on a baking tray and bake in an oven preheated to 180°C/350°F/Gas 4 for 15–20 minutes, until the fish is cooked through. Serve the parcels sealed, allowing diners to open their own.

PATRANI MACHCHI

Baked fish wrapped in banana leaves (India)

This is the Indian version of what the people of Java call Pepes Ikan (see opposite). I would not be surprised if this is another of the many dishes that have travelled from Persia via India to Indonesia. Serve with vegetables of your choice and rice. See page 134 for illustration.

INGREDIENTS

4 fillets of plaice or turbot, 150–175g (5–6oz) each
½ tsp salt
juice of 1 small lemon
4 tbsp grated fresh coconut (see page 133),
or 3 tbsp desiccated coconut
3 tbsp finely chopped fresh coriander leaves
fresh banana leaves (see page 20), or foil
For the paste
1 tbsp coriander seeds, roasted (see page 155),
roughly crushed
1 tsp cumin seeds, roasted (see page 155), roughly crushed
2 cloves garlic, chopped
2 tsp white poppy seeds (see page 23), roughly crushed
2 tbsp tamarind water (see page 101),
or distilled white vinegar
1 tsp sugar
1 fresh green and 1 red chilli, deseeded and chopped
2 tbsp groundnut oil
½ tsp salt, plus extra to taste

PREPARATION

1 Rub the fish fillets all over with the salt and lemon juice, and leave to stand in a cool place for 30 minutes.
2 Put all the paste ingredients into a blender and blend until as smooth as possible. Transfer the paste mixture to a bowl and stir in the grated fresh or desiccated coconut and the fresh coriander leaves. Add more salt, if necessary.
3 If using banana leaves, cut them to cover a large piece of foil about 40cm (16in) square. Alternatively, just use a double layer of foil. Arrange the fish fillets in a single layer on top of the leaves or foil and rub each piece well, on both sides, with the paste mixture.
4 Fold the banana leaves and foil over the fillets to enclose them, securing the banana leaves with bamboo skewers and turning the edges of the foil over to seal and make a loose parcel. Put the parcel directly on a shelf of an oven preheated to 190°C/375°F/Gas 5 and bake for 15–20 minutes.
5 Unwrap the parcel and transfer the fish, along with the cooking juices, to a large flameproof dish. Place under a preheated hot grill for 2–3 minutes, to lightly brown the tops, then serve immediately.

LACHAP LONGLEI GUIN

Deep-fried sole with chilli bean sauce and asparagus (China)

I watched chef Simon Yung of the Dorchester Hotel, London, prepare this classic Cantonese dish. Naturally, as a professional chef, his presentation is impressive, with the fish skeleton formed into a boat shape and deep-fried until crisp. Making it at home, I use only the fish fillet. Serves 2 as a main course or 4 as an appetizer.

INGREDIENTS

2 skinned Dover sole fillets, each 250–300g (8–10oz),
each cut into 4 thin slices on the diagonal (see page 150)
1 tsp light soy sauce
few drops of sesame oil
4 large fresh shiitake mushrooms or chestnut mushrooms,
stalks removed and caps sliced
30g (1oz) canned sliced bamboo shoots, cut into fine
julienne strips (see page 154)
30g (1oz) carrot, cut into fine julienne strips
(see page 154)
3 spring onions, cut into 2cm (¾in) lengths
2 tsp cornflour
salt and freshly ground black pepper, to taste
about 300ml (½ pint) vegetable oil for deep-frying
6 asparagus spears, about 7cm (3in) long
2 tbsp chopped fresh coriander leaves, to garnish
For the sauce
2 tbsp chilli bean sauce
¼ green pepper, deseeded and finely diced
1 clove garlic, crushed and finely chopped
1–2 tsp rice vinegar (see page 29)
3 tbsp hot water

PREPARATION

1 Sprinkle the fish slices with the soy sauce and sesame oil. Divide the mushrooms, bamboo shoots, carrot and spring onions into 8 equal portions and arrange each portion on a slice of fish. Roll up each slice with the vegetables inside.
2 Sprinkle some of the cornflour and a little salt and pepper over each roll and rub it in gently. The cornflour helps to seal the rolls.
3 Mix the sauce ingredients in a small pan. Heat the oil in a wok until very hot. Add the fish rolls and fry for 2 minutes only. Remove the rolls from the wok with a slotted spoon. Transfer to a heated serving platter and keep warm.
4 Heat the sauce in the pan and, at the same time, fry the asparagus in the wok for 10 seconds. Remove the asparagus from the wok and drain on kitchen paper. Pour the hot sauce over the fish rolls and arrange the asparagus around it. Sprinkle with the coriander, to garnish, then serve immediately.

PLEA TRAY
Fish salad (Cambodia)

*Every Asian community seems to have its own favourite
fish salad, and if life were longer it would be fascinating
to travel around and collect all of them. Luckily, all the
ones I have found so far, including this one by Rosine Ek
of Chez Rosine Cuisine du Cambodge, Paris, can be made
with fish that are readily available in the West
without losing the flavour of Asia.*

INGREDIENTS
4 tbsp fresh lime juice
2 tsp finely chopped fresh lemongrass, centre only
1 tsp finely chopped fresh galangal (see page 27)
1–3 fresh red bird's eye chillies, finely chopped
1 tsp sugar
2 tsp fish sauce (nuoc mam), (see page 28)
¼ tsp salt, plus extra to taste
*375g (12oz) salmon fillet, cut into thin strips
(see page 150)*
½ medium cucumber or 1 mini cucumber, peeled
2 shallots, very finely sliced
1 red pepper, deseeded and cut into very fine strips
handful each of 2 types of fresh mint leaves
2–3 iceberg lettuce leaves, finely shredded

PREPARATION

1 Mix the lime juice, lemongrass, galangal, chillies,
sugar, fish sauce and salt together in a bowl. Add
the strips of fish, turning them until well coated,
then leave to marinate in a cool place for 2–3 hours.
2 Cut the cucumber in half, lengthways, and
scoop out and discard the seeds, using a teaspoon.
Slice the cucumber into very thin half moon shapes.
3 Put the cucumber slices into a glass serving
bowl. Add the shallots, red pepper, both types of
mint and the lettuce, and mix together well.
4 Remove the strips of fish from the marinade
and transfer to the salad. Season the marinade
with more salt, if desired, and pour over the salad.
Toss all the ingredients together until well mixed,
then serve immediately.

FISH TERIYAKI
Glazed grilled fish (Japan)

Teriyaki is a grilled (yaki) dish with a sauce that forms a glaze (teri) during cooking. Traditionally, teriyaki is arranged on a platter lined with chrysanthemum leaves, decorated with a flower carved from daikon (mooli) and served with a small pile of shredded pink pickled ginger. As I have never managed to carve this flower successfully, I simply pile up fine matchsticks of daikon and ginger next to the fish. Serve the fish hot, followed by plain boiled Japanese rice with some vegetables or a salad, if desired.

INGREDIENTS

*4 halibut steaks, 150–175g (5–6oz) each,
cut about 5cm (2in) thick
1 tsp coarse sea salt
4 tbsp groundnut oil
2 tbsp finely shredded pink pickled ginger
(see page 31), to garnish
125g (4oz) mooli (see page 20), cut into tiny julienne
strips (see page 154), soaked in iced water, to garnish*
For the marinade / glaze
*2 tbsp sake (see page 29)
2 tbsp mirin (see page 29)
75ml (5 tbsp) dark soy sauce
1 tbsp sugar*

PREPARATION

1 Rub the fish steaks all over with the salt and leave to stand for 30 minutes. Rinse well under cold running water, then dry on kitchen paper.
2 Combine the ingredients for the marinade in a glass bowl. Add the fish steaks and leave to stand for 1–2 hours, turning several times.
3 Remove the fish steaks from the marinade and arrange, side by side, on a grill pan. Cook under a preheated hot grill, for 5–8 minutes, turning once, until golden brown all over.
4 Pour the marinade into a small pan and heat for 2–3 minutes, or until it has thickened and caramelized. Using the back of a spoon, glaze the fish steaks all over with the mixture. Return the fish to the grill and cook for 2–3 minutes more.
5 Arrange the teriyaki on a serving platter and garnish with a small pile of shredded pink pickled ginger and another of mooli.

IKAN MASAK TAUCO
Fish in black bean sauce (Malaysia)

Here I recommend plaice and black bean sauce, but you could use yellow bean sauce and the freshest fillets of any white fish. Serve with rice or noodles, or simply with salad for a light lunch.

INGREDIENTS

*4 skinned fillets of plaice, 175–200g (6–7oz) each,
or cod or monkfish
½ tsp salt
1 tsp freshly ground black pepper
1 tbsp demerara sugar
2 tbsp plain flour
4 tbsp groundnut oil or soya oil
6 shallots or 1 large onion, very finely sliced
2–5 fresh green chillies, deseeded and thinly sliced
250g (8oz) small button mushrooms, thinly sliced
1 tsp light soy sauce
3 spring onions, cut into thin rounds*
For the paste
*2 tbsp black bean sauce or yellow bean sauce
2 cloves garlic, chopped
5cm (2in) piece of fresh ginger root, chopped
¼ tsp chilli powder
1 tbsp tamarind water (see page 101), or lemon juice
2 tbsp groundnut oil or soya oil*

PREPARATION

1 Rub the fish fillets all over with the salt and pepper. Mix the sugar and flour together in a small bowl and rub over one side of the fillets. Roll up the fillets, floured side on the outside, then secure with a wooden cocktail stick and set aside.
2 Put the paste ingredients into a blender and blend until as smooth as possible. Transfer the paste mixture to a small bowl.
3 Heat the oil in a large non-stick frying pan. Add the fish rolls and fry, turning frequently, for 2–3 minutes. Remove from the pan with a slotted spoon and transfer to a plate, then carefully remove the cocktail sticks.
4 Reheat the oil. Add the shallots or onion and cook, stirring almost continuously, for 2 minutes. Add the paste, green chillies and mushrooms and cook, stirring frequently, for 2–3 minutes. Increase the heat and stir in the soy sauce and spring onions.
5 Return the fish rolls to the pan and stir carefully until well coated with the black bean sauce. Lower the heat, then cover the pan and cook for 1 minute only. Remove the pan from the heat and leave to stand, still covered, for 2 minutes then serve immediately.

IKAN MASAK LADA

Pan-fried fillet of cod coated in chillies
(Malaysia)

Chilli lovers will appreciate this popular Malaysian
dish. It does not need to be blisteringly hot, because if you
choose the right chillies – large red ones – they are quite
mild. Serve with rice or noodles and salad.

INGREDIENTS

4 pieces of cod fillet, 150–175g (5–6oz) each
½ tsp salt, plus extra to taste
½ tsp freshly ground white pepper, plus extra to taste
75ml (5 tbsp) groundnut oil or vegetable oil
10 large fresh red chillies or 2 red peppers, deseeded
and finely chopped
4 shallots, very finely chopped
2 cloves garlic, finely chopped
2 tsp finely chopped fresh ginger root
2 tsp ground coriander
1 tbsp tamarind water (see page 101)

PREPARATION

1 Rub the fish all over with the salt and pepper,
and leave to stand for 10–15 minutes.
2 Heat the oil in a frying pan. Add the fish fillets
in a single layer and fry over a medium heat for
2 minutes. Turn the fillets over with a fish slice
and cook for 2 minutes more.
3 Remove the fish from the pan and transfer to
a plate. Add the chillies or red peppers, shallots
and garlic to the pan and cook, stirring almost
continuously, for 6 minutes. Add the ginger and
ground coriander. Season to taste and cook,
stirring continuously, for 2 minutes.
4 Add the tamarind water to the pan, then raise
the heat and cook, stirring continuously, for 2
minutes. Add 2 tablespoons of hot water to the
mixture if it looks too dry.
5 Arrange the fish fillets on top of the chilli
mixture, cook for 1 minute, then turn them over
and cook for 1 minute more. Remove the pan
from the heat, then cover and leave to stand
for 2 minutes before serving.

SUZUKI SASHIMI

Raw sea bass with vegetables and
dipping sauce (Japan)

I admit I have only made this dish once, but it was a
great success. My fish was caught at 4 o'clock in the
morning off the coast of Cornwall, delivered to my house
in London at 11am, and eaten that evening. I would not
attempt to prepare sashimi with anything less fresh.
Good sashimi is unbeatable, so I have included this
recipe for those who are lucky enough to live by the sea
where truly fresh fish is easily available. Make the
dipping sauce well in advance; it will keep refrigerated
in an airtight jar for 2–3 days.

INGREDIENTS

½ medium cucumber, halved lengthways
500g (1lb) very fresh sea bass fillet, cut into
very thin slices (see page 150)
1 lemon, cut into wedges
handful of fresh mint leaves, to garnish
wasabi paste (see page 31), to serve
For the dipping sauce
125ml (4fl oz) dark soy sauce
1 tbsp sake (see page 29)
1 tbsp mirin (see page 29)
2 tbsp tamari soy sauce (see page 28)
30g (1oz) bonito flakes (see page 30)

PREPARATION

1 For the dipping sauce, combine the dark soy
sauce, sake and mirin in a small pan. Bring to the
boil, then simmer for 5 minutes. Remove the pan
from the heat and add the tamari soy sauce and
bonito flakes. Leave to stand for about 5 hours.
2 Scoop out and discard the seeds of the cucumber
using a teaspoon, then cut the cucumber into
julienne strips (see page 150).
3 To serve, arrange the fish slices on 4 plates,
place the cucumber julienne and lemon wedges on
top, and garnish with the mint. Put the wasabi and
the dipping sauce into separate small bowls, so
each guest has their own.
4 To eat, the lemon is squeezed over the fish. A
slice of fish is picked up with chopsticks and dipped
into the wasabi, then into the dipping sauce. The
fish is eaten alternately with a little cucumber.
5 Alternatively, the fish can be eaten like a salad,
with a knife and fork, and mixed with salad leaves,
if desired, with the wasabi and the dipping sauce
mixed together and poured over.

NGA WEHIN

Basic fish curry (Burma)

Some Burmese curries are similar to Thai curries; others are more closely related to Indian curries. It is hard to tell which side of the family this one favours, for it is a basic curry that contains neither coconut milk nor yogurt. It is worth using the whole fish, with bones and head, as this gives a tasty sauce. Serve with rice and vegetables.

INGREDIENTS

½ grouper or sea-perch or 2 pomfrets,
1–1.25kg (2–2½ lb) in total
900ml (1½ pints) water
5cm (2in) piece of fresh ginger root, thinly sliced
1 tsp ground turmeric
½ tsp salt, plus extra to taste
1 tbsp fish sauce (nam pla), (see page 28)
1 stem of fresh lemongrass, cut into 3 pieces
freshly ground black pepper, to taste
3 tbsp chopped fresh coriander leaves, to garnish
For the paste
5 shallots, chopped
3 cloves garlic, chopped
2–6 small dried red chillies
1 tsp finely chopped fresh lemongrass, centre only
2 tbsp tamarind water (see page 101)
3 tbsp vegetable oil
1 tbsp fish sauce (nam pla), (see page 28)
2 red tomatoes, skinned and chopped

PREPARATION

1 Put the fish in a pan with the water, ginger, turmeric, salt, fish sauce and lemongrass. Bring to the boil, then simmer for 8–10 minutes.
2 Remove the fish from the pan and leave to cool. Take the fish off the bones in large pieces and set aside. Return the skin, bones and head to the stock and simmer for 20 minutes more. Strain the stock into a bowl and discard the solids.
3 Put the paste ingredients into a blender and blend until as smooth as possible. Transfer the paste mixture to a pan and bring to the boil. Cook, stirring frequently, for 3 minutes.
4 Add the strained stock and cook for another 15–20 minutes, until the sauce is reduced. Season to taste and add the fish. Heat through for 3–4 minutes, then sprinkle with the coriander leaves to garnish, and serve immediately.

HOJAN HSIN TAIJI

Stir-fried scallops in oyster sauce (China)

When prepared in a Chinese restaurant kitchen, this classic Cantonese dish is stir-fried for only a few seconds over a fierce heat. At home, the flame under my wok is much less powerful, so this dish takes me about 5 minutes to cook. It is important to have every ingredient prepared in advance and ready to hand. See page 96 for illustration.

INGREDIENTS

12 raw scallops, corals separated and reserved,
white meat cut in half horizontally
1 tsp cornflour
1 tbsp light soy sauce
¼ tsp freshly ground white pepper, plus extra to taste
1 tbsp Shaohsing wine (see page 29), or dry sherry
4 tbsp groundnut oil
1 small celery heart with the leaves, roughly chopped
6 fresh shiitake mushrooms, stalks removed
and caps quartered
3 spring onions, cut into 1cm (½in) lengths on the diagonal
2 ripe tomatoes, skinned, deseeded and quartered, optional
salt, to taste
For the sauce
2 tbsp oyster sauce
1 tbsp Shaohsing wine (see page 29), or dry sherry
2 tsp very finely chopped fresh ginger root
1 tsp very finely chopped garlic
½ tsp cornflour
1 tbsp light soy sauce
½ tsp sesame oil

PREPARATION

1 Place the white scallop meat in a bowl and rub with the cornflour, soy sauce, white pepper and Shaohsing wine. Leave to stand in a cool place.
2 Put the ingredients for the sauce, except the sesame oil, in a bowl. Mix together, then set aside.
3 Heat a wok until hot and add the groundnut oil. When the oil starts to smoke, add the halved scallops and stir-fry for 1 minute. Remove from the wok with a slotted spoon and transfer to a bowl.
4 Add the celery and mushrooms to the wok and stir-fry for 1–2 minutes. Remove from the wok with the slotted spoon and transfer to a plate. Discard the oil remaining in the wok.
5 Reheat the wok, pour in the sauce mixture and cook, stirring continuously, for 1–2 minutes. Raise the heat and add the spring onions and tomatoes, if using, and stir-fry for 30 seconds.
6 Add the scallops along with any cooking juices, the reserved corals, the celery and mushrooms. Stir-fry for another 30 seconds, then stir in the sesame oil. Season to taste and serve immediately.

HOMOK TALAY

Mixed seafood in coconut milk (Thailand)

Asia offers dozens, if not hundreds, of variations on the hot pot, but the main ingredients are usually fish and shellfish or meat and vegetables. Serve with rice.

INGREDIENTS

2 squid, about 250g (8oz) each, cleaned (see page 150) and cut into bite-sized pieces, tentacles discarded
8–12 live mussels, scrubbed and washed
8 raw scallops, corals separated, white meat cut in half
8 raw tiger prawns, legs removed
4 ready-cooked crab claws
handful each of fresh mint leaves and basil leaves
salt and freshly ground black pepper, to taste
8 small fresh red chillies, to garnish
For the sauce
3 tbsp vegetable oil
4 shallots or 1 medium onion, chopped
3 cloves garlic, chopped
1–3 large fresh red chillies, deseeded and finely chopped
2 tsp finely chopped fresh ginger root
½ tsp ground turmeric
seeds of 3 green cardamom pods
2 tbsp tamarind water (see page 101)
2 fresh kaffir lime leaves (see page 26)
1 stem of fresh lemongrass, cut into 3 pieces
1 tsp salt
1 tsp sugar
900ml (1½ pints) very thick coconut milk (see page 141)
1 tsp fish sauce (nam pla), (see page 28), optional

PREPARATION

1 Add the squid pieces to a pan of lightly salted boiling water and cook for 4–5 minutes. Drain in a colander and set aside.

2 Pick over the mussels and discard any with broken shells or those that do not close when lightly tapped. Put the mussels in a pan of boiling water and cook for 1 minute.

3 Remove the pan from the heat and leave the mussels to stand for a few minutes, until the shells open. Discard any mussels that remain closed and rinse the open ones to rid them of any sand.

4 For the sauce, heat the oil in a large heavy-based pan. Add the shallots, garlic, chillies and ginger, and fry, stirring continuously, for 2 minutes.

5 Add the turmeric, cardamom seeds, tamarind water, lime leaves, lemongrass, salt and sugar. Stir once and add the coconut milk. Bring to the boil, then lower the heat a little and cook, stirring frequently, for 30–40 minutes, or until the sauce is reduced by half.

Vegetable oil

Small red chillies

Black pepper

Salt

Basil

Mint

Squid

Scallops   Tiger prawns   Crab claws   Mussels

6 Add all the seafood, the mint and basil leaves, and cook for 4–5 minutes. Season to taste, then remove the lime leaves and lemongrass, and garnish with the chillies.

Fish sauce

Coconut milk

Sugar

Lemongrass

Kaffir lime
leaves

Tamarind
water

Cardamom
pods

Ground
turmeric

Fresh
ginger

Large red
chillies

Garlic

Shallots

PEELING & DEVEINING PRAWNS

1 Remove and discard the head and shell of the prawn. Make a short cut along the back of the prawn to reveal the black vein or intestine.

2 Using the tip of a knife, pull out and discard the intestine. By keeping the cut along the back short, the prawn will remain straight when cooked.

3 To make the prawn curl, or "butterfly", during cooking, make a longer cut all the way down the back of the prawn when removing the intestine.

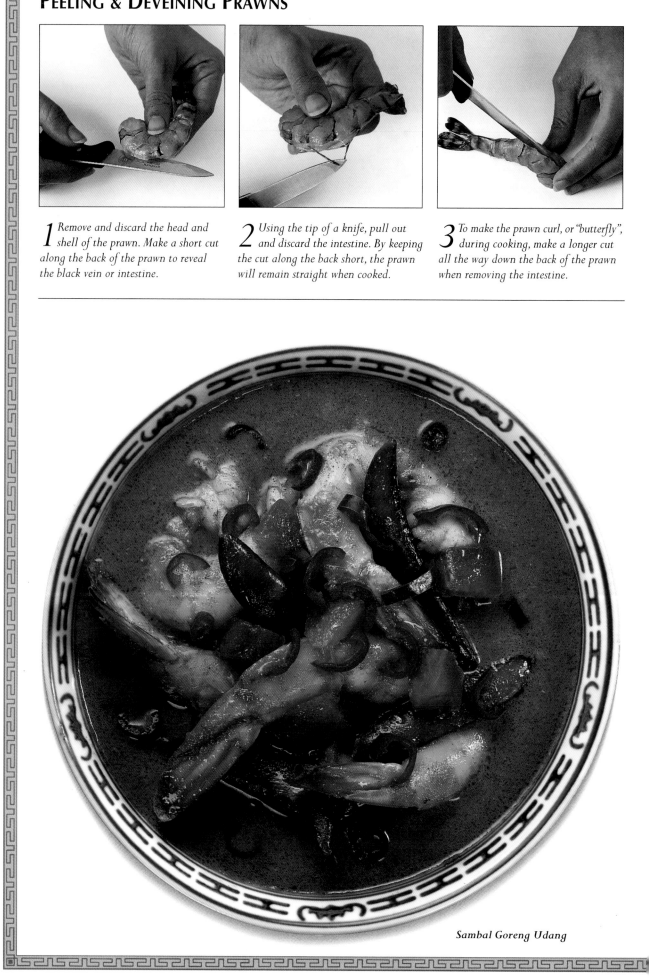

Sambal Goreng Udang

SAMBAL GORENG UDANG

Prawns in rich coconut sauce (Indonesia)

For centuries, this has been a classic and very popular dish throughout Java. It has now become one of the better-known dishes in Indonesian cuisine. Serve with rice and accompany with stir-fried vegetables or a salad.

INGREDIENTS

450ml (¾ pint) hot water
2 fresh kaffir lime leaves (see page 26), or bay leaves
5cm (2in) piece of fresh lemongrass
125g (4oz) creamed coconut, broken into pieces
16–20 raw king prawns, peeled and deveined (see steps opposite)
2 ripe tomatoes, skinned, deseeded and chopped
125g (4oz) mangetout or sugar snap peas
For the paste
3 shallots or 1 small onion, chopped
2 cloves garlic, chopped
5cm (2in) piece of fresh ginger root, peeled and sliced
3 large fresh red chillies, deseeded and chopped
1 tsp dried shrimp paste (see page 31), optional
2 candle nuts (see page 22), or macadamia nuts, or blanched almonds, chopped
1 tsp ground coriander
1 tsp paprika
½ tsp salt, plus extra to taste
1 tbsp tamarind water (see page 101), or lemon juice
2 tbsp groundnut oil or vegetable oil
3 tbsp cold water

PREPARATION

1 Put all the paste ingredients into a blender and blend until as smooth as possible. Transfer the paste mixture to a pan, bring to the boil and cook for 4 minutes, stirring frequently. Add the hot water, lime leaves or bay leaves and lemongrass. Return to the boil, then simmer for 20 minutes.
2 Add the creamed coconut and stir until dissolved. Simmer, stirring continuously, for 3–4 minutes more. Season with more salt, if desired.
3 Bring the sauce to a rolling boil. Add the prawns and cook, stirring continuously, for 2 minutes.
4 Add the tomatoes and mangetout or sugar snap peas, and simmer for another 2 minutes only. Do not cook the mixture for any longer or the prawns will become tough and tasteless. Discard the lime leaves and lemongrass or bay leaves before serving.

JINGHA KARI

Prawn curry (India)

This curry is very similar to one cooked for me by a Burmese friend long ago in central Java – it was quite delicious. The difference is that my friend used finely chopped young coconut flesh which is, I suppose, the alternative to the yogurt used here. Serve with a rice pilaff, such as Navratan Pullao (see page 126 for recipe).

INGREDIENTS

4 tbsp groundnut oil or vegetable oil
2 medium onions, finely sliced
2 fresh green chillies, deseeded and finely sliced
5cm (2in) piece of cinnamon stick
8–10 cloves
4 tbsp hot water
4 tbsp low-fat natural yogurt, lightly whisked
salt and freshly ground black pepper, to taste
16–20 raw king prawns, peeled and deveined (see steps opposite)
3 tbsp chopped fresh flat-leaf parsley or coriander, to garnish
For the paste
6 cloves garlic, chopped
2 tsp finely chopped fresh ginger root
½ tsp chilli powder
½ tsp ground turmeric
1 tsp ground coriander
1 tbsp tamarind water (see page 101), or lemon juice
4 tbsp cold water

PREPARATION

1 Put all the paste ingredients into a blender and blend until as smooth as possible. Transfer the paste mixture to a bowl and set aside.
2 Heat the oil in a pan. Add the onions and fry, stirring frequently, for 8 minutes. Remove from the pan with a slotted spoon and transfer to a bowl.
3 Pour off the oil from the pan, leaving about 1 tablespoon. Return the pan to the heat, add the chillies, cinnamon and cloves, and stir-fry for 1 minute. Return the onions to the pan, add the paste mixture and stir-fry for 1 minute.
4 Stir in the hot water and simmer for 5 minutes. Add the yogurt and seasoning and cook, stirring, for 1–2 minutes. Increase the heat and add the prawns. Stir until they are well coated with the sauce, then cover the pan and cook over a medium heat for 3 minutes.
5 Remove the pan from the heat and leave to stand, tightly covered, for 2 minutes. Discard the cinnamon stick and cloves. Transfer the curry to a heated serving dish and sprinkle with the chopped parsley or coriander, to garnish.

ALIMANGO TAUSI
Stuffed crab with yellow bean sauce
(Philippines)

To give substance to the stuffing in this dish, Filipinos like to use fruit, typically guava. But other fruit, such as apple or quince, are also delicious. This dish is usually deep-fried or steamed. Here, however, it is baked in the oven. Serve with rice or noodles, or just a mixed green salad.

INGREDIENTS

4 small whole cooked crabs, about 375g (12oz) each
1 medium guava or apple or quince, peeled and quartered, then deseeded or cored
3 tbsp groundnut oil
2 shallots, finely sliced
2 cloves garlic, finely sliced
1 tbsp yellow bean sauce
2 small dried red chillies
2 tsp finely chopped fresh ginger root
1 tbsp light soy sauce
3 eggs, lightly beaten
2 tbsp chopped spring onions
salt and freshly ground black pepper, to taste

PREPARATION

1 Plunge the crabs into a large pan of boiling water and simmer for 5 minutes. Remove from the pan and leave to cool on a tray.
2 When cold, prepare and clean the crabs (see page 151). Clean and reserve the shells. Thinly slice the quartered guava or apple or quince crossways, into a bowl of lightly salted water.
3 Heat the oil in a wok. Add the shallots, garlic, yellow bean sauce, chillies and ginger, and stir-fry for 2 minutes. Add the drained slices of fruit and stir-fry for another 2 minutes.
4 Add the soy sauce, then cover the wok and cook over a low heat for 2 minutes. Stir in the beaten eggs and spring onions and season to taste. Cook, stirring continuously, for 1–2 minutes.
5 Divide the crab meat among the crab shells and spoon the fruit and egg mixture equally over the crab. Arrange the shells on a baking tray and bake in an oven preheated to 180°C/350°F/Gas 4 for 10–15 minutes, until the egg starts to brown. Place the crabs under a preheated hot grill to brown further, if desired.

JUI JIN JEUN HO HAI
Deep fried soft-shell crab (China)

Soft-shell crabs (small blue crabs that have just moulted) are a delicacy, especially on the east coast of the United States where they are extremely popular. I suggest you buy frozen ones, because they have been thoroughly cleaned before freezing. Serves 2 on its own or 4 as part of a main course with 2 other dishes.

INGREDIENTS

4 frozen soft-shell crabs, defrosted and rinsed
1 egg yolk, lightly beaten
1 tbsp cornflour blended with 2 tbsp cold water
about 300ml (½ pint) oil for deep-frying
2 tsp finely chopped garlic
1 fresh large red chilli, deseeded and chopped, or ½ tsp dried red chilli flakes
1 tsp light soy sauce
For the marinade
½ tsp each salt and freshly ground white pepper
1 tsp sugar
2 tbsp Shaohsing wine (see page 29), or dry sherry

PREPARATION

1 Combine the marinade ingredients in a bowl, add the crabs and turn to coat. Leave to marinate for 10 minutes.
2 Remove the crabs from the marinade and transfer to a plate. Reserve the marinade. Brush the crabs with the egg yolk, then coat with the cornflour mixture and set aside for a few minutes.
3 Heat a wok until hot, then add the oil and heat to about 160°C (325°F). Add the crabs and fry for 1 minute. Remove from the heat for 1 minute. Return the wok to the heat and fry the crabs for 3–4 minutes, or until golden.
4 Remove the crabs from the wok with a slotted spoon and transfer to a plate, to drain. Carefully pour off the oil from the wok.
5 Place the wok over a medium heat. Add the garlic and chilli, and stir-fry for a few seconds. Add the soy sauce and the reserved marinade, and stir-fry for a few seconds more. Return the crabs to the wok and stir until they are well coated with the sauce.

DHALLO BADUN
Fried squid curry (Sri Lanka)

Long-cooking seems to be preferred in Asia, especially for curry. This is because the curry sauce needs to reduce slowly which improves the flavour and also makes it look more appetizing. In this recipe, however, instead of cooking the squid for an hour in the curry sauce, I fry raw squid for just a few minutes and add it to the long-cooked sauce just before serving. Serves 6–8 as a main course with plain boiled rice or a rice pilaff, plus 2 other dishes.

INGREDIENTS

1kg (2lb) small squid, cleaned (see page 150) and cut into thin rings, tentacles cut into 5cm (2in) lengths
175ml (6fl oz) groundnut oil or vegetable oil for frying
6 shallots or 1 large onion, finely sliced
4 cloves garlic, finely chopped
2 tsp finely chopped fresh ginger root
1 stem of fresh lemongrass, cut into 3 pieces
5 fresh or dried curry leaves (see page 26), optional
½–1 tsp chilli powder
1 small cinnamon stick
1 tsp ground coriander
½ tsp ground cumin
½ tsp fenugreek seeds
½ tsp fennel seeds
2 cloves
2 green cardamom pods
60ml (2fl oz) hot water
2 tbsp distilled white vinegar
salt and freshly ground black pepper, to taste
600ml (1 pint) coconut milk (see page 141)

PREPARATION

1 Rinse the squid rings and tentacles under cold running water, then transfer to a colander and leave to drain completely.
2 Heat 3 tablespoons of the oil in a pan. Add the shallots or onion and fry, stirring frequently, until they begin to brown. Add the garlic, ginger, lemongrass, curry leaves and all the dried spices, and cook, stirring frequently, for 2 minutes.
3 Add the hot water and vinegar, then season to taste. Bring to the boil, then simmer for 5 minutes. Stir in the coconut milk and bring almost to the boil. Reduce the heat and simmer, uncovered, for about 1 hour. Adjust the seasoning, if necessary.
4 Heat the remaining oil in a wok. Add the drained squid in 2 or 3 batches and fry for 3 minutes per batch. Remove the squid from the wok with a slotted spoon and transfer to the simmering sauce. Simmer, stirring once or twice, for 2 minutes more, then serve immediately.

HOY LAI PHAD NAM PRIK PHAO
Braised clams with basil (Thailand)

In Thailand there are at least three different kinds of basil. For this dish you can use any of them, though it is perhaps easier to find anise basil or Thai basil. Alternatively, ordinary sweet basil will do very well. See page 111 for illustration.

INGREDIENTS

1kg (2lb) live clams, soaked in cold water
3 tbsp groundnut oil or vegetable oil
3 shallots, finely sliced
3 cloves garlic, finely chopped
2 large fresh green chillies, deseeded and cut on the diagonal into 3 slices
1 tsp chilli sauce (see page 28), optional
1 tbsp fish sauce (nam pla), (see page 28)
handful of fresh Thai basil leaves (see page 26)
2 fresh red chillies, deseeded and diced, to garnish

PREPARATION

1 Scrub the clams well in their soaking water, then rinse under cold running water. Set the clams aside in a colander, discarding any with broken shells, or those that do not close when lightly tapped.
2 Heat the oil in a pan, add the shallots, garlic and green chillies, and stir-fry for 1 minute. Add the chilli sauce, if using, and stir in the clams. Increase the heat and stir-fry for 4 minutes, or until the clams open. Discard any clams that remain closed.
3 Stir in the fish sauce and most of the basil leaves. Scatter over the remaining basil leaves and red chillies, to garnish, and serve immediately.

POULTRY

The domestic hen is descended from the jungle fowl of Southeast Asia, and anyone who has driven along country roads in Indonesia will know that these fowl retain many of their wild, unpredictable ways. Ducks are migrants, domesticated in China and Europe; they are, strictly, exotics in places like Bali, where you may see a flock marching to the rice fields behind a boy with a white flag.

TSOI PE TSA JI GAI

Deep-fried crispy-skin chicken (China)

The preparation of this Cantonese dish is very much like that for Peking Duck (see page 46 for recipe). However, the crispness of the skin here is the result of deep-frying twice.

INGREDIENTS

1 tbsp five-spice powder (see page 27)
1 tsp salt
1 tsp sugar
1 chicken, 1.5–1.75kg (3–3½lb), scalded with boiling water (see page 152)
2 tbsp rice vinegar (see page 29)
3 tbsp clear honey
about 1.25 litres (2 pints) vegetable oil for deep-frying
3 spring onions, each cut into 3 pieces
3 thick slices of peeled fresh ginger root

PREPARATION

1 Mix the five-spice powder, salt and sugar together and rub over the scalded chicken, and inside the body cavity. Mix the vinegar with the honey and rub all over the chicken skin.
2 Secure the chicken on a duck hook (see page 152), then hang in a cool, airy place for 2–3 hours.
3 Heat a large wok, and when hot pour in the vegetable oil. Heat the oil until it reaches about 160°C (325°F). Put the spring onions and ginger into the cavity of the chicken.
4 Add the chicken to the wok and fry until the skin is golden, about 8 minutes. Remove the chicken from the wok, transfer to a colander and drain well.
5 Just before serving, reheat the oil. Prick the chicken skin all over with a fork and return the chicken to the oil. Deep-fry for about 10 minutes, until the chicken is well cooked and the skin is just a little browner and crisper than before. Remove from the wok and drain well on kitchen paper. Cut the chicken into quarters and serve.

OSENG OSENG AYAM DENGAN SAYURAN

Stir-fried chicken with vegetables (Indonesia)

This kind of stir-fry — a little meat with plenty of vegetables — is typical of many Southeast Asian countries, where meat is expensive, and vegetables are cheap and abundant. Beef, pork or lamb can be used instead of chicken. Serves 4–6 with rice. See page 73 for illustration.

INGREDIENTS

3 tbsp groundnut oil
3 shallots, finely sliced
1 tsp finely sliced fresh ginger root
1 large fresh red chilli, deseeded and sliced
1 tsp grated palm sugar (see page 30), or demerara sugar
1 tsp dried shrimp paste (see page 31), optional
1 skinless chicken breast, cut into thick slices
1 tbsp light soy sauce
90ml (6 tbsp) hot water
175g (6oz) fine asparagus, tips separated from stems and stems cut in half on the diagonal
175g (6oz) baby button mushrooms
175g (6oz) baby corn cobs, halved lengthways
1 large yellow pepper, deseeded and cut into 8–10 strips
125g (4oz) mangetout, halved on the diagonal if large
salt and freshly ground black pepper, to taste

PREPARATION

1 Heat the oil in a wok. Add the shallots, ginger and chilli, and stir-fry for 1–2 minutes. Add the sugar and shrimp paste, if using, and stir briefly.
2 Add the slices of chicken and stir-fry for 3–4 minutes. Stir in the soy sauce and hot water, and simmer for 3 minutes.
3 Add the asparagus stems, mushrooms and baby corn cobs, and stir again. Lower the heat, then cover and simmer for 3 minutes.
4 Add the asparagus tips, yellow pepper and mangetout. Stir-fry for 2 minutes and season to taste. Stir-fry for 2 minutes more, then serve.

KYET THAR HIN

Chicken curry with limes (Burma)

The use of lime in this dish indicates that it is more closely related to the curries of Thailand than India.

INGREDIENTS

3 tbsp vegetable oil
1 tsp sesame oil
3 medium onions, finely chopped
2 cloves garlic, chopped
1 tsp ground turmeric
1 tbsp ground coriander
2 cinnamon sticks
4 cloves
3 fresh kaffir lime leaves (see page 26)
4 boned and skinned chicken breasts and
4 boned and skinned thighs
3 tbsp Balachaung (see page 132 for recipe)
1 stem of fresh lemongrass, cut into 3 pieces
175g (6oz) can chopped tomatoes
1 tsp freshly ground black pepper
1 tbsp fish sauce (see page 28)
juice of 2 limes
salt, to taste
1 lime cut into wedges, to garnish

PREPARATION

1 Mix the vegetable oil and sesame oil together in a bowl, then transfer to a large ovenproof casserole and place over a medium heat. Add the onions and fry, stirring frequently, for 5 minutes.
2 Stir in the garlic, ground turmeric and coriander, cinnamon sticks, cloves and lime leaves. Add the chicken pieces and stir until they are well coated.
3 Add the Balachaung and stir-fry for 2 minutes. Add the lemongrass and tomatoes, then cover and simmer for 30 minutes.
4 Uncover the dish and increase the heat a little. Add the black pepper, fish sauce and lime juice. If the mixture is too thick add a little hot water.
5 Cook the chicken for 10 minutes more, adding salt, if necessary. Serve the curry immediately or cook it further, until the chicken is very tender and almost falling off the bones.
6 To cook the curry longer, cover the dish and place in an oven preheated to 160°C/325°F/Gas 3. Cook for 20 minutes, then reduce the temperature to 110°C/225°F/Gas ¼ and cook for up to 1 hour longer, if desired.
7 Remove the cinnamon sticks, cloves, lime leaves and lemongrass. Skim off some of the oil from the sauce and garnish with the lime wedges, to serve.

GAENG PED KAI

Red curry of chicken (Thailand)

There are three main types of curry in Thailand: green, red and massaman. The green and red curries are "city" curries as opposed to the latter, a "jungle" curry, which is much stronger and spicier. Serve with plain boiled rice.

INGREDIENTS

750g (1½lb) boned chicken breasts and thighs, cut into 2cm (¾in) cubes
1.25 litres (2 pints) coconut milk (see page 141)
250g (8oz) baby new potatoes
For the paste
4 shallots, finely chopped
3 cloves garlic, finely chopped
5cm (2in) piece of fresh lemongrass, outer leaves removed, centre chopped
2cm (¾in) piece of fresh galangal (see page 27), finely chopped
1 tsp grated kaffir lime rind (see page 22)
1 tsp ground black pepper
1 tbsp coriander seeds, roasted (see page 155), roughly crushed
1 tsp cumin seeds, roasted (see page 155), roughly crushed
½ tsp each of ground mace and nutmeg
5 fresh red chillies, deseeded and chopped
1 red pepper, deseeded and chopped, optional
1 tsp salt, plus extra to taste
½ tsp dried shrimp paste (see page 31)
2 tbsp each of water and vegetable oil
2 tbsp tamarind water (see page 101)
For the garnish
1 tbsp chopped fresh red chillies
1 tbsp chopped fresh coriander leaves
2 tbsp roasted peanuts, roughly chopped

PREPARATION

1 Put all the paste ingredients into a blender and blend until as smooth as possible. Transfer the paste mixture to a large pan and simmer, stirring frequently, for 4 minutes.
2 Add the chicken and stir until well coated. Cover and simmer for 4 minutes. Add the coconut milk to the pan and simmer, stirring frequently, for 30 minutes. Season to taste.
3 Add the potatoes and cook, stirring frequently, for 10–15 minutes, or until tender. Garnish with the chillies, coriander leaves and peanuts.

PIPIAN

Chicken and pork in peanut sauce (Philippines)

Normally served as a very thick rice-flour porridge with meat and peanut butter, this lighter version of Pipian includes sliced boiled chicken, pork and ham and a peanut sauce. Serves 8–10 with rice.

INGREDIENTS

1 chicken, about 1.5kg (3lb), halved lengthways
1kg (2lb) pork leg meat, in one piece, skin removed
500g (1lb) uncooked ham, in one piece, skin and fat removed
1 large onion, halved
4 cloves garlic
2.5 litres (4 pints) water
For the peanut sauce
3 tbsp vegetable oil
4 shallots, finely sliced
3 cloves garlic, finely sliced
2 tsp paprika
½ tsp ground turmeric
½ tsp freshly ground white pepper, plus extra to taste
125g (4oz) shelled peanuts, fried and ground to a powder
2 tbsp tamarind water (see page 101), or lemon juice
salt, to taste

PREPARATION

1 Put the chicken, pork and ham in a large pan with the onion, garlic and water. Bring to the boil, then let it bubble gently for 1–1¼ hours.
2 Remove the meat from the stock and leave to cool in a bowl. Strain 600ml (1 pint) of the stock into another bowl and skim well.
3 Remove the chicken from the bones in large pieces, discard the fat from the pork and trim the ham. Slice all the meat thinly and set aside.
4 For the sauce, heat the oil in a pan or wok. Add the shallots and garlic and fry, stirring continuously, for 2 minutes. Add the paprika, ground turmeric and pepper, and stir again.
5 Add the measured stock, bring to the boil, then simmer for 2 minutes. Add the ground peanuts, stir once and simmer for 5 minutes. Add the tamarind water or lemon juice, and season to taste.
6 Stir the meat into the sauce and simmer for 3 minutes, until heated through, then serve immediately. Alternatively, arrange the cold meat on a platter and serve the sauce separately.

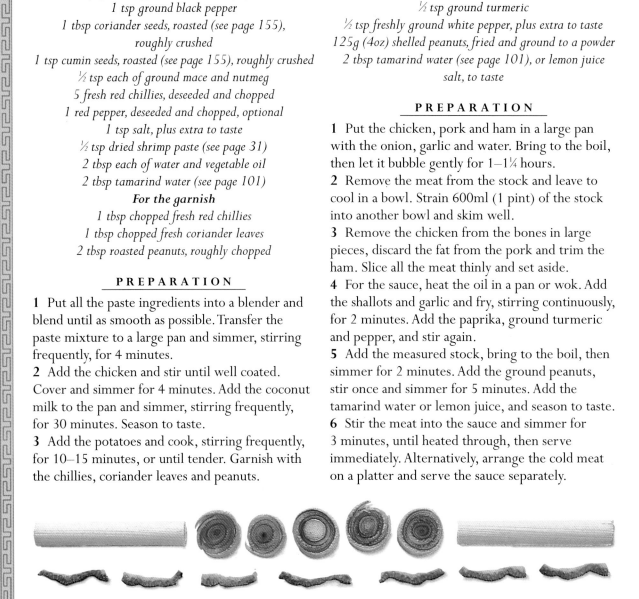

DUI GA NHOI THIT
Stuffed boned chicken legs (Vietnam)

*Traditionally, this dish is made with a whole chicken,
boned from the neck so the skin remains intact.
The result is quite impressive, but it takes time
and skill. This short-cut version uses only chicken legs.
Serve hot as a main course, or cold, thinly sliced, as
an appetizer with Nuoc Cham (see page 128 for recipe)
as a dipping sauce.*

INGREDIENTS

*4 large chicken legs (drumstick and thigh in one piece),
boned in one piece (see page 152)
juice of half a lemon
salt and freshly ground black pepper, to taste
2 tbsp vegetable oil or clarified butter*
For the stuffing
*2 boned and skinned chicken thighs, chopped
175g (6oz) pork fillet, chopped
2 large fresh red chillies, deseeded and chopped
3 shallots, chopped
2 cloves garlic, chopped
2 stems of fresh lemongrass, outer leaves
removed, centre chopped
1 tsp sugar
2 tbsp fish sauce (nuoc mam), (see page 28)
2 tbsp vegetable oil
30g (1oz) wood ears, rehydrated (see page 155)
60g (2oz) cellophane noodles (see page 25), soaked in
hot water for 5 minutes, then drained*

PREPARATION

1 Put the boned legs in a bowl and rub with
the lemon juice and salt and pepper. Cover and
refrigerate while preparing the stuffing.
2 For the stuffing, put the chopped chicken and
pork in a food processor and process for a few
seconds. Transfer to a bowl.
3 Put all the remaining stuffing ingredients,
except the wood ears and noodles, into the food
processor and process to a paste. Add to the
ground meat and mix well.
4 Slice the wood ears into thin strips and cut the
noodles into short lengths with a pair of scissors,
then mix into the stuffing mixture.
5 Heat a little of the oil in a frying pan, add a
teaspoon of the stuffing mixture and fry until
cooked through. Taste, then add salt and pepper
to the remaining stuffing mixture, if required,
mixing well.
6 Using a spoon, press some of the stuffing into
the centre of each drumstick and then the thigh,
working carefully so that the meat and skin can be
folded over neatly to hold the stuffing in place.

7 Arrange the legs in an ovenproof dish, then
brush all over with the remaining oil. Place in an
oven preheated to 160°C/325°F/Gas 3 and roast
for 45–50 minutes. Serve the chicken, hot or cold,
cut into thick slices.

DHANSAK
Chicken cooked with lentils and vegetables (India)

*This is an adaptation, somewhat simplified, of a grand
Parsee dish. It is usually served with rice only, as
vegetables are already included.*

INGREDIENTS

*2 tbsp vegetable oil
1 tsp cumin seeds
1 medium onion, finely sliced
8 boned and skinned chicken thighs
1 tsp finely chopped fresh ginger root
6 cloves garlic
1 medium aubergine, cut across into 4 slices,
then each piece quartered
2 tbsp chopped fenugreek leaves (see page 26), optional
1½ tsp salt, plus extra to taste
¼ tsp ground black pepper
1 tsp garam masala (see page 156)*
For the lentils
*2 tsp ground coriander
½ tsp ground cumin
½ tsp chilli powder
½ tsp mustard powder
¼ tsp fenugreek seeds, ground
½ tsp ground turmeric
125g (4oz) green lentils, rinsed
600ml (1 pint) cold water
1 medium potato, cut into 8 pieces*

PREPARATION

1 Put all the ingredients for the lentils into a large
pan. Bring to the boil, then cover and simmer for
20 minutes. Remove the pan from the heat and
mash the lentils and potatoes a little with a spoon
or potato masher.
2 Heat the oil in another pan. Add the cumin
seeds and onion and cook, stirring frequently,
for 2–3 minutes. Add the chicken and ginger,
and cook, stirring, for a further 2 minutes.
3 Add the garlic, aubergine, fenugreek leaves,
salt and pepper to the chicken. Cover and cook
for 20 minutes. Stir in the lentil mixture, cover
and simmer for 5 minutes. Stir in the garam masala
and more salt, if necessary. Transfer the Dhansak
to a platter and serve immediately.

SZE CHUAN JAR GAI

Fried chicken Szechuan-style (China)

For this Szechuan dish the dark meat from the drumstick and thigh is preferred. Red and green chillies are normally used, but here I have substituted red chillies and green pepper to make it less fiery. Serve with rice.

INGREDIENTS

4 boned chicken drumsticks and 4 boned thighs, cut into 2cm (¾in) cubes, skin left on
1 small egg white
1 tbsp cornflour
1 tbsp dark soy sauce
125ml (4fl oz) vegetable oil
3 large fresh red chillies, deseeded and cut into 1cm (½in) pieces
1–2 tbsp crushed garlic
1 large green pepper, deseeded and cut into 1cm (½in) pieces
handful of fresh flat-leaf parsley
2 tbsp rice wine (see page 29), or medium-dry sherry
1 tsp sesame oil
For the sauce
2 tbsp light soy sauce
½ tsp salt
1 tsp sugar
¼ tsp chilli powder or ground black pepper
2 tsp rice vinegar (see page 29)
1 tsp cornflour
2 tbsp cold water

Green pepper

Garlic

Red chilli

Vegetable oil

Dark soy sauce

Cornflour

Egg white

PREPARATION

1 Put the chicken pieces into a glass bowl and add the egg white, cornflour and dark soy sauce. Stir well to mix thoroughly. Leave to stand in a cool place for 20 minutes.

2 Mix all the sauce ingredients together in another bowl. Heat a wok over a high heat. Add the oil and heat until very hot.

3 Add the chicken pieces to the wok in 2 batches and fry, stirring quickly, for 2 minutes per batch. Remove the chicken with a slotted spoon and transfer to a plate.

4 Add the chillies to the wok and stir-fry for 2 minutes. Remove with the slotted spoon and scatter over the chicken. Carefully pour off most of the oil, leaving about 3 tablespoons in the wok.

5 Reheat the oil in the wok, add the garlic and fry for a few seconds, stirring vigorously. Add the green pepper and stir-fry for 1 minute, then add the parsley and the chicken with the chillies.

6 Stir in the wine or sherry over a high heat. Pour in the sauce mixture, stir-fry for 1 minute, then add the sesame oil and serve immediately.

Chicken drumsticks   *Chicken thighs*

Sesame
oil

Rice wine

Light soy
sauce

Salt

Sugar

Chilli
powder

Rice vinegar

Flat-leaf
parsley

MURGH SALAR JUNG
Chicken in cashew and coconut sauce (India)

*This is an adaptation of a recipe by my friend
Joyce Westrip. Serve with rice.*

INGREDIENTS
4 skinless chicken breasts
120ml (4fl oz) vegetable oil
3 large onions, finely sliced
400ml (¾ pint) coconut milk (see page 141)
2 tbsp Serundeng (see page 133 for recipe), to garnish
For the marinade
300ml (½ pint) natural yogurt, lightly whisked
¼ tsp each of ground cloves and ground cinnamon
½ tsp salt
*½ tsp crumbled saffron strands, soaked in 3 tbsp
warm milk for 15 minutes*
For the paste
2 tsp white poppy seeds (see page 23), roughly crushed
10 cashew nuts, chopped
2 shallots, chopped
3 tsp finely chopped fresh ginger root
1 tsp finely chopped garlic
2–3 dried red chillies, chopped
*1 tsp coriander seeds, roasted (see page 155),
roughly crushed*
½ tsp cumin seeds, roasted (see page 155), roughly crushed
2 green cardamom pods, roughly crushed
1 tsp fennel seeds, roughly crushed
6 black peppercorns, roughly crushed
½ tsp salt, plus extra to taste
3 tbsp vegetable oil
125ml (4fl oz) hot water

PREPARATION
1 Mix all the marinade ingredients together in a
bowl. Add the chicken and marinate for 4 hours in
a cool place, or overnight in a refrigerator.
2 Put all the paste ingredients into a blender and
blend until as smooth as possible.
3 Heat the vegetable oil in a wok, add the onions
and fry until well browned. Remove half the
onions with a slotted spoon and transfer to a large
pan. Drain the remaining onions on kitchen paper.
4 Reheat the onions in the pan. Stir in the paste
mixture and bring to the boil. Reduce the heat and
simmer for 6–8 minutes, stirring frequently.
5 Add the chicken and marinade to the pan,
turning the meat until well coated. Simmer for
10 minutes, then add the coconut milk.
6 Bring to the boil, then cook over a medium heat
for 25–30 minutes. Season to taste. Transfer to a
warm platter, sprinkle with the reserved fried
onions and the Serundeng, then serve.

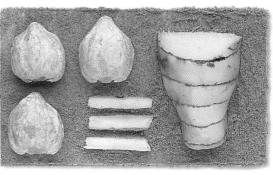

AYAM GORENG JAWA
Javanese fried chicken (Indonesia)

*If you prefer not to deep-fry the chicken, simply serve it
at the end of the cooking time in step 3 – it tastes just
as good. Serve with rice and a vegetable dish such as
Orak-arik (see page 113 for recipe).*

INGREDIENTS
600ml (1 pint) coconut milk (see page 141)
*1 chicken, about 1.75kg (3½lb), cut into
8–10 pieces (see page 153)*
salt, optional
about 600ml (1 pint) vegetable oil for deep-frying
For the paste
6 shallots, chopped
1 tsp ground coriander
*3 candle nuts (see page 22), or 5 blanched
almonds, chopped*
1 large fresh red chilli, deseeded and chopped
¼ tsp ground turmeric
*1cm (½in) piece of fresh galangal (see page 27),
peeled and chopped*
*5cm (2in) piece of fresh lemongrass, outer leaves
removed, centre chopped*
1 tsp salt
1 tsp grated palm sugar (see page 30), or demerara sugar

PREPARATION
1 Put all the paste ingredients, plus 90ml (3fl oz) of
the coconut milk, into a blender and blend until as
smooth as possible. Transfer the mixture to a large
pan and simmer, stirring frequently, for 6 minutes.
2 Add the chicken pieces to the pan and stir until
well coated with the paste mixture. Add the
remaining coconut milk and bring to the boil.
3 Lower the heat and simmer, uncovered, for
1 hour or until all the liquid is absorbed. Season
with salt, if required. Remove from the heat and
serve, if desired, or leave until cold.
4 Heat the oil in a large wok. Add half the chicken
pieces and fry, moving them about occasionally, for
10–12 minutes, until the skin is golden and crisp.
Remove from the pan and drain on kitchen paper.
Fry the remaining chicken, then serve hot or warm.

BEBEK BETUTU
Traditional long-cooked Balinese duck (Indonesia)

Here, I use kale or spinach as an alternative to the usual stuffing of cassava leaves, but the recipe still includes the traditional mix of Balinese spices. Serves 4–6 with rice.

INGREDIENTS
175–250g (6–8oz) curly kale or spinach, blanched in boiling water for 2 minutes, squeezed dry and shredded
1 duck, 1.75–2kg (3½–4lb)
For the paste
5 shallots or 2 medium onions, chopped
4 cloves garlic, chopped
5 fresh red chillies, deseeded and chopped
2 candle nuts (see page 22), or macadamia nuts, chopped (optional)
2 tsp coriander seeds, roughly crushed
1 tsp cumin seeds, roughly crushed
2 cloves, roughly crushed
2 green cardamom pods, roughly crushed
2.5cm (1in) piece of cinnamon stick, roughly crushed
¼ tsp ground or grated nutmeg
½ tsp ground turmeric
¼ tsp ground white pepper, plus extra to taste
1cm (½in) piece of fresh galangal (see page 27), peeled and chopped
5cm (2in) piece of fresh lemongrass, outer leaves removed, centre chopped
1 tsp dried shrimp paste (see page 31)
3 tbsp tamarind water (see page 101), or lime juice
2 tbsp each of groundnut oil and water
1 tsp salt, plus extra to taste

PREPARATION
1 Put all the paste ingredients into a blender and blend until as smooth as possible. Transfer the paste mixture to a pan and simmer for 6–8 minutes, stirring frequently. Season to taste, then transfer the paste to a glass bowl and leave to cool.
2 Mix half the cold paste with the shredded kale or spinach. Rub the remaining paste over the duck, inside and out. Stuff the shredded greens into the duck. Loosely wrap the duck in 2 or 3 layers of foil, folding the foil over at the top to seal.
3 Put the duck in a roasting tin and place in the centre of an oven preheated to 160°C/325°F/ Gas 3. Cook for 2 hours, then reduce the oven temperature to 120°C/250°F/Gas ½ and cook for a further 3–4 hours.
4 Unwrap the duck and transfer to a large dish. Spoon off and discard the oil from the cooking juices. For the sauce, pour the juices into a pan, add the stuffing from the duck and heat through.

5 Carve the duck – it will be very tender so the meat will come off the bones very easily – then transfer the meat to a heated serving platter. Serve the duck immediately, with the sauce poured over it or served separately in a bowl.

HAK TJIN TJAN NAH HIU
Stir-fried duck with black pepper (China)

I find that a stir-fry like this tastes much better if the slices of meat are marinated first. Frying the duck in plenty of very hot oil helps to make it more tender.

INGREDIENTS
4 duck breasts, each cut into 6 thin slices on the diagonal
125ml (4fl oz) vegetable oil
8 spring onions, each cut into 3 pieces
2 tbsp Shaohsing wine (see page 29), or dry sherry
1 tbsp dark soy sauce
salt and freshly ground black pepper, to taste
For the marinade
1 tbsp light soy sauce
1 tbsp Shaohsing wine (see page 29), or dry sherry
1 tsp ginger juice (see page 155)
½ tsp chilli oil
¼ tsp ground black pepper

PREPARATION
1 Mix all the marinade ingredients together in a large bowl. Add the slices of duck, turning them until well coated, then leave to marinate in a cool place for 2–3 hours.
2 Heat a wok and pour in the oil. When the oil is very hot, add the duck slices and stir-fry for 2 minutes. Remove from the wok with a slotted spoon and transfer to a plate.
3 Carefully pour off most of the oil, leaving about 1 tablespoon in the wok. Reheat the oil in the wok and add the spring onions. Stir-fry for 30 seconds, then add the duck.
4 Pour the wine or sherry over the meat, then carefully swirl the wok and tip it slightly so that the alcohol catches alight and flames the duck. Alternatively, light it with a match. Once the flames have died down, add the soy sauce and salt and pepper, to taste. Stir-fry the duck for about 30 seconds more, then serve immediately.

KALIO BEBEK

Duck pieces in rich coconut sauce (Indonesia)

In other Asian countries Kalio is known as "Indonesian curry". In fact it is not a true curry, since it does not use all the spices that are usually present in a curry paste.

INGREDIENTS

*1 duck, about 2kg (4lb), cut into 8–10 pieces
(see page 153), most of the fat removed
2 tbsp distilled white vinegar
2 litres (3 pints) boiling water
2 litres (3 pints) coconut milk (see page 141)
5 shallots, finely chopped
4 cloves garlic, finely chopped
2–6 large fresh red chillies, deseeded and finely chopped
½–1 tsp chilli powder, optional
2 tsp finely chopped fresh ginger root
1 tsp ground turmeric
2cm (¾in) piece of fresh galangal (see page 27)
1 stem of fresh lemongrass, cut across into 2 pieces
1 tsp salt, plus extra to taste
freshly ground black pepper, to taste*

PREPARATION

1 Wash the duck pieces in cold water and place in a bowl. Rub with the vinegar, then pour over the boiling water and leave to stand for 5 minutes. (The vinegar helps to remove the duck odour, while the boiling water melts the fat under the skin.) Drain the duck in a colander.

2 Put all the remaining ingredients in a large pan and add the duck. Bring to the boil, then lower the heat until the coconut milk bubbles gently.

3 Cook uncovered for 1½ hours, stirring frequently, until the sauce is quite thick and the meat is tender. Season to taste and discard the galangal and lemongrass before serving.

BATAKH VINDALOO

Duck curry (India)

A variation of the classic pork vindaloo from Goa, this curry uses plenty of garlic and chillies and has little fat. Serve with rice.

INGREDIENTS

4–6 duck breasts, skinned, each cut across into 5 pieces
90ml (6 tbsp) vegetable oil
2 large red onions, finely sliced
125ml (4fl oz) hot water
salt and freshly ground black pepper, to taste
For the marinade
3 tbsp red wine vinegar
½ tsp chilli powder
½ tsp salt
For the paste
3 shallots, chopped
5–8 cloves garlic, chopped
1cm (½in) piece of fresh ginger root, peeled and chopped
4–8 large fresh red chillies, deseeded and chopped
1 medium red pepper, deseeded and chopped
1 tsp cumin seeds, roughly crushed
2 tsp coriander seeds, roughly crushed
1cm (½in) piece of cinnamon stick, roughly crushed
2 cloves, roughly crushed
1 tsp grated palm sugar (see page 30), or demerara sugar
2 tbsp vegetable oil
1 tbsp distilled white vinegar
2 tbsp tamarind water (see page 101)

PREPARATION

1 Mix the marinade ingredients together. Put the duck pieces into a bowl. Pour the mixture over the duck and rub it well into the meat. Leave to marinade for 10 minutes.
2 Put all the paste ingredients into a blender and blend until as smooth as possible.
3 Heat the oil in a wok, add the onions and fry, stirring frequently, for 6–8 minutes or until they begin to brown. Remove the onions with a slotted spoon and transfer to a large pan.
4 Add half the duck pieces to the wok and cook for 3 minutes, stirring frequently. Remove with the slotted spoon and transfer to a bowl. Fry the remaining duck pieces.
5 Reheat the onions in the pan and stir for a few seconds. Add the paste mixture and simmer, stirring frequently, for 8 minutes.
6 Add the duck, along with any juices that have accumulated in the bowl. Stir once or twice, then add the hot water. Cover the pan, bring to the boil, then simmer for 40 minutes. Season to taste. Cook, uncovered, for 10–15 minutes, then serve hot.

SECH TEA ANG-KRUENG

Roasted and grilled duck with spices (Cambodia)

Rosine Ek, the chef proprietor of Chez Rosine Cuisine du Cambodge, Paris, gave me this recipe. It can be made with pork, lamb or beef but my favourite is the recipe that uses duck breasts, as described here. Serve with rice and a green salad or a selection of raw vegetables.

INGREDIENTS

4 duck breasts
For the marinade
2 tsp finely chopped lemongrass, centre part only
1 clove garlic, finely chopped
2 shallots, finely chopped
2 tsp dark soy sauce
½ tsp freshly ground black pepper
2 tsp fish sauce (nuoc mam), (see page 28)
2 tbsp coconut milk (see page 141)
For the sauce
125ml (4fl oz) water
2 tsp fish sauce (nuoc mam), (see page 28)
1 tbsp distilled white vinegar
½ tsp sugar
2–3 tbsp ground roasted peanuts
4 tbsp coconut milk (see page 141)
salt, to taste

PREPARATION

1 Mix the marinade ingredients together in a glass bowl. Add the duck breasts and leave to stand for 2 hours or overnight in the refrigerator.
2 For the sauce, mix the water, fish sauce, vinegar and sugar in a medium pan. Bring to the boil, then simmer for 5 minutes. Remove the pan from the heat and set aside.
3 Remove the duck breasts from the marinade and arrange on a rack in a roasting tin. Place in an oven preheated to 180°C/350°F/Gas 4 and roast for 20–25 minutes, turning once. Remove the duck from the oven and place under a preheated hot grill to brown further.
4 Cut each duck breast diagonally into 4 slices and arrange on a serving platter. Reheat the sauce and bring to the boil. Add the ground peanuts and cook, stirring, for 1 minute. Add the coconut milk and salt, if necessary, and simmer for 2 minutes. Pour the sauce over the duck and serve immediately.

CHINA

The philosophy of yin and yang underlies the ancient Chinese classification of foods into "cold" and "hot". These must be balanced if a meal is to be spiritually correct, healthy and delicious. Even the colours of these classic dishes suggest which ones are vigorous and assertive, and which are cooling and contemplative.

HOJAN HSIN TAIJI
Stir-fried scallops in oyster sauce.
(See page 79 for recipe.)

CHAR SIU PAAIH GWAT
Pork spare ribs in barbecue sauce.
(See page 102 for recipe.)

*HAHNG
YAHN DAUH FUH*
Almond float. (See page
137 for recipe.)

*LO HAN CHAI
Buddha's delight.
(See page 115 for recipe.)*

MEAT

It is only recently that people in Asia have bred animals just for their meat. Years ago, for most of us, fresh meat was holiday food, and usually pretty tough. For that reason, Asian women became experts at preparing and cooking meat in a variety of ways – cutting it into thin slices, marinating it, adding herbs and spices, or slow-cooking it in coconut milk – to produce tender and aromatic results. I have kept the traditional flavours of these dishes, but have adapted the recipes to suit the well-bred meat we are now used to in the West.

CHAR SIU

Roast strips of pork (China)

This is a classic Cantonese dish. Serve hot, as you would serve traditional roast pork, or mix cold slices with stir-fried vegetables, fried rice or fried noodles.

INGREDIENTS

1kg (2lb) boneless pork with some fat, from the neck end or leg, cut into 4 strips
2 tbsp clear honey
For the marinade
2 tbsp sugar
1 tbsp light soy sauce
2 tbsp yellow bean sauce
2 tbsp hoisin sauce
1 tbsp oyster sauce, optional
1 tsp five-spice powder (see page 27)
1 tbsp Shaohsing wine (see page 29), or dry sherry
½ tsp salt

PREPARATION

1 Mix the marinade ingredients together in a glass bowl. Add the meat and rub all over with the mixture. Marinate for 4–5 hours, turning the meat several times and rubbing it with the marinade.
2 Remove the pork strips from the marinade and place on a wire rack, side by side without touching. Place over a roasting tin half-filled with cold water.
3 Put the pork in an oven preheated to 190°C/375°F/Gas 5 and roast for 30 minutes. Remove the meat from the oven and dip the strips back into the marinade, turning them until well coated.
4 Arrange the pork on the rack again and return to the oven. Lower the temperature to 180°C/350°F/Gas 4 and cook for 30–35 minutes. Transfer the pork to a serving plate and brush with the honey. Cut the meat into thin slices and serve immediately.

MOO WAN

Sweet pork with marigold (Thailand)

Quite often a dish that is easy to make turns out to be the most popular. Here, the addition of kapi (Thai dried shrimp paste) gives the pork an authentic flavour. The marigold petal garnish is simple but effective.

INGREDIENTS

500g (1lb) pork fillet, cut into bite-sized pieces
1 tbsp dark soy sauce
¼ tsp salt, plus extra to taste
2 tbsp groundnut oil or vegetable oil
1 onion, finely chopped
2 tbsp grated palm sugar (see page 30), or dark soft brown sugar
2 tbsp fish sauce (nam pla), (see page 28)
1 tbsp light soy sauce
½ tsp ground white pepper
¼ tsp freshly ground black pepper, plus extra to taste
120ml (8 tbsp) hot water
1 tsp dried shrimp paste (kapi), (see page 31)
2 tbsp chopped fresh coriander leaves, to garnish
handful of fresh or dried marigold petals (see page 22), to garnish

PREPARATION

1 Place the pork in a glass bowl and rub with the dark soy sauce and salt. Leave to stand.
2 Heat the oil in a wok. Add the onion and fry until soft. Add the sugar and fish sauce, and stir vigorously until the sugar is caramelized.
3 Add the pork, stir-fry for 3 minutes, then add the light soy sauce, white and black pepper and hot water. Stir-fry over a high heat for 3 minutes.
4 Add the shrimp paste and stir-fry for 1–2 minutes more. Season to taste and sprinkle with the chopped coriander and marigold petals, to garnish.

PAD SOM SIN MOO

Pork in coconut milk with pickled onions (Laos)

*Like their Thai neighbours, the Lao use a lot
of coconut milk in their cooking. Serve with
plain steamed rice.*

INGREDIENTS

*4 large boneless pork chops, the lean meat cut into 1cm
(½ in) cubes, the fat reserved and roughly chopped
6 cloves garlic, finely sliced
1 tsp ground white pepper, plus extra to taste
2 tsp salt, plus extra to taste
600ml (1 pint) thick coconut milk (see page 141)
20 small red onions or pickling onions, peeled
juice of 1–2 limes
1 tbsp sugar
4 tbsp water
1 tbsp fish sauce (nam pla), (see page 28)
2 tbsp chopped spring onions, the green part only
4 tbsp chopped fresh coriander leaves*

PREPARATION

1 Put the reserved chopped pork fat in a pan and
heat until it becomes oily. Add the cubes of meat
and the sliced garlic and cook, stirring frequently,
for 3 minutes.

2 Remove and discard the pieces of fat. Add the
ground pepper and half the salt to the pan, stir
once, then add the coconut milk.

3 Bring the mixture to the boil, then reduce the
heat until the coconut milk bubbles slowly, and
cook uncovered for a further 30–35 minutes, or
until the coconut milk is quite thick.

4 Put the small red onions or pickling onions in
a pan with the lime juice, sugar, water and the
remaining salt. Simmer until all the liquid has
evaporated and the onions are caramelized.

5 Add the fish sauce to the thickened coconut
milk, increase the heat and stir-fry for 3 minutes.
Season to taste, then add the spring onions,
chopped coriander leaves and the caramelized
onions, and serve immediately.

CHA DUM
Pork loaf (Vietnam)

For the tastiest loaf it is best to use really good-quality ham. If all you can find is the ready-sliced, watery kind, it is better to leave it out. Serve with a green salad and Nuoc Cham (see page 128 for recipe). The loaf can also be added to casseroles or used as a sandwich filling.

INGREDIENTS

250g (8oz) fresh shiitake mushrooms, or 10 dried shiitake mushrooms, rehydrated (see page 155), stalks removed and caps thinly sliced
750g (1½ lb) minced lean pork
125–175g (4–6oz) good-quality ham, finely diced, optional
5 spring onions, finely chopped
1 tbsp fish sauce (nuoc mam), plus extra to taste
½ tsp salt, plus extra to taste
1 tsp freshly ground black pepper
3 large eggs, lightly beaten

PREPARATION

1 In a large bowl, mix the mushrooms with all the remaining ingredients, kneading them together for a few seconds. Fry a small spoonful of the mixture in a little oil and taste for seasoning. Add more salt or fish sauce to the remaining loaf mixture, if desired.
2 Pack the mixture into a well-greased 1kg (2lb) loaf tin, pressing it down with the back of a spoon. Cover the tin with several layers of foil, then place in the top of a steamer. Cover with the lid and steam over boiling water for 60–80 minutes, or until the centre of the loaf is cooked through.
3 Alternatively, stand the loaf tin in a roasting tin. Pour enough warm water around the loaf tin to come halfway up the sides. Place in an oven preheated to 180°C/350°F/Gas 4 and cook for 60–80 minutes, or until the centre of the loaf is cooked through.
4 Remove the loaf tin from the steamer or roasting tin and leave to cool slightly. Turn the loaf out of the tin on to a serving platter and leave until cold. Serve thinly sliced.

ADOBONG BABOY
Red stew of pork (Philippines)

I am told that Adobo, or "Adobong", has long held an honoured place in the cuisine of the Philippines. There, a red stew usually takes its colour from annatto seed, but here I use the more widely available paprika and ground turmeric instead. Serves 6–8 with plenty of rice.

INGREDIENTS

1.5kg (3lb) pork leg meat, cut into 2cm (¾ in) cubes
6–8 cloves garlic, finely chopped
125ml (4fl oz) distilled white vinegar, or rice vinegar (see page 29)
1.25 litres (2 pints) water
2 fresh kaffir lime leaves (see page 26), or bay leaves
1 tsp salt, plus extra to taste
3 tbsp vegetable oil
3 shallots, chopped
2 cloves garlic, crushed
1–2 large fresh red chillies, deseeded and chopped
1 tsp paprika
1 tsp ground turmeric
175ml (6fl oz) very thick coconut milk (see page 141)
2 tbsp fish sauce (nam pla), (see page 28)
freshly ground black pepper, to taste

PREPARATION

1 Put the pork, garlic, vinegar and water into a large pan. Bring to the boil, then boil gently for 40 minutes, skimming occasionally. Add the lime leaves or bay leaves and salt, and cook for 5 minutes.
2 Remove the meat from the pan with a slotted spoon and transfer to a colander to drain. Boil the stock for a further 30 minutes, skimming the froth frequently. Strain 600ml (1 pint) of the stock into a bowl.
3 Heat the oil in a large pan. Add the shallots, garlic and chillies, and fry for 2 minutes. Add the paprika and turmeric, and stir for a few seconds. Add about 5 tablespoons of the coconut milk and stir again, once or twice.
4 Add the meat and stir until the pieces are coloured with the paprika and turmeric. Add the measured stock and the fish sauce and cook for 30 minutes. Add the remaining coconut milk and cook over a medium heat for 20 minutes. Season to taste and serve.

MAKING TAMARIND WATER

1 Place a block of tamarind pulp in a large bowl. Add enough hand-hot water to cover, then squeeze the pulp between your fingers until it has separated from the seeds and the water is brown.

2 Pour the mixture into a sieve set over a pan. Strain off the liquid, mashing the pulp against the sides of the sieve. Bring the liquid in the pan to the boil, then simmer for 10 minutes. Leave to cool.

3 Spoon 1 tablespoon of liquid into each section of an ice-cube tray, then freeze. Remove the cubes from the tray and store in freezer bags. Use one cube for each tablespoon of tamarind water.

VINDALOO

Pork cooked in chilli-hot and sour sauce (India)

This is a traditional Goan dish. It can be short-cooked using pork fillet, or long-cooked using pork leg meat. Serves 6–8 with rice. See page 135 for illustration.

INGREDIENTS

*1.5kg (3lb) pork fillet or lean leg meat,
cut into 1cm (½in) cubes
120ml (8 tbsp) vegetable oil
3 large red or white onions, finely sliced
6 fresh or dried curry leaves (see page 26), optional
175ml (6fl oz) or 900ml (1½ pints) hot water
salt and freshly ground black pepper, to taste*
For the marinade
*3 tbsp red wine vinegar
1 tsp salt
½ tsp chilli powder*
For the paste
*4 shallots, chopped
6–8 cloves garlic, chopped
4–8 large fresh red chillies, deseeded and chopped
1 large red pepper, deseeded and chopped
2cm (¾in) piece of peeled fresh ginger root, chopped
1 tbsp coriander seeds, roughly crushed
2 tsp cumin seeds, roughly crushed
2 cloves, roughly crushed
1cm (½in) piece of cinnamon stick, roughly crushed
1 tsp grated palm sugar (see page 30), or soft brown sugar
2 tbsp vegetable oil
2 tbsp distilled white vinegar
2 tbsp tamarind water (see steps above)*

PREPARATION

1 Mix the marinade ingredients together. Put the cubed pork into a bowl and rub all over with the marinade. Leave to marinate for 10 minutes.
2 Put all the paste ingredients into a blender and blend until as smooth as possible.
3 Heat the vegetable oil in a wok, add the onions and fry, stirring frequently, for 8–10 minutes. Remove from the wok with a slotted spoon.
4 Add the meat to the wok in 3 or 4 batches and fry for 3 minutes per batch. Remove the meat from the wok with the slotted spoon.
5 Put the onions into a large pan. Place over a medium heat and reheat, stirring for a few seconds. Add the paste mixture and simmer, stirring frequently, for 8 minutes. Add the meat and the curry leaves, if using, and stir until well coated.
6 If using pork fillet, add 175ml (6fl oz) hot water. For leg meat, add 900ml (1½ pints) hot water. Bring to the boil, then cover, and simmer for 20 minutes for the fillet, or 1 hour and 20 minutes for the leg meat. Season to taste, cook uncovered for 1 minute more, then serve immediately.

TWAEJIGOGI SAEKTCHIM

Stuffed pork with vegetables (Korea)

At first glance this dish looks complicated to make. In fact it is quite straightforward and after cooking it a few times I find I enjoy it more and more. Serve with rice.

INGREDIENTS

500–625g (1–1¼lb) pork fillet, cut into 4 crossways
1 tsp each of salt and freshly ground black pepper
4 tbsp vegetable oil
2 tbsp pine nuts, roasted (see page 155), to garnish

For the filling
2–3 tbsp vegetable oil
1 tsp sesame oil
1 large carrot, cut into julienne strips (see page 154)
2 small courgettes, cut into julienne strips
(see page 154)
8 button mushrooms, finely sliced
6 dried shiitake mushrooms, rehydrated (see page 155),
stalks removed and caps finely sliced

For the sauce
2 tbsp dried shrimps (see page 31)
2 tbsp chopped fresh ginger root
1 clove garlic, chopped
¼ tsp sugar or 1 tbsp mirin (see page 29)
1 tbsp light soy sauce
pinch of salt
4 tbsp water

PREPARATION

1 Rub the pork with the salt and pepper, and leave to stand for 5 minutes. Heat the oil in a frying pan, add the pieces of pork and cook for 3–4 minutes, turning frequently. Remove from the pan and set aside. Wipe the pan clean.
2 For the filling, mix the vegetable oil and sesame oil together and heat in the frying pan. Add the carrot, stir-fry for 1 minute, then remove from the pan. Cook the remaining vegetables in separate batches for 1 minute each.
3 Put the sauce ingredients into a blender and blend until as smooth as possible. Transfer the mixture to a small pan and simmer for 4 minutes. Pass the sauce through a sieve into a small bowl.
4 Make 4 parallel cuts across each piece of meat, taking care not to cut right through. Place the pork in a heatproof dish deep enough to hold the juices that form during cooking.
5 Stuff some of the carrots into a cut in one portion of the meat. Fill the remaining cuts with some of the other vegetables, keeping each type separate.
6 Stuff the other pieces of pork in the same way. Arrange the remaining vegetables on top of the meat, so that the colours match those of the stuffing.

7 Pour the sauce evenly over the vegetables and pork. Place the dish in a steamer, cover, and steam over rapidly boiling water for 10–12 minutes. Remove the dish from the steamer, sprinkle with the pine nuts, to garnish, and serve immediately.

CHAR SIU PAAIH GWAT

Pork spare ribs in barbecue sauce (China)

Here is the Chinese original of the Thai steamed and grilled spare ribs (see opposite). The ribs can be eaten with rice or noodles, or just by themselves with salad. See page 96 for illustration.

INGREDIENTS

2 litres (3 pints) water
½ tsp salt
1kg (2lb) pork spare ribs, cut into
7–8cm (3–3½in) lengths
3 tbsp vegetable oil
2 tsp finely chopped fresh ginger root
6 shallots, finely chopped
2 tbsp dark soy sauce
2 tbsp light soy sauce
2 tbsp hoisin sauce
1 tsp sugar
1 tsp freshly ground black pepper
4 tbsp hot water
2 tbsp Shaohsing wine (see page 29), or dry sherry
90ml (6 tbsp) chicken stock
spring onion brushes (see page 155), to garnish

PREPARATION

1 Boil the water in a large pan and add the salt. Add the ribs to the pan and simmer for 4 minutes. Drain the ribs and pat dry with kitchen paper.
2 Heat the oil in a large heavy-based casserole. Add the ribs and stir-fry for 3 minutes. Add the ginger and shallots, and stir-fry for 2 minutes.
3 Add the two types of soy sauce, the hoisin sauce, sugar and black pepper. Increase the heat, stir-fry for 30 seconds, then add the hot water. Stir again and cover the pot.
4 Place the casserole in an oven preheated to 160°C/325°F/Gas 3 and cook for 1–1¼ hours. Stir in the Shaohsing wine or sherry, then remove the ribs from the sauce and arrange them, side by side, in a large roasting tin.
5 Return the ribs to the oven, increase the temperature to 200°C/400°F/Gas 6 and cook for 10–15 minutes more. Transfer the remaining sauce from the casserole to a small pan. Add the chicken stock and reheat. Arrange the ribs on a plate, garnish with the spring onions and serve with the sauce.

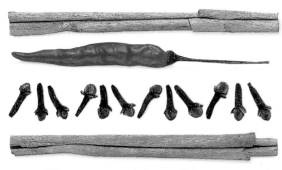

GRADOOK MOO NUENG TAO JEAW

Steamed and grilled spare ribs with yellow bean sauce (Thailand)

This is one of the many popular Thai dishes with a strong Chinese influence. The Thai version has bird's eye chillies and tamarind added to the sauce.

INGREDIENTS

1kg (2lb) pork spare ribs, cut into 7.5cm (3in) lengths
125ml (4fl oz) hot water
salt and freshly ground black pepper, to taste
For the marinade/sauce
4 tbsp yellow bean sauce
2 cloves garlic, crushed
2–6 fresh red bird's eye chillies, crushed
¼ tsp ground cloves
¼ tsp ground cinnamon
2 tbsp ginger juice (see page 155)
2 tbsp tamarind water (see page 101)
1 tbsp dark soy sauce
2 tsp fish sauce (nam pla), (see page 28)
1 tsp grated palm sugar (see page 30), or soft brown sugar

PREPARATION

1 Mix the marinade ingredients together in a glass bowl. Put the ribs into another bowl, then coat well with a third of the marinade. Leave in a cool place for 2 hours, or refrigerate overnight.
2 Transfer the remaining marinade to a pan. Add the hot water and boil, stirring frequently, for 5 minutes. Season to taste, then leave to cool.
3 Bring the ribs back to room temperature, then place in a steamer and cook for 1 hour. Remove the ribs from the steamer and leave until cold. (Up to this point everything can be prepared well in advance and refrigerated.)
4 Allow the ribs and sauce to come back to room temperature. Pour half the sauce into a pan and bring to the boil to reheat.
5 Arrange the ribs on a grill pan and place under a preheated hot grill. Cook for 4–5 minutes, turning frequently and brushing with the remaining sauce. Pour the reheated sauce into a bowl and serve as a dipping sauce with the ribs.

MASSAMAN

Beef curry (Thailand)

The original recipe for this dish travelled with Islam from the Middle East to Asia. The Thais have put their signature to this Massaman – that is, Muslim – curry by adding their own favourite ingredients of coriander root, kaffir lime rind and fish sauce.

INGREDIENTS

3 tbsp vegetable oil
2 large onions, finely sliced
1kg (2lb) brisket or chuck steak, most of the fat removed, cut into 2cm (¾ in) cubes
2 pieces of dried galangal (see page 27)
3–5 pieces of dried kaffir lime rind (see page 22)
2 stems of fresh lemongrass, halved
3 cloves
3cm (1½ in) piece of cinnamon stick
1 tsp salt, plus extra to taste
900ml (1½ pints) hot water
600ml (1 pint) coconut milk (see page 141)
375g (12oz) small new potatoes
2 tbsp tamarind water (see page 101)
1–2 tsp grated palm sugar (see page 30), or brown sugar
2 tbsp roasted peanuts, chopped, to garnish
For the paste
2–6 large fresh red chillies, deseeded and chopped
4 cloves garlic, chopped
2 tbsp coriander seeds, roasted (see page 155), roughly crushed
1 tbsp cumin seeds, roasted (see page 155), roughly crushed
¼ tsp grated nutmeg
3 coriander roots (see page 26), or stems, chopped
1 tbsp fish sauce (nam pla), (see page 28)

PREPARATION

1 Heat the oil in a pan. Add the onions and fry, stirring continuously, for 6–8 minutes, until they begin to brown. Add the meat, stir for 2–3 seconds, then add the galangal, lime rind, lemongrass, cloves and cinnamon. Stir again and add the salt and hot water. Bring to the boil, cover, and cook over a medium heat for 55–60 minutes, stirring frequently.
2 Put all the paste ingredients, plus 4 tablespoons of the coconut milk, into a blender and blend until as smooth as possible. Transfer the paste to a small pan and simmer, stirring frequently, for 8 minutes.
3 Remove the galangal, lime rind, lemongrass, cloves and cinnamon from the meat. Add the new potatoes and stir in the paste, blending well.
4 Simmer, uncovered, for 5 minutes. Add the rest of the coconut milk, the tamarind water and sugar. Cook, uncovered, for 30 minutes. Add more salt, to taste, and sprinkle with the peanuts, to garnish.

HUHNG SIU NGAUH

Red-cooked beef with broccoli (China)

*In Chinese cookery, the term "red-cooked" refers to any
food that is long-cooked in soy sauce. Long cooking is a
convenient way of catering for large numbers, as the dish
can be prepared well in advance and reheated when
required without any deterioration of the flavour or
texture. Serves 6–8 with steamed or boiled white rice.*

INGREDIENTS

2kg (4lb) piece of rolled brisket, cut in half across
2 litres (3 pints) water
1 tsp salt, plus extra to taste
1 large onion, roughly chopped
3 slices of peeled fresh ginger root
3 tbsp vegetable oil
2 tsp finely chopped fresh ginger root
*1 tsp freshly ground black pepper, plus
extra to taste*
4 tbsp dark soy sauce
*1cm (½in) piece of cassia bark (see page 27),
or cinnamon stick*
1 star anise
900ml (1½ pints) hot water
*4 tbsp Shaohsing wine (see page 29),
or dry white wine*
500–750g (1–1½lb) broccoli, cut into small florets

PREPARATION

1 Put the beef, water, salt, onion and sliced ginger
in a large pan and bring to the boil. Lower the heat
a little, then cover and boil gently for 1 hour.
2 Remove the beef from the stock and transfer to
a chopping board. Strain the stock into a bowl and
skim well. Measure and reserve 600ml (1 pint) of
the stock. Cut the beef into 2.5cm (1in) cubes and
pat dry with kitchen paper.
3 Heat the oil in a large casserole, add the cubed
beef and stir-fry for 2 minutes. Add the chopped
ginger, the black pepper, soy sauce, cassia bark
or cinnamon stick and the star anise, and stir-fry
for a few seconds.
4 Add the hot water and stir once. Cover the
casserole, place in an oven preheated to 150°C/
300°F/Gas 2 and cook for 1 hour and 20 minutes.
5 Remove the casserole from the oven and add the
wine and the reserved stock. Stir once and season
to taste. Remove the cassia bark or cinnamon stick
and star anise. Cover the casserole and return to
the oven. Lower the temperature to 120°C/250°F/
Gas ½ and cook for 1 hour.
6 Remove the casserole from the oven and place
over a medium heat. Add the broccoli florets,
simmer uncovered for 8–10 minutes, then serve.

Vegetable oil

Fresh ginger

Onion

Salt

Rolled brisket

Black pepper

Dark soy sauce

Cassia bark

Star anise

Shaohsing
wine

Broccoli

SUKIYAKI

Beef and vegetable hot pot (Japan)

This recipe is based on recollections of a magnificent sukiyaki prepared by a visiting Japanese professor at my university in central Java. He cooked it in a proper sukiyaki pot (see page 149) at the dining table, while his wife passed around the guests' bowls as they were filled and refilled. Chopsticks are normally used to cook and eat with, but where hot oil is concerned you may feel safer with a spoon and fork or tongs. Serve with Japanese rice.

INGREDIENTS

4 eggs, optional
soy sauce, to serve
200g (7oz) shirataki (see page 24), optional
about 4 tbsp vegetable oil
750g (1½lb) very thinly sliced beef sirloin (see page 152)
6 spring onions, thinly sliced on the diagonal
500g (1lb) firm tofu (see page 24), cut into 16 cubes
125–175g (4–6oz) fresh shiitake mushrooms
or chestnut mushrooms, thinly sliced
175g (6oz) watercress
For the broth
about 600ml (1 pint) clear beef or chicken stock
3 tbsp dark soy sauce
1 tbsp mirin (see page 29)
4 tbsp sake (see page 29)
1–2 tsp sugar, optional

PREPARATION

1 Mix the broth ingredients in a pan. Bring to simmering point and keep hot, so it can be taken to the table in a bowl. Alternatively, pour the broth into a fondue pot, so it can simmer at the table.
2 Arrange a sukiyaki pot (see page 149) or an electric frying pan on the dining table, and turn on the heat. Provide each diner with a small bowl of cooked rice, an empty soup bowl and a pair of chopsticks. Place an unbroken egg on a small plate by the side of each empty bowl. On the table there must also be a small bowl of soy sauce.
3 If using the shirataki, cook them in a large pan of boiling salted water for 3–4 minutes. Drain well in a colander, then rinse under cold running water and drain again.
4 To serve, put 1–2 tablespoons of the oil into the hot sukiyaki pot or frying pan. When it is hot, add 4–8 slices of the meat and fry, turning several times.
5 Add a few pieces of spring onion, 4 pieces of tofu, a few slices of mushroom and sprigs of watercress to the pot or pan. Stir for 1–2 minutes, then add a ladle of simmering broth and some of the shirataki, if using, and heat through.

6 Everybody helps themselves from the pot or pan: the egg, if desired, is broken over the food in the soup bowl, then some of the simmering broth is spooned over. The egg is stirred until it scrambles in the hot stock, then a few drops of soy sauce are added.
7 The cook adds more ingredients and broth to the pot as they become depleted. The rice is eaten between the meat and vegetables or by itself at the end of the meal.
8 The broth remaining in each bowl is drunk like tea from a cup, but if preferred a soup spoon can be used.

BOXAO MANG

Beef with bamboo shoots (Vietnam)

You can find Indonesian, Malaysian, Singaporean and Filipino variations of this classic Southeast Asian dish. Serves 2 with rice or noodles.

INGREDIENTS

4 tbsp groundnut oil or soya oil
375g (12oz) rump steak, cut across the grain into 2cm (¾in) wide strips (see page 152)
200g (7oz) canned bamboo shoots, drained and rinsed, sliced lengthways into thin strips
4 spring onions, thinly sliced on the diagonal
3 tbsp sesame seeds, roasted (see page 155), crushed with a pestle and mortar
For the Nuoc Cham
2 tbsp fish sauce (nuoc mam), (see page 28)
2 cloves garlic, crushed
1–2 small dried red chillies, finely chopped
juice of half a lime or lemon
large pinch of salt
large pinch of sugar, optional

PREPARATION

1 Put the ingredients for the Nuoc Cham in a small glass bowl and mix together well with a teaspoon.
2 Heat a wok until very hot, then add half the oil and heat until smoking. Add the beef and stir-fry quickly for 1 minute. Remove the beef with a slotted spoon and transfer to a plate.
3 Add the remaining oil to the wok and heat until smoking. Add the bamboo shoots and stir-fry for 1 minute, then add the spring onions and fry for 1 minute more.
4 Add the Nuoc Cham to the wok and stir-fry over a very high heat for 30 seconds. Add the beef and the crushed sesame seeds. Cook for another 30 seconds to heat the beef through, then serve immediately.

GULE KAMBING
Aromatic lamb stew (Indonesia)

In central Java Gule Kambing is made with goat meat. I use lamb, usually the best end of neck, the saddle or fillet end of leg. Serves 6–8 with plenty of plain boiled or steamed white rice.

INGREDIENTS

*1.5–2kg (3–4lb) lean lamb, cut into
1.5cm (½in) cubes
600ml (1 pint) hot water
5cm (2in) piece of cinnamon stick
1 stem of fresh lemongrass, cut into 3 pieces
2 fresh kaffir lime leaves (see page 26), or bay leaves
250–375ml (8–12fl oz) thick coconut milk
(see page 141)
salt and freshly ground black pepper, to taste
2 tbsp Crisp-fried Onions (see page 132
for recipe), to garnish
handful of fresh flat-leaf parsley, to garnish*
For the paste
*5 shallots or 1 onion, chopped
4 cloves garlic, chopped
3 candle nuts (see page 22), or macadamia nuts,
roughly chopped
2–4 large fresh red chillies, deseeded and chopped
¼ tsp ground white pepper
2 tsp chopped fresh ginger root
1 tsp chopped fresh galangal (see page 27)
1 tsp ground turmeric
2 tsp ground coriander
2 cloves, roughly crushed
1 tsp salt
4 tbsp tamarind water (see page 101)
3 tbsp vegetable oil*

PREPARATION

1 Put all the paste ingredients into a blender and blend until as smooth as possible. Transfer the paste mixture to a large pan and simmer, stirring frequently, for 6–8 minutes.
2 Add the meat to the pan and cook, stirring continuously, for 2 minutes. Add the hot water, cinnamon stick, lemongrass and lime leaves or bay leaves. Cover and simmer for 30 minutes.
3 Add the coconut milk to the pan and cook, uncovered, over a low heat for 30–40 minutes, stirring frequently. The exact cooking time will depend on the desired consistency of the sauce.
4 Season to taste, then remove the cinnamon stick, lemongrass and lime leaves or bay leaves.
5 Transfer the stew to a serving bowl and sprinkle with the Crisp-fried Onions and chopped fresh parsley, to garnish.

KAMBING KORMA
Lamb curry with coconut milk (Malaysia)

This curry is very similar to the Muslim lamb korma of central India, except that it is not made with yogurt. Often, as in India, it is served with roti (bread), especially at lunchtime. For an evening meal, it is served with rice. Serves 6–8 with roti or rice.

INGREDIENTS

*1kg (2lb) mutton or lamb leg meat,
cut into 2cm (¾in) cubes
1 tsp salt, plus extra to taste
75ml (5 tbsp) ghee (see page 29), or vegetable oil
5 shallots or 1 large red onion, finely chopped
6 cloves garlic, finely chopped
2 tsp chopped fresh ginger root
2 tsp finely chopped fresh lemongrass, centre only
5cm (2in) piece of cinnamon stick
2 fresh or dried curry leaves (see page 26), or bay leaves
600ml (1 pint) hot water
250ml (8fl oz) very thick coconut milk (see page 141)
freshly ground black pepper, to taste*
For the dry spice mixture
*2 tsp coriander seeds
1 tsp cumin seeds
1 tsp fennel seeds
seeds of 3 green cardamom pods
4 cloves
10 black peppercorns*

PREPARATION

1 Roast the dry spice mixture (see page 155) for 3 minutes, then leave to cool. Grind to a fine powder in a spice mill or using a pestle and mortar.
2 Place the cubes of meat in a large glass bowl. Sprinkle with the ground spices and the salt, and mix together well. Leave to stand in a cool place for 15–20 minutes.
3 Heat the ghee or oil in a wok or large shallow pan. Add half the meat and fry for 5 minutes, stirring continuously. Remove the meat from the wok with a slotted spoon and transfer to a plate. Fry the remaining meat and remove from the wok.
4 Reheat the wok, add the shallots or onion and stir-fry for 5 minutes. Add the garlic, ginger and lemongrass, and stir-fry for 2 minutes more.
5 Return the meat to the wok, add the cinnamon stick and curry leaves or bay leaves and stir once. Add the hot water, then cover and simmer for 40–45 minutes.
6 Stir in the coconut milk and simmer for 20 minutes, stirring frequently. Season to taste, and remove the cinnamon stick and curry leaves or bay leaves before serving.

ALOO GOSHT

Meat curry with potatoes (India)

Lamb is the usual meat for this curry, but you will also find this dish made with beef or chicken, depending on where you are in Asia. Serve with roti (bread) or rice.

INGREDIENTS

*4 medium potatoes, cut in half crossways,
each half quartered
4 large or 8 small lamb chops
200g (7oz) can of chopped tomatoes
120ml (4fl oz) hot water
4 tbsp natural yogurt
salt and freshly ground black pepper, to taste*
For the paste
*4 shallots, chopped
2 cloves garlic, chopped
8 white peppercorns, roughly crushed
¼ tsp chilli powder
1 tbsp coriander seeds, roughly crushed
2 tsp cumin seeds, roughly crushed
1 tsp ground turmeric
¼ tsp salt
3 tbsp vegetable oil
4 tbsp water*

PREPARATION

1 Put the potatoes in a large bowl of lightly salted cold water until ready to use.

2 Put the paste ingredients into a blender and blend until as smooth as possible. Transfer the paste mixture to a pan and simmer, stirring frequently, for 4–5 minutes.

3 Add the lamb chops to the pan and cook, turning frequently, until brown all over. Drain the potato pieces, add them to the pan and cook, stirring continuously, for 2–3 minutes.

4 Add the chopped tomatoes, cover, and simmer for 15 minutes. Add the hot water, cover, and cook over a medium heat for 20 minutes, or until the potatoes are tender.

5 Add the yogurt, a spoonful a time, stirring briskly. Simmer for 5 minutes, season and serve.

DALCHA
Lamb cooked with lentils (India)

*This everyday Indian dish is simple to make and the
ingredients are readily available. Any dhal or lentils
can be made into Dalcha, but my own favourite
is red lentils. Serve with rice.*

INGREDIENTS

500g (1lb) lean lamb leg meat, cut into 2cm (¾in) cubes
1 medium onion, finely sliced
1 tsp ground cumin
2 tsp finely chopped fresh ginger root
1½ tsp salt, plus extra to taste
3 tbsp tamarind water (see page 101)
*2 medium purple aubergines, halved crossways,
each half quartered*
125g (4oz) French beans, halved
4 ripe tomatoes, skinned and quartered
½ tsp chilli powder
handful of fresh coriander leaves, to garnish
For the lentils
1 tsp ground coriander
¼ tsp chilli powder
½ tsp mustard powder
½ tsp fenugreek seeds, ground
½ tsp ground turmeric
250g (8oz) red lentils, washed and drained
600ml (1 pint) water
For the fried ingredients
4 tbsp vegetable oil
1 large onion, sliced
2–3 dried chillies, each cut into 3 pieces
1 clove garlic, crushed
½ tsp each of yellow mustard seeds and cumin seeds
4 fresh or dried curry leaves (see page 26), optional
large pinch of asafoetida (see page 30), optional

PREPARATION

1 For the lentils, put all the ingredients into a
large pan. Bring to a boil, then cover and
simmer for 15 minutes.
2 Add the cubed lamb and onion. Stir, then add the
cumin, ginger and salt. Cook, stirring continuously,
for 1–2 minutes until all the ingredients are well
mixed. Stir in the tamarind water, then cover and
cook over a low heat for 20 minutes.
3 Add the aubergines and beans and cook, covered,
for 8 minutes. Add the tomatoes and chilli powder
and simmer for 4 minutes. Taste and season with
more salt, if desired.
4 For the fried ingredients, heat half the vegetable
oil in a heavy-based frying pan. Add the onion and
fry until golden brown. Remove the onion with a
slotted spoon and drain on kitchen paper.

5 Pour the rest of the oil into the frying pan. Add
the chillies, garlic, mustard and cumin seeds, curry
leaves and asafoetida, if using. Stir-fry for 1 minute.
6 Transfer the Dalcha to a serving platter and
spoon the fried ingredients over it, along with half
the oil in the pan. Sprinkle with the fried onions
and the fresh coriander, to garnish.

KHOUA SIN FAHN
Venison in rich coconut sauce (Laos)

*I am told that in Laos, as in several Asian countries, what
we call venison is the meat of a much smaller animal
than the Western deer. The meat is cooked in thick coconut
milk until the water evaporates, so that by the end of
cooking the meat is fried in the oil. Serves 6–8.*

INGREDIENTS

2 litres (3 pints) thick coconut milk (see page 141)
*1.5kg (3lb) venison, from the saddle or haunch,
cut into 2cm (¾in) cubes*
1 tsp salt, plus extra to taste
4 tbsp chopped spring onions
For the paste
4 cloves garlic, chopped
2–4 large fresh red chillies, deseeded and chopped
5 shallots, chopped
3 fresh kaffir lime leaves (see page 26), chopped

PREPARATION

1 Put the paste ingredients, plus 90ml (3fl oz) of
the coconut milk, into a blender and blend until
as smooth as possible.
2 Transfer the paste mixture to a large pan. Add
the venison, salt and the remaining coconut milk
and stir well.
3 Bring the mixture to the boil, then reduce the
heat a little so that the coconut milk bubbles gently.
Cook for 1½ hours, stirring occasionally, until the
coconut milk has reduced and thickened.
4 Transfer the mixture to a wok and cook until
the sauce becomes oily. Cook, stirring frequently,
for 15 minutes, until the sauce is thick. Season to
taste and add the spring onions. Cook, stirring
continuously, for 1 minute, then serve.

THAILAND

The Thai cook lets every ingredient speak for itself, using vegetables, herbs and fruit in the same dish as salty fish sauce, dried shrimps and pungent spices. Against these are set fragrant rice, noodles and delicately flavoured seafood.

YAM WOON SEN
Spicy salad of cellophane vermicelli, prawns and pork.
(See page 119 for recipe.)

YAM PLA
MUEK MAMUANG
Green mango and squid salad.
(See page 119 for recipe.)

HOY LAI PHAD
NAM PRIK PHAO
*Braised clams with
basil. (See page 85
for recipe.)*

VEGETABLES & SALADS

In Western cookery books, recipes for vegetable dishes and salads are often found in separate chapters. But in Asia we have never made much of a distinction between cooked and raw garden produce. We like to harvest our vegetables when they are young and tender and need little or no cooking, so raw and cooked can be mixed together in warm salads. They have to be as appealing to the senses as anything else on the table, varied in colour and texture as well as flavour.

KAJITCHIM

Steamed stuffed aubergines (Korea)

Traditionally, these aubergines have minced beef mixed into the stuffing. This recipe is a vegetarian version to be eaten with rice or noodles.

INGREDIENTS

4 purple aubergines, about 12–15cm (5–6in) long
3 large onions, sliced
½ tsp salt
75ml (5 tbsp) warm water
3 tbsp vegetable oil
For the stuffing
2 cloves garlic, finely chopped
2 tsp sesame seeds
½ tsp coarse sea salt
250–300g (8–10oz) Chinese-style tofu
2 tbsp vegetable oil
1 tsp sesame oil
3 shallots, finely chopped
1 large fresh red chilli, deseeded and finely chopped
125g (4oz) fresh shiitake mushrooms, stalks removed and caps thinly sliced
250g (8oz) button mushrooms, thinly sliced
1 tsp very finely chopped fresh ginger root
1 tbsp light soy sauce
2 tbsp chopped spring onions
2 tbsp chopped fresh flat-leaf parsley or celery leaves
salt and freshly ground black pepper, to taste

PREPARATION

1 Cut 4 slits in each aubergine, as if cutting in quarters lengthways, but leaving the ends intact. Set aside while preparing the stuffing.
2 For the stuffing, crush the garlic, sesame seeds and salt to a paste, using a pestle and mortar.
3 Put the tofu in a bowl and cover with boiling water. Leave to stand for 10 minutes, then drain it in a colander and leave to cool. When cool enough to handle, wrap the tofu in a piece of muslin or a clean tea towel and squeeze out all the excess water.
4 Heat the vegetable oil and sesame oil in a wok. Add the shallots and fry, stirring continuously, for 2 minutes. Stir in the garlic and sesame seed paste and the chopped chilli. Add both types of mushrooms and the ginger and cook, stirring frequently, for 4 minutes.
5 Add the tofu, crushing it with the back of a spoon, and stir the mixture until everything is thoroughly blended. Stir in the soy sauce, spring onions and parsley, and season to taste.
6 Spoon the stuffing into the slits in each aubergine. Spread the sliced onions in the bottom of a large pan. Sprinkle with the salt and pour the warm water over them. Arrange the stuffed aubergines on top of the onions in a single layer.
7 Cover and cook over a low heat for 1 hour. Check the pan regularly, to make sure that the onions have not dried out and started to burn. Add more water if necessary. Alternatively, arrange all the ingredients in a large casserole and bake in an oven preheated to 160°C/325°F/Gas 3 for 1½ hours.
8 Transfer the aubergines to a warm serving platter. Add the vegetable oil to the onions in the pan or casserole and fry, stirring continuously, for 3–4 minutes, or until browned. Spoon the onions over the aubergines and serve.

YAM MAKHUA PHAO

Sweet and sour aubergines (Thailand)

For this dish, small round aubergines are normally used; they are available in Thai and some Chinese shops. Here, however, I have used large purple aubergines and have roasted them instead of the usual boiling or steaming.

INGREDIENTS

2 large purple aubergines
30g (1oz) dried shrimps (see page 31)
2 tbsp chopped fresh coriander leaves
For the dressing
2 shallots, very finely sliced
1–2 bird's eye chillies, finely chopped
3 tbsp fish sauce (nam pla), (see page 28)
3 tbsp lime or lemon juice
1 tbsp sugar
75ml (5 tbsp) water

PREPARATION

1 Place the whole aubergines on a baking tray and roast in an oven preheated to 190°C/375°F/Gas 5 for 35–40 minutes. Transfer the hot aubergines to a plastic bag and leave until cool enough to handle.
2 Peel off the skin from the warm aubergines, then cut each one into large chunks and transfer to a salad bowl. Roast the dried shrimps for 2–3 minutes (see page 155), then leave to cool. Grind to a coarse powder with a pestle and mortar and set aside.
3 Put the dressing ingredients into a small pan and simmer for 2 minutes. Pour over the aubergines, then sprinkle with the ground shrimps and the chopped coriander. Toss the ingredients together, to mix well, and serve at room temperature.

ORAK-ARIK

Stir-fried cabbage with eggs (Indonesia)

I am not exaggerating if I say that virtually everybody in Java knows how to cook this very simple and homely dish, and everybody likes it. Serves 4–6 as a side dish.

INGREDIENTS

3–4 tbsp vegetable oil
4 shallots, finely sliced
2 cloves garlic, finely chopped
1 tsp finely chopped fresh ginger root, optional
500–750g (1–1½ lb) white cabbage, finely shredded
1 tsp salt, plus extra to taste
75ml (5 tbsp) hot water
¼–½ tsp ground white pepper, plus extra to taste
2–3 eggs, lightly beaten

PHOOL GOBI AUR ALOO KI BHAJI

Cauliflower with potatoes (India)

In most Asian cuisines potatoes are considered a vegetable, not a staple. Serves 4–6.

INGREDIENTS

2 large waxy potatoes, about 300g (10oz) each
1 cauliflower, about 750g (1½ lb), cut into small florets
2 tsp coriander seeds
1–2 small dried red chillies
2 tsp cumin seeds
75–90ml (5–6 tbsp) ghee (see page 29), or vegetable oil
1 tsp yellow mustard seeds
1 large fresh green chilli, deseeded and finely chopped
½ tsp ground turmeric
1 tsp salt, plus extra to taste
¼ tsp freshly ground black pepper

PREPARATION

1 Boil the potatoes in their skins for 18–20 minutes, until tender. Leave to cool. Peel, quarter and cut each into 2 or 3 pieces. Blanch the cauliflower in boiling water for 1 minute, then drain.
2 Roast the coriander seeds, dried chillies and half the cumin seeds for 3–4 minutes (see page 155), then grind to a powder using a pestle and mortar.
3 Heat 75ml (5 tablespoons) of the ghee in a large, non-stick shallow pan or wok. Add the mustard seeds and remaining cumin seeds, and stir until they start to pop. Add the green chilli and turmeric.
4 Stir for a few seconds, then add the cauliflower and stir-fry for 2 minutes. Add the potatoes, the powdered spices, salt and pepper, and stir-fry for 2–3 minutes, until heated through. Add the rest of the ghee and more salt if necessary, then serve.

PREPARATION

1 Heat the oil in a wok. Add the shallots, garlic and ginger and stir-fry for 2–3 minutes.
2 Add the shredded cabbage and salt, and stir-fry for 3 minutes. Add the hot water and ground white pepper, stir again, then cover the wok and simmer for 2–3 minutes.
3 Uncover the wok, increase the heat and stir the cabbage continuously for 1 minute. Add the beaten eggs, stir and turn them vigorously until they are scrambled and cooked through. Season to taste and serve immediately.

REBONG CHAR

Bamboo shoots, prawns and pork in

a spicy sauce (Singapore)

This dish is a very popular example of Nonya cooking: typically Chinese in origin, but with some Malaysian-influenced hot chilli to give it an extra lift. Garnish with fresh coriander and serve with boiled or fried rice.

INGREDIENTS

8–12 raw king prawns, peeled and deveined (see page 82), halved lengthways, shells reserved

450ml (¾ pint) water

1 tsp plain flour

1 tbsp light soy sauce

250g (8oz) boneless pork chops with a little fat, thinly sliced

3 tbsp pork fat or lard or vegetable oil

1cm (½in) piece of fresh ginger root, finely chopped

2 large fresh red chillies, deseeded and finely chopped

2 cloves garlic, finely chopped

2 star anise

1 tbsp yellow bean sauce

175–250g (6–8oz) canned bamboo shoots (drained weight), rinsed and thinly sliced

salt and freshly ground black pepper, to taste

PREPARATION

1 Rinse and wash the prawn shells and place in a pan with the water. Bring to the boil, then cover and simmer for 20 minutes. Strain the stock through a fine sieve and discard the shells.

2 Blend the flour and the soy sauce and rub into the pork slices. Set aside for a few minutes.

3 Heat the pork fat, lard, or oil in a wok. Add the ginger, chillies and garlic, and stir-fry for 1–2 minutes. Add the pork slices and stir-fry over a very high heat for 2 minutes.

4 Add the star anise, yellow bean sauce and the prawn stock. Keep the wok over a high heat and let the mixture bubble for 2–3 minutes.

5 Add the prawns and bamboo shoots, and stir-fry for 2 minutes. Season to taste, stir again, and cook for 1 minute more, then serve immediately.

BANDAKKA CURRY
Okra curry (Sri Lanka)

Similar curries to this are made all over the Indian subcontinent as well as in Malaysia. This one tastes very good with Ikan Masak Molek (see page 36), the classic Malaysian fish curry. If you eat them together, you do not need to make the sauce for the okra, because the fish curry has enough for both dishes. Serves 4 as a side dish or 2 as a main course with rice.

INGREDIENTS

500g (1lb) okra, trimmed and thinly sliced crossways
½ tsp ground turmeric
½ tsp chilli powder or paprika
½ tsp salt
125ml (4fl oz) vegetable oil for frying
For the curry sauce
2 tbsp vegetable oil
1 small onion, finely sliced
2 large fresh green chillies, deseeded and finely sliced
large pinch of ground turmeric
1 tsp ground coriander
½ tsp ground cumin
1cm (½in) piece of cinnamon stick
4 fresh or dried curry leaves (see page 26), optional
1 tsp salt, plus extra to taste
175ml (6fl oz) coconut milk (see page 141)
freshly ground black pepper, to taste

PREPARATION

1 For the curry sauce, heat the oil in a pan. Add the onion and stir-fry for 4 minutes. Add all the remaining sauce ingredients, except the coconut milk, and stir-fry for 1 minute.
2 Add the coconut milk to the pan, bring to the boil, then lower the heat and simmer for 10 minutes. Season to taste and set aside.
3 In a bowl, toss the sliced okra with the ground turmeric, chilli powder or paprika and salt.
4 Heat the oil in a wok or frying pan. Add the okra and fry, stirring frequently to prevent them from burning, for 3 minutes or until crisp. (Cook the okra in two batches if necessary, to avoid overcrowding the pan.)
5 Remove the okra from the wok with a slotted spoon and drain on kitchen paper.
6 The okra can be served crisp, or soft, according to taste. If you prefer the latter, heat the sauce almost to boiling point and add the fried okra. Simmer for 1 minute and serve hot. For crisp okra, serve the sauce separately.

LO HAN CHAI
Buddha's delight (China)

This is adapted from a recipe by my friend Deh-ta Hsiung. The 18 principal ingredients of the original recipe represented the 18 disciples of Buddha, hence the name "Buddha's delight". Serves 4–6 as a side dish. See page 97 for illustration.

INGREDIENTS

15g (½oz) golden needles (see page 27), optional
15g (½oz) wood ears (see page 21), optional
60g (2oz) dried shiitake mushrooms
125g (4oz) cellophane vermicelli (see page 25)
175g (6oz) mangetout
175g (6oz) baby sweetcorn, halved lengthways
2 tbsp groundnut oil
4 spring onions, sliced on the diagonal
15g (½oz) fresh ginger root, peeled and chopped
250g (8oz) canned straw mushrooms (drained weight), rinsed, or 250g (8oz) small button mushrooms
1 tsp sugar
2 tbsp light soy sauce
250g (8oz) fried tofu (see page 24), sliced
90–125g (3–4oz) canned ginkgo nuts (see page 22), (drained weight), optional
½ tsp sesame oil
salt and freshly ground black pepper, to taste

PREPARATION

1 Soak the golden needles in boiling water for 10 minutes, then drain. Trim off the hard edges from the buds and cut each needle into 2 pieces.
2 Rehydrate the wood ears (see page 155), then cut into small pieces. Rehydrate the dried shiitake for 30 minutes (see page 155), reserving the soaking liquid. Remove and discard the stalks of the shiitake and cut the caps in half.
3 Soak the cellophane vermicelli in hot water for 5 minutes. Drain, then with scissors, snip them into short pieces.
4 Blanch the mangetout and baby sweetcorn in boiling water for 1 minute, then refresh under cold running water and drain.
5 Heat the groundnut oil in a wok or casserole. Add the spring onions and ginger, and stir-fry for 20 seconds. Add all the mushrooms and the golden needles, and stir-fry for 30 seconds.
6 Add the sugar, soy sauce, fried tofu, mangetout and baby corn. Add 125ml (4fl oz) of the shiitake soaking liquid, cover and simmer for 3 minutes.
7 Uncover the wok or casserole, and add the vermicelli, ginkgo nuts, if using, and the sesame oil. Stir-fry for 2 minutes more, then season to taste and serve hot.

ALOO BAIGAN KORMA

Braised mixed vegetables with yogurt (India)

*This is a vegetarian dish with potatoes and aubergines
as the main ingredients, but with other vegetables
added to make a satisfying one-dish meal.
Serve with rice or bread.*

INGREDIENTS

3 tbsp vegetable oil
1 large onion, finely chopped
2 tbsp ground coriander
2 tbsp ground cumin
1 tsp ground turmeric
2 cloves garlic, finely chopped
2 tsp finely chopped fresh ginger root
120ml (8 tbsp) natural yogurt, lightly whisked
2 tbsp ground almonds
4 ripe tomatoes, skinned, deseeded and
roughly chopped
120ml (4fl oz) hot water
6 medium new potatoes, scrubbed and
quartered lengthways
2 medium purple aubergines, halved across, then
each half cut into 8 pieces
1 tsp salt, plus extra to taste
1–2 large fresh red chillies, deseeded and
finely chopped
10 whole baby carrots or 4–5 medium carrots,
sliced on the diagonal
250g (8oz) yard-long beans (see page 21), or
French beans, cut into 5cm (2in) lengths
4 tbsp chopped fresh coriander leaves, to garnish

PREPARATION

1 Heat the oil in a large heavy-based pan. Add the
onion and fry, stirring continuously, for 6 minutes.
2 Add the ground coriander, ground cumin and
turmeric, and fry, stirring continuously, for about
1 minute. Stir in the garlic and ginger.
3 Gradually add the yogurt to the pan and cook,
stirring continuously, for 1–2 minutes. Add the
ground almonds, half the chopped tomatoes and
the hot water. Stir again, then add the potatoes,
aubergines and salt. Lower the heat, cover the pan
and simmer for 7 minutes.
4 Add the chillies, the whole or sliced carrots
and the beans. Stir once, then cover the pan and
simmer very gently for about 15 minutes, or until
all the vegetables are tender.
5 Add more salt, if necessary, and stir in the
remaining chopped tomatoes. Cook for 1 minute
more, to heat the tomatoes through, then remove
from the heat and sprinkle with the chopped fresh
coriander, to garnish.

Ground
almonds

Natural
yogurt

Fresh ginger

Garlic

Ground turmeric

Ground cumin

Ground
coriander

Onion

Vegetable oil

Tomatoes

New
potatoes

Aubergine

Salt

Red
chillies

Baby
carrots

Yard-long
beans

Fresh
coriander

CHAI SIU NGO
Vegetarian goose (China)

This is a classic vegetarian dish; when cooked, the beancurd skin resembles that of roast goose or duck. If it has been deep-fried, the skin will also be crisp. Serves 4 as an appetizer or as part of a dim sum meal.

INGREDIENTS

8 dried shiitake mushrooms, rehydrated (see page 155), soaking liquid reserved, stalks removed
1 tbsp light soy sauce
1 tsp sesame oil
3 beancurd sheets (see page 25)
2 carrots, cut into very fine julienne strips (see page 154)
2–3 celery sticks, cut into very fine julienne strips (see page 154)
1–2 tbsp dark soy sauce
1 tbsp sugar
about 300ml (½ pint) vegetable oil for deep-frying

PREPARATION

1 Strain the mushroom soaking liquid into a jug and add the soy sauce and sesame oil. Dice the mushroom caps.
2 Put the beancurd sheets on a plate, pour the mushroom liquid over them and leave to soak for 5 minutes, to make them more pliable.
3 Spread out one beancurd sheet on a large tray. Place some carrot and celery julienne on the left half of the sheet. Spoon over a little of the dark soy sauce and the sugar. Fold the right half of the sheet over the filling and scatter over some of the diced mushrooms and a little more soy sauce.
4 Fold the whole sheet in half again, in the same way. The width of the folded sheet should now be about 5–7cm (2–3in). Repeat with the remaining beancurd sheets and vegetables. Brush or dab dark soy sauce on the outside of each roll. Do not seal.
5 Heat the oil for deep-frying in a wok or large pan to 150°C (300°F). To shallow fry, heat about 2 tablespoons of oil in a frying pan. Add one roll to the wok or frying pan and fry for 2–3 minutes, turning it several times, until the outside of the roll is quite crisp and golden.
6 Remove the roll from the pan with a slotted spoon and drain on kitchen paper. Keep hot in a warm oven while the remaining rolls are fried. Cut each roll crossways into sections about 5–7cm (2–3in) long. Serve immediately, as the beancurd will toughen once cold.

SHIRA AE
Mixed vegetable salad with sesame dressing (Japan)

Sesame dressing can be served with any seasonal vegetables – cooked, raw or a mixture of both. It also makes an excellent dip for crudités. Serves 4–6 as a side dish or as an appetizer.

INGREDIENTS

4–8 asparagus spears, trimmed and thinly sliced on the diagonal
125g (4oz) cauliflower, cut into small florets
1 medium yellow courgette, cut into very fine julienne strips (see page 154)
4 red radishes, cut into very fine julienne strips (see page 154), and soaked in cold water
1 small red pepper, deseeded, and cut into very fine julienne strips (see page 154)
For the dressing
4 tbsp sesame seeds
1 tbsp sugar
1 tsp salt
2 tsp light soy sauce
2 tbsp rice vinegar (see page 29)
3 tbsp bonito stock (see page 30), or other stock
1 tbsp mirin (see page 29)
¼ tsp freshly ground white pepper, optional
300–375g (10–12oz) silken tofu

PREPARATION

1 For the dressing, put all the ingredients, except the tofu, into a blender and blend until smooth.
2 Add the tofu to the sesame mixture and blend until well mixed with the paste. Season to taste, then transfer the dressing to a glass bowl and refrigerate until serving time.
3 Cook the sliced asparagus in boiling water for 4 minutes, then transfer to a colander to drain. Refresh under cold running water and drain again.
4 Blanch the cauliflower florets for 3 minutes and refresh, then blanch the courgette strips for 1 minute and refresh. Drain the radishes.
5 To serve, divide the vegetables among 4 or 6 serving plates, arranging each vegetable separately around the edge, then spoon some sesame dressing into the centre of each plate.

YAM WOON SEN

Spicy salad of cellophane vermicelli,
prawns and pork (Thailand)

Similar salads to this are also popular in Vietnam and
Korea, and make a refreshing cold lunch or appetizer.
Serves 4–6 as a lunch by itself, or 6–8 as an appetizer.
See page 110 for illustration.

INGREDIENTS

7g (¼oz) wood ears (see page 21), optional
200g (7oz) cellophane vermicelli (see page 25)
3 tbsp vegetable oil
30g (1oz) dried shrimps (see page 31)
15g (½oz) dried sliced garlic
350g (12oz) lean pork, coarsely minced or hand-chopped
salt and freshly ground black pepper, to taste
45g (1½oz) shallots, sliced
60g (2oz) small onions, thinly sliced into rings
1 spring onion, thinly sliced on the diagonal
45g (1½oz) fresh celery leaves (the tender inner leaves)
4 tbsp fish sauce (nam pla), (see page 28)
4 tbsp lemon juice
30g (1oz) sugar
4–6 small fresh red chillies, deseeded and finely chopped
16 cooked peeled king prawns
125g (4oz) fresh coriander leaves, about half chopped
red chilli flowers (see page 155), to garnish, optional

PREPARATION

1 Rehydrate the wood ears in 450ml (¾ pint) of
warm water (see page 155). Rinse, then slice into
thin strips and set aside.
2 Pour hot water over the noodles, leave to stand
for 5 minutes, then drain. Using scissors, cut the
noodles into 7–10cm (3–4in) lengths.
3 Heat 2 tablespoons of the oil in a pan. Add the
dried shrimps and fry until just crisp. Remove
from the pan with a slotted spoon and leave to
drain on kitchen paper.
4 Reheat the oil and fry the garlic for 1–2 minutes,
or until golden brown and crisp. Drain on kitchen
paper. Heat the remaining oil in another pan and
stir-fry the pork over a high heat for 3–4 minutes,
or until cooked through. Season to taste.
5 In a glass bowl, mix together the shallots, onions,
spring onion, celery leaves and wood ears, if using.
Add the fish sauce, lemon juice, sugar and chillies.
6 About 10 minutes before serving, toss the
noodles, mushroom mixture, pork, prawns and
coriander together in a large bowl to mix well.
7 Arrange the noodle mixture on a large serving
plate and sprinkle with the crisp-fried shrimps and
garlic. Garnish with the chilli flowers if desired,
and serve at room temperature.

YAM PLA MUEK MAMUANG

Green mango and squid salad (Thailand)

Some green, unripe mangoes may be too sour, but
unfortunately you will not know until you taste them.
Those that are too sour need salting and sugaring before
using, as described below. Serves 4–6 as an appetizer.
See page 111 for illustration.

INGREDIENTS

2 small green, unripe mangoes (see page 23), peeled,
flesh cut into thin slices or small matchsticks
750g (1½lb) small squid, cleaned and cut into
rings (see page 150), tentacles discarded
handful of fresh coriander leaves
handful of fresh Thai basil leaves (see page 26)
lettuce leaves, to serve, optional
For the dressing
juice of 2 limes
1 tbsp sugar
2 tbsp fish sauce (nam pla), (see page 28)
1–3 fresh red bird's eye chillies, finely chopped
1cm (½in) piece of fresh lemongrass, centre
only, finely chopped
1 shallot, finely chopped
2 tbsp warm water
1 clove garlic, finely chopped, optional
1 tbsp finely chopped fresh coriander leaves

PREPARATION

1 Taste the sliced mango; if it is too sour, put it
in a colander and sprinkle with 1 tablespoon of
salt and 1 tablespoon of sugar. Leave to stand for
1–2 hours, then rinse thoroughly under cold
running water and drain well.
2 Cook the squid rings in lightly salted boiling
water for 4 minutes. Drain in a colander and leave
to cool. Mix all the ingredients for the dressing in
a glass bowl.
3 About 1 hour before serving, add the squid,
mango, coriander and basil leaves to the dressing.
Mix well and leave to stand at room temperature.
To serve, arrange some lettuce leaves, if using, on a
plate. Spoon the salad on top and serve immediately.

NOODLES & RICE

Without noodles, without rice, Asia would be an inconceivably different place. Not every Asian lives on them; other staples – maize, sago and cassava – are still supreme in some less-populated areas. But anyone who was brought up on rice will confirm that it is the most versatile and satisfying of all foods. Only noodles come close to it, but noodles are a product of city life; rice, however refined and polished, is always a reminder of the countryside.

UDON SUKI

Hot pot with udon noodles (Japan)

This is a kind of Japanese fondue, with the broth simmering in a fire-pot or electric frying pan in the centre of the table. Alternatively, the hot-pot can be heated in a casserole and served in individual bowls at the table.

INGREDIENTS

375g (12oz) dried udon noodles (see page 24)
2 medium carrots, cut into thin rounds
12–16 mangetout
375g (12oz) spinach leaves or broccoli florets
8 leaves from a head of Chinese leaves
4 fresh shiitake mushrooms or chestnut mushrooms,
stalks removed and caps halved
8–12 raw king prawns, peeled and
deveined (see page 82)
250–375g (8–12oz) lean chicken, thinly sliced
½ tsp salt
2 tsp lemon juice
For the broth
1.5 litres (2½ pints) bonito stock (see page 30),
or chicken stock
60–90ml (4–6 tbsp) light soy sauce
2 tbsp mirin (see page 29)
For the condiments
4 spring onions, finely chopped
1 tbsp finely chopped or grated fresh ginger root
1 lemon, cut into 4 wedges

PREPARATION

1 Cook the noodles in plenty of boiling water for 18 minutes. Drain in a colander, then rinse under cold running water and leave to drain.
2 Blanch the carrots in lightly salted boiling water for 3 minutes. Refresh in cold water. Blanch the mangetout for 2 minutes, then refresh and drain.

3 Boil the spinach or broccoli for 2 minutes, then refresh in cold water and drain well. Compress the spinach in the palm of your hand and squeeze out any remaining excess water. Cut the dry spinach into 4 portions.
4 Blanch the Chinese leaves for 2 minutes and refresh in cold water. Drain well, then roll the leaves up inside a bamboo rolling mat or tea towel (see page 149) and cut each roll into 4 sections.
5 Arrange the prepared vegetables, mushrooms and cooked noodles on a large serving platter. Cook the prawns in boiling water for 2 minutes, then drain and arrange on a smaller plate. Sprinkle the chicken slices with the salt and lemon juice, then rub gently to coat evenly. Arrange with the prawns.
6 To serve in a fire-pot or electric frying pan, arrange the vegetables and noodle platter, the prawns and chicken and all the prepared condiments at the table. Place a deep soup bowl and chopsticks in front of each diner.
7 Mix the ingredients for the broth in a pan, bring to a rolling boil, then transfer to the heated pan.
8 Allow diners to help themselves to the vegetables, noodles, prawns and chicken, and "cook" them in the central pan. The mushrooms and chicken should be cooked for 3 minutes, the rest of the ingredients are simply reheated for about 2 minutes.
9 Diners transfer what they have cooked to their own bowls, ladle over some broth and help themselves to condiments. In Japanese households, where only chopsticks are used, the broth is drunk from the bowls, like tea.
10 Alternatively, heat the broth in a large casserole. Add the chicken, cook for 3 minutes, then add the raw prawns and simmer for 1 minute. Add the vegetables and noodles and cook for a further 2 minutes. Bring the dish to the table and serve the hot pot in individual bowls.

CHAR KWEE TEOW

Rice stick noodles with pork and prawns
(Singapore)

Chinese in origin, this dish long ago became popular
street food in Singapore and Malaysia.

INGREDIENTS

2 litres (3 pints) cold water
1 tsp salt
250g (8oz) rice stick noodles (see page 25),
5–10mm (¼–½ in) wide
75ml (5 tbsp) vegetable oil
3 shallots, finely sliced
2 tbsp yellow bean sauce
1 tsp ground coriander
½ tsp ground cumin
large pinch of ground turmeric
¼ tsp chilli powder
2 tbsp hot water
2 tbsp lard or vegetable oil
125g (4oz) pork fillet, thinly sliced crossways
8–12 raw king prawns, peeled and deveined (see page 82)
3 cloves garlic, finely sliced
1 tsp finely chopped fresh ginger root
1 large fresh red chilli, deseeded and thinly
sliced on the diagonal
60g (2oz) fresh beansprouts, rinsed and trimmed
1 tbsp dark soy sauce
1 tbsp light soy sauce
3 tbsp hot water or stock
5 spring onions, cut into 2cm (1in) lengths
salt and freshly ground black pepper, to taste

PREPARATION

1 Boil the water with the salt in a large pan. Add the noodles, stir well, and boil for 2–3 minutes. Drain the noodles in a colander, then rinse under cold running water until cold and leave to drain.
2 Heat 2 tablespoons of the oil in a wok. Add the shallots and fry for 2 minutes. Stir in the yellow bean sauce, all the spices and the hot water, and stir-fry for 1–2 minutes.
3 Add the noodles to the wok, stirring and tossing them until heated through. Transfer the mixture to a large platter, cover with foil and keep hot in a warm oven.
4 Wipe the wok clean with kitchen paper. Heat the lard and remaining oil in the wok. Add the pork and fry, stirring frequently, for 3 minutes. Remove the pork with a slotted spoon and drain on kitchen paper.
5 Reheat the oil, add the prawns and stir-fry for 3 minutes. Remove the prawns with the slotted spoon and drain on kitchen paper.

6 Add the garlic and ginger to the wok and stir-fry for a few seconds. Add the chilli, beansprouts, the dark and light soy sauce and hot water or stock, and simmer for 2 minutes.
7 Return the pork and prawns to the wok. Add the spring onions, stir-fry for 1 minute, then season to taste. Spoon the mixture over the noodles to serve.

PANCIT GUISADO

Fried noodles with mixed meat (Philippines)

Pancit Guisado differs from other Asian fried noodles
mainly in its use of chorizo, the Spanish sausage. It
can be made with egg noodles or rice noodles and
is ideal as a one-dish meal.

INGREDIENTS

2.5 litres (4 pints) water
½ tsp salt, plus extra to taste
375–500g (12oz–1lb) egg noodles or rice noodles
3 tbsp lard or olive oil
1 medium red onion, chopped
3 cloves garlic, chopped
1cm (½ in) piece of fresh ginger root, finely chopped
1 large fresh red chilli, deseeded and finely chopped
175–250g (6–8oz) pork fillet, thinly sliced crossways
1 large chicken breast, thinly sliced crossways
250–375g (8–12oz) uncooked spicy chorizo sausage,
sliced about 1cm (½ in) thick
125g (4oz) white cabbage or Chinese leaves, thickly sliced
2 medium carrots, sliced into thin rounds
75ml (5 tbsp) hot water or chicken stock
1 tsp dried shrimp paste (see page 31), optional
2 tbsp light soy sauce
60g (2oz) Chinese chives (see page 26),
cut into 2cm (¾ in) lengths
3 spring onions, cut into 2cm (¾ in) lengths
freshly ground black pepper, to taste

PREPARATION

1 Boil the water with the salt in a large pan. Add the noodles, stir well, and cook for 3 minutes. Drain the noodles in a colander, then rinse under cold running water until cold and leave to drain.
2 Heat the lard or oil in a wok. Add the onion, garlic, ginger and chilli, and stir-fry for 2 minutes. Add the pork and stir-fry for 2 minutes. Add the chicken and chorizo, and stir-fry for 2–3 minutes.
3 Add the cabbage and carrots, stir and add the water or stock, the shrimp paste and soy sauce. Cook for 3 minutes, stirring frequently.
4 Add the noodles, chives and spring onions. Stir and toss the noodles until heated through. Season to taste and serve immediately.

CHAPCHAE

Warm rice noodles with vegetables (Korea)

This was originally a noodle dish with beef, vegetables and mushrooms, but, as so often in Asia, the meat is used very sparingly and cut, like the vegetables, into tiny strips. As a result the meat and mushrooms are almost indistinguishable. My vegetarian version, here, keeps the textures and flavours of the original dish without using any meat at all. Serves 4 as an appetizer, or 2 as a light lunch.

INGREDIENTS

200g (7oz) rice vermicelli (see page 25)
2 tbsp light soy sauce
1 tsp sesame oil
2 tbsp groundnut oil or vegetable oil
2 shallots, finely sliced
2–4 small dried red chillies, chopped, or salt and freshly ground black pepper, to taste
2 medium carrots, cut into fine julienne strips, (see page 154)
1–2 leeks, rinsed thoroughly, cut into fine julienne strips, (see page 154)
125g (4oz) fresh shiitake mushrooms, or 60g (2oz) dried shiitake, rehydrated (see page 155), stalks removed and caps thinly sliced
For the garnish
250g (8oz) baby spinach leaves, rinsed and drained, or large spinach leaves, blanched
2 eggs, beaten, made into 1 flat omelette, cut into strips
2 tsp sesame seeds, roasted (see page 155)

PREPARATION

1 Cover the rice vermicelli with warm water and leave to stand for 20 minutes. Drain well in a colander and set aside.

2 Heat the soy sauce and sesame oil in a wok. Add the drained noodles, stir-fry for 2 minutes, then transfer to a large bowl. Wipe the wok clean with kitchen paper.

3 Heat the groundnut or vegetable oil in the wok. Add the shallots and dried chillies, if using, and stir-fry for 2 minutes. Add the carrots and leeks, and stir-fry for a further 2 minutes. Add the mushrooms and cook, stirring frequently, for 2–3 minutes more.

4 Season with salt and pepper, if not using the dried chillies, and remove the wok from the heat. Add the vegetables to the warm noodles and toss all the ingredients together to mix well.

5 Line individual serving plates with the raw baby spinach or the blanched large spinach and arrange portions of the noodles and vegetables on top. Garnish with the omelette and sprinkle over the roasted sesame seeds. Serve warm or cold.

Shallots

Groundnut oil

Sesame oil

Light soy sauce

Rice vermicelli

Carrots

Leeks

Shiitake
mushrooms

Baby spinach

Omelette

Sesame seeds

Dried red
chillies

HAI JO MAH JI MEE

Yifu noodles with crabmeat sauce (China)

*The combination of dried fish, crabmeat and straw
mushrooms is typical of southern China. Fresh egg
noodles can be used instead of dried yifu noodles, but
they need to be deep-fried for a few minutes before
they are softened in the hot stock.*

INGREDIENTS

*60g (2oz) dried anchovies (see page 30),
or dried shrimps (see page 31)
375–425g (12–14oz) dried yifu noodles (see page 24),
or 500g (1lb) fresh egg noodles
about 300ml (½ pint) vegetable oil for deep-frying
(only if using fresh egg noodles)
600ml (1 pint) boiling chicken stock, or boiling water
plus 1 tbsp ginger juice (see page 155)
4 tbsp chicken stock
1 tbsp oyster sauce
½ tsp freshly ground black pepper
1 tbsp dark soy sauce
125g (4oz) fresh crabmeat, white meat only
½ tsp sesame oil
125g (4oz) canned straw mushrooms (drained weight),
rinsed and halved, or 175g (6oz) fresh oyster mushrooms,
blanched in hot stock for 1 minute, sliced
4–6 spring onions, thinly sliced on the diagonal
salt, to taste*

PREPARATION

1 Place the dried anchovies or dried shrimps on
a baking sheet and bake in an oven preheated to
160°C/320°F/Gas 3 for 6–8 minutes, or until
crisp. Leave to cool, then grind to a powder in a
blender or using a pestle and mortar.
2 Put the dried yifu noodles in a bowl. If using
fresh egg noodles, heat the oil in a wok or deep-fat
fryer, add the noodles and fry for 2–3 minutes or
until crisp. Remove the noodles from the oil with
a slotted spoon and transfer to a bowl.
3 Pour the boiling stock or ginger-flavoured water
over the yifu noodles or the fried noodles, leave to
stand for 2–3 minutes, then drain in a colander.
4 Heat a dry wok for 2 minutes, then add the
ground fish or shrimps, followed immediately by
the 4 tablespoons of chicken stock. Swirl the stock
around, then stir in the oyster sauce, black pepper,
dark soy sauce, crabmeat and sesame oil.
5 Add the mushrooms and noodles to the wok.
Stir again and toss the noodles with chopsticks
until all the ingredients are thoroughly mixed
and heated through. Add the spring onions and
salt, if necessary. Stir and toss again for 1 minute,
then serve immediately.

KHAO PAD KHAI HORAPHA

Fried rice with chicken and basil (Thailand)

*In this classic fried rice dish the basil is deep-fried for
a few minutes, so that it becomes crisp when cold.*

INGREDIENTS

*125ml (4fl oz) vegetable oil
handful of fresh Thai basil leaves (see page 26)
3 shallots, finely sliced
2 cloves garlic, finely sliced
1 large fresh red chilli, deseeded and finely chopped
375g (12oz) chicken, thinly sliced into small pieces
500g (1lb) cooked jasmine rice (see page 156)
1 tbsp chopped spring onions
2 tsp fish sauce (nam pla), (see page 28)
salt, to taste*

PREPARATION

1 Heat the oil in a wok, add the basil leaves and
fry for 1–2 minutes. Remove from the wok with
a slotted spoon and drain on kitchen paper.
2 Add the shallots to the wok and stir-fry for 2–3
minutes or until just beginning to brown. Remove
from the wok with the slotted spoon and drain
well on kitchen paper.
3 Remove all but 2 tablespoons of the oil from
the wok. Reheat the wok, add the garlic and chilli,
and stir-fry for 1 minute. Add the chicken and
stir-fry for 3 minutes. Add the rice and spring
onions, and stir until thoroughly heated. Add the
fish sauce and salt, if necessary.
4 Stir half the fried basil into the rice and arrange
on a serving dish. Sprinkle with the remaining basil
and the fried shallots, then serve immediately.

NASI KEBULI

Savoury rice with fried chicken (Indonesia)

Originally a Middle Eastern pilaff, this recipe has travelled far and evolved over the centuries. Serves 6.

INGREDIENTS

about 300ml (½ pint) vegetable oil for deep-frying
500g (1lb) basmati rice, soaked in cold water for
1 hour, then drained
For the stock
1 chicken, 1.75–2kg (3½–4lb), cut into
8–10 pieces (see page 153)
3 shallots or 1 medium onion, chopped
2 cloves garlic, chopped
1 tbsp ground coriander
1 tsp ground cumin
1cm (½in) piece of fresh galangal (see page 27)
5cm (2in) piece of fresh lemongrass
1 small cinnamon stick
2 cloves
¼ tsp grated nutmeg
2 tsp salt
2 litres (3 pints) cold water
For the garnish
½ cucumber, sliced
2 tbsp Crisp-fried Onions (see page 132 for recipe)
handful of fresh flat-leaf parsley

PREPARATION

1 For the stock, put all the ingredients in a large pan. Bring to the boil and boil gently for 50 minutes. Remove the chicken pieces and drain in a colander. Simmer the stock for 10 minutes more, then strain into a bowl and discard the solids. Reserve 900ml (1½ pints) of the stock and skim well.
2 Put 2 tablespoons of the oil in a separate pan. Heat the remaining oil in a wok or deep-fat fryer to 180°C (350°F). Add half the chicken pieces and fry for 10–15 minutes, moving them around with a slotted spoon, until the skin is evenly brown and crisp.
3 Remove the chicken from the oil and drain on kitchen paper. Fry the rest of the chicken.
4 While the chicken is cooking, heat the reserved oil. Add the rice and stir until coated. Add the measured stock, then stir and cook over a medium heat for 8–10 minutes, until the stock is absorbed.
5 Cover the pan, reduce the heat to minimum and cook undisturbed for 10–12 minutes. Remove the pan from the heat and place it, still covered, on a wet tea towel. Leave for 5 minutes.
6 Pile the rice in the centre of a large platter and place the chicken around it. Arrange the cucumber slices over the rice and sprinkle the Crisp-fried Onions and parsley over all.

BRINJAL PULLAO

Spicy pilaff with aubergines (Southern India)

This dish has been a favourite of mine since I learned how to make it years ago from a charming South Indian chef working in New Delhi. It is easy to make, spicy and chilli-hot. Serves 2.

INGREDIENTS

2 tbsp split mung beans (see page 31), roasted
for 5 minutes (see page 155)
2–4 small dried red chillies, roasted for 5 minutes,
(see page 155)
about 300ml (½ pint) vegetable oil for frying
8 whole baby aubergines or 1 medium purple aubergine,
cut into large cubes
2 tbsp ghee (see page 29) or groundnut oil
½ tsp yellow mustard seeds
1 tsp chopped fresh ginger root
¼ tsp ground turmeric
375g (12oz) cooked basmati rice (see page 156)
1 tsp lemon juice
salt and freshly ground black pepper, to taste

PREPARATION

1 Crush the roasted mung beans and chillies into a coarse powder using a pestle and mortar.
2 Heat the oil in a wok or frying pan. Add the whole baby aubergines or the cubed large aubergine and fry for 5–6 minutes. Remove the aubergine from the wok with a slotted spoon and drain on kitchen paper.
3 If using baby aubergines, cut each one in half lengthways, leaving the halves joined at the stalk. Carefully drain the oil from the wok.
4 Heat the ghee in the wok. Add the mustard seeds and fry, stirring continuously, for 1–2 minutes. Stir in the ginger and turmeric. Add the rice and stir until thoroughly heated through.
5 Add the lemon juice and the fried aubergines to the wok, stir and turn the rice with a large spoon. Season to taste, then stir in the crushed mung bean and chilli mixture before serving.

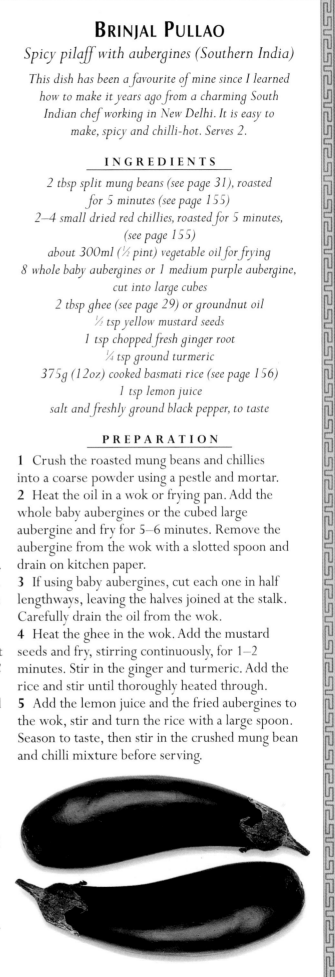

NAVRATAN PULLAO
Mixed vegetable pilaff (India)

*The name of this dish is sometimes translated as the
"nine jewels" pilaff. The nine jewels or navratan symbolize
nine brilliant ministers at the court of the great Moghul
Emperor Akbar in the sixteenth century. Here the
"jewels" are represented by nine different vegetables.
Serves 6–8 as a one-dish meal, or more as part of
a buffet. See page 134 for illustration.*

INGREDIENTS

*90g (3oz) each of carrot, turnip, pumpkin, mushrooms,
French beans, cauliflower, broccoli, broad beans, peas; or
about 750g (1½ lb) ready-prepared mixed vegetables
3 tbsp vegetable ghee or vegetable oil
1 large onion, very finely sliced
½ tsp black cumin seeds (see page 27)
3 green cardamom pods
2 cloves
2.5cm (1in) piece of cinnamon stick
¼–½ tsp chilli powder
3 fresh or dried curry leaves (see page 26), or bay leaves
salt and freshly ground black pepper, to taste
500g (1lb) basmati rice, rinsed, soaked in cold
water for 30 minutes, then drained
900ml (1½ pints) water*

PREPARATION

1 To prepare the whole vegetables, cut the carrot,
turnip and pumpkin into small cubes. Slice the
mushrooms, cut the beans into short lengths, and
divide the cauliflower and broccoli into small florets.
2 Heat the ghee or oil in a large pan. Add the onion
and fry, stirring frequently, for 5 minutes. Add all
the spices and the curry leaves or bay leaves, and
cook, stirring frequently, for 30 seconds.
3 Add all the vegetables, stir for a few seconds,
then cover the pan and cook the vegetables in their
own juices for 4 minutes. Season to taste.
4 Add the rice and stir for 10 seconds. Stir in the
water and bring to a rolling boil. Stir again, then
immediately lower the heat. Cover the pan and
simmer undisturbed for 20 minutes.
5 Remove the pan from the heat and place it, still
covered, on a wet tea towel. Leave for 5 minutes.
Transfer the pilaff to a serving platter and serve.

NASI KUNING
Savoury yellow rice (Indonesia and Malaysia)

*In many parts of Asia, yellow is considered a lucky or
even a royal colour – after all, it is the colour of gold.
This dish is served at any celebration, small or large: the
birth of a baby, the building of a new house, success in an
exam. The yellow colour comes from ground turmeric.
See page 73 for illustration.*

INGREDIENTS

*3 tbsp vegetable oil
3 shallots, finely sliced
500g (1lb) basmati rice, rinsed, soaked in cold
water for 1 hour, then drained
1 tsp ground turmeric
1 tsp ground coriander
1 tsp ground cumin
1 cinnamon stick
2 cloves
2 fresh kaffir lime leaves (see page 26),
or bay leaves
1 tsp salt
900ml (1½ pints) coconut milk (see page 141),
or chicken stock*

PREPARATION

1 Heat the oil in a large pan. Add the shallots
and fry, stirring frequently, until they are just
beginning to brown.
2 Add the rice and stir until all the grains are well
coated. Add the spices, lime leaves or bay leaves
and salt, and stir again. Add the coconut milk or
stock and bring to the boil.
3 Reduce the heat a little and cook, uncovered,
until all the liquid is absorbed. Cover the pan
tightly and reduce the heat to minimum. Cook
undisturbed for 10–12 minutes.
4 Remove the pan from the heat and place it, still
covered, on a wet tea towel. Leave for 5 minutes.
Transfer the rice to a serving bowl, remove the
cinnamon, cloves and lime or bay leaves, and serve.

NASI GORENG

Fried rice (Indonesia)

For good Nasi Goreng, the rice should be cooked about 2–3 hours before it is fried, so that it has time to become cold. Serves 4–6 as an accompaniment.

INGREDIENTS

500g (1lb) long-grain rice, washed in 2 changes of water, drained
600ml (1pint) cold water
3 tbsp groundnut oil
3 shallots or 1 small onion, very finely chopped
1–3 large fresh red chillies, deseeded and cut into thin rounds, or ½ tsp chilli powder
1 tsp chopped fresh ginger root
2 medium carrots, finely diced
60g (2oz) white cabbage, finely shredded
125g (4oz) button mushrooms, quartered
1 tsp paprika
2 tsp tomato purée or tomato ketchup
1 tbsp light soy sauce
salt, to taste
For the garnish
½ cucumber, sliced
2 tbsp Crisp-fried Onions (see page 132 for recipe)
few sprigs of watercress

PREPARATION

1 Place the drained rice and cold water in a large pan. Bring to the boil, uncovered, then simmer for 10–12 minutes, until all the water is absorbed. Stir once with a wooden spoon, then reduce the heat to low. Cover the pan and leave to cook undisturbed for 10–12 minutes.

2 Remove the pan from the heat and place it, still covered, on a wet tea towel. Leave for 5 minutes. Spoon the rice into a bowl, cover with a damp tea towel and leave to stand for 2–3 hours, or until completely cold.

3 Heat the oil in a wok. Add the shallots or onion, fresh chillies or chilli powder and the ginger, and stir-fry for 1–2 minutes. Add the carrots and cabbage, and stir-fry for a further 2 minutes.

4 Add all the remaining ingredients, except the rice and garnishes, and stir-fry for 6 minutes, or until all the vegetables are cooked through.

5 Add the cold rice and mix it thoroughly with the vegetables over a low heat, until it is heated through and takes on the reddish tinge of the paprika and tomato purée. Do not allow the rice to burn. Transfer the mixture to a heated serving dish and arrange the garnishes on top and around the dish.

SAUCES & ACCOMPANIMENTS

Dinner time in an Asian household has always been the domestic equivalent of the rush-hour, even if no guests are expected. In my childhood home in Sumatra, up to twenty family members were catered for each day. Among a large number of people there will always be differences in appetite and taste, so everyone is expected to help themselves to what they want from all the dishes and accompaniments the cook has provided. In this way, the flavour of each dish is matched to each person's taste.

SAMBAL ULEK

Basic chilli sauce (Indonesia)

This plain chilli sauce will keep refrigerated for several weeks and saves you deseeding and chopping fresh chillies every time you need one or two for a recipe. One teaspoon of this sauce is the equivalent of 1 large chilli. Makes 300ml (½ pint).

INGREDIENTS

250g (8oz) large fresh red chillies
1 tsp salt
3 tbsp vegetable oil
1 tbsp tamarind water (see page 101),
or distilled white vinegar
2 tbsp hot water

PREPARATION

1 Put the chillies in a large pan of boiling water and cook for 2 minutes. Remove from the heat and drain well in a sieve.
2 Put the chillies into a blender, add the remaining ingredients and blend until as smooth as possible. Transfer the sauce to a pan and cook over a low heat, stirring frequently, for 8 minutes.
3 Remove the pan from the heat and leave until cold. The sauce can be kept refrigerated in an airtight jar for up to 4 weeks.

NUOC CHAM

Dipping sauce (Vietnam / Laos)

Almost every appetizer and savoury snack in Vietnam is served with this sauce. It is supposed to be salty, chilli-hot, garlicky, sweet and sour. Feel free to adjust the quantity of each ingredient to suit your own taste and the food you are going to eat with it. The carrots, apart from adding colour, are very useful for those who do not like their dip too hot or too salty.

INGREDIENTS

4 tbsp fish sauce (nuoc mam), (see page 28)
2 tbsp lime juice or lemon juice
2 tsp sugar
2–5 small fresh red chillies, finely chopped
1–2 cloves garlic, crushed
1 carrot, finely shredded
1–2 tsp finely chopped fresh coriander leaves

PREPARATION

1 Combine the fish sauce, lime juice, sugar, chillies and garlic in a glass bowl. Stir to mix well, then cover and refrigerate.
2 About 2–3 hours before serving, stir in the shredded carrot and fresh coriander leaves. Keep the sauce refrigerated until serving time. Use on the day of making.

Ajad

Namjeem

NAMJEEM

Sweet chilli sauce (Laos / Thailand)

A delicious dipping sauce for spring rolls. The consistency can be adjusted by adding more water to thin it down, or it can be cooked longer until thickened.

INGREDIENTS

175ml (6fl oz) water
12 large fresh red chillies, chopped
4 cloves garlic
2 tsp sugar
½ tsp salt, plus extra to taste
1 tbsp fish sauce (nam pla), (see page 28)
1 tbsp distilled white vinegar or rice vinegar
1 tbsp groundnut oil or vegetable oil
1 tsp sesame oil, optional

PREPARATION

1 Put all the ingredients in a pan. Bring to the boil, then cover and simmer for 15 minutes. Transfer to a blender and blend until fairly smooth.
2 Return the sauce to the pan and simmer for 2–3 minutes. Add more salt, if needed. Serve at once, or keep refrigerated in an airtight jar for up to 7 days.

AJAD

Cucumber relish (Thailand)

Ajad is usually very hot as well as sour and sweet. It is used as relish for spring rolls or satay, for those who do not like or are allergic to peanut sauce.

INGREDIENTS

1 medium cucumber, peeled and halved lengthways
2–6 fresh red bird's eye chillies, finely chopped
2 tbsp fish sauce (nam pla), (see page 28)
2 tbsp distilled white vinegar
1 tbsp sugar
¼ tsp salt
1 tbsp chopped fresh chives or spring onions
1 tbsp chopped fresh coriander leaves

PREPARATION

1 Remove the seeds from the cucumber with a teaspoon, then thinly slice the cucumber into half moon shapes.
2 Transfer the cucumber slices to a glass serving bowl and stir in all the remaining ingredients. Serve the relish at once, or keep refrigerated in an airtight jar for up to 2 days.

SAMBAL KACANG

Peanut sauce (Malaysia / Indonesia / Singapore)

Most satay, except for the Japanese Yakitori, are eaten with peanut sauce. It should be deep brown in colour, so do not peel off the peanut skins before they are fried. Serve the sauce hot or warm. Makes about 600ml (1 pint).

INGREDIENTS

175ml (6fl oz) vegetable oil
375g (12oz) shelled peanuts
1.25 litres (2 pints) cold water
2 tbsp dark soy sauce
1 tbsp lemon juice
salt and freshly ground black pepper, to taste
For the paste
4 shallots, chopped
4 cloves garlic, chopped
4 large fresh red chillies, deseeded and chopped
2.5cm (1in) piece of fresh ginger root, peeled and chopped
2 tsp ground coriander
3 candle nuts (see page 22), or 6 blanched almonds, chopped
1 tsp paprika
2 tbsp tamarind water (see page 101)
2 tbsp groundnut oil
1 fresh kaffir lime leaf (see page 26), optional
5cm (2in) piece of fresh lemongrass, outer leaves removed, centre chopped

PREPARATION

1 Heat the oil in a wok. Add the peanuts and deep-fry, stirring frequently, for 3–4 minutes, or until golden. Remove from the wok with a wire scoop and leave to drain on kitchen paper.
2 Put all the paste ingredients into a blender and blend until as smooth as possible. Transfer the paste mixture to a pan and bring to the boil. Boil for 2 minutes, stirring continuously, then add the cold water. Return the mixture to the boil, then simmer for 10 minutes.
3 Grind the fried peanuts in an electric spice mill or a food processor until they become a fairly fine powder. Add to the pan and stir until evenly incorporated into the sauce.
4 Add the dark soy sauce and lemon juice to the sauce and season to taste. Simmer, stirring frequently, until reduced and thickened to the consistency you require. The sauce should be quite thick but still pourable.
5 The sauce can be frozen for up to 2 months. Defrost completely then reheat, adding a cup or so of hot water. (The sauce usually becomes very thick after freezing.) Simmer the sauce until it has reduced to the consistency you require.

MANGAI ACHAR

Mango pickle (India)

The unripe green mangoes used to make this pickle are available in Indian and some other Asian shops. They are small and the skin is thin, so they do not need to be peeled. Serve as an accompaniment to curries or with cold meat. Makes about 425g (14oz).

INGREDIENTS

12 small unripe green mangoes (see page 23)
2 tbsp salt, plus extra to taste
4 tbsp corn oil or vegetable oil
2–8 hot fresh green chillies, deseeded and chopped
2 tbsp brown mustard seeds
½ tsp ground turmeric
large pinch of asafoetida powder (see page 30), optional
2 tsp sugar
2 tsp distilled white vinegar

PREPARATION

1 Wash the mangoes well, then cut off the flesh from either side of the large central stone in two sections. Cut each piece into quarters. Trim the remaining flesh from the sides of the stone.
2 Put the mango pieces into a colander and rub with the salt. Leave to stand for 1 hour, then rinse well under cold running water and leave to drain.
3 Heat the oil in a non-corrosive pan. Add the chillies and stir-fry for about 2 minutes. Add the mustard seeds and stir-fry, about 1 minute. Stir in the mango slices, then cover the pan and simmer for 6–8 minutes.
4 Add the remaining ingredients and simmer, uncovered, for 4–5 minutes, stirring occasionally. Add more salt, if necessary. Remove the pan from the heat and leave the mixture until cold.
5 Transfer the pickle to an airtight glass jar and leave to mature for at least 5 days before eating. Can be kept refrigerated for up to 4 weeks.

ACAR KUNING

Mixed vegetable pickle (Malaysia / Indonesia)

Acar Kuning can be bought ready-made, however the commercial products often contain more cabbage than other vegetables, so, in the summer, I like to preserve my own vegetables this way. Serve cold as an accompaniment to curry and rice, or serve hot or warm as a vegetable, with grilled meat or fish. Makes 875g–1kg (1¼–2lb).

INGREDIENTS

175ml (6fl oz) water
10–12 small pickling onions, peeled
250g (8oz) French beans, cut into 2–3 pieces
250g (8oz) carrots, cut into thin sticks 2cm (¾in) long
250g (8oz) cauliflower, cut into small florets
2–8 small dried red chillies
1 tsp mustard powder
1 tsp sugar
1 tsp salt, plus extra to taste
freshly ground black pepper, to taste
For the paste
3 shallots, chopped
2 cloves garlic, chopped
2 large fresh red chillies, deseeded and chopped
3 candle nuts (see page 22), or 5 blanched
almonds, chopped
1 tsp ground turmeric
3 tbsp distilled white vinegar
2 tbsp olive oil or vegetable oil

PREPARATION

1 Put the paste ingredients into a blender and blend until as smooth as possible. Transfer the paste mixture to a non-corrosive pan. Bring to the boil, then simmer, stirring frequently, for 2 minutes. Add the water and simmer for 3 minutes.
2 Add the onions to the pan, cover, and cook for 3 minutes. Add the beans and carrots, and cook, covered, for 3 minutes. Add all the remaining ingredients. Stir once or twice, then simmer, uncovered, for 4 minutes or until the vegetables are tender and have absorbed most of the sauce.
3 Season to taste and remove from the heat. Serve hot, warm or cold. Can be kept refrigerated in airtight jars for up to 4 weeks.

VAMBOTU PAHI

Aubergine pickle (Sri Lanka)

Like the Indian Mango Pickle (see opposite), this pickle can be made mild or very hot by simply adjusting the amount of chillies added. I like to make this with good olive oil, though I know it is not the oil used in Sri Lanka. As well as serving this pickle as an accompaniment to curry, I like it as a sandwich filling, either by itself or with ham or bacon. Makes 875g–1kg (1¼–2lb).

INGREDIENTS

3–4 medium purple aubergines, about 1kg (2lb) in total
1 tbsp salt, plus extra to taste
175ml (6fl oz) virgin olive oil or vegetable oil,
plus extra to cover
3 shallots, finely chopped
2 cloves garlic, chopped
2–8 fresh hot green chillies, finely sliced
2 tsp mustard seeds, crushed
1 tsp ground turmeric, optional
2 tsp ground coriander
1 tsp ground cumin
1 tsp ground fennel seeds
¼ tsp chilli powder
2 tsp sugar
125ml (4fl oz) water
4 tbsp tamarind water (see page 101),
or distilled white vinegar

PREPARATION

1 Halve the aubergines lengthways, then cut each half across into 5mm (¼in) slices. Put the slices in a colander, rub with the salt, and leave to stand for about 1 hour. Rinse the slices under running water, then pat dry with kitchen paper.
2 Heat the oil in a non-stick frying pan. Add the aubergine slices in batches and fry for 3–4 minutes per batch. Remove the slices from the pan with a slotted spoon and transfer to a plate. Repeat with the remaining batches.
3 Pour the oil remaining in the frying pan into a non-corrosive pan and reheat it. Add the shallots, garlic and chillies and fry, stirring continuously, for 2 minutes. Add the mustard seeds and all the ground spices and the sugar, and cook, stirring frequently, for 1–2 minutes. Add the water and tamarind water, and simmer for 5 minutes.
4 Add more salt, if necessary, then add the sliced aubergine and all the cooking juices from the plate. Stir once, then simmer the mixture for 5–8 minutes. Remove the pan from the heat and leave until cold.
5 Transfer the cold pickle to airtight glass jars. Top up with a little more olive oil, if desired. Can be kept refrigerated for up to 4 weeks.

KIMCHEE

Pickled cabbage (Korea)

Kimchee is widely available in Asian supermarkets. But if you cannot buy it and if you like preserving, here is how to make it at home. It takes several days to "cure", so make it well in advance. Makes 875g–1kg (1¼–2lb).

INGREDIENTS

30g (1oz) small dried red chillies
1 tsp dried shrimps (see page 31)
1kg (2lb) Chinese leaves
1½ tbsp salt
3 cloves garlic, crushed
1 bunch spring onions, green part only, chopped
2 tsp sugar

PREPARATION

1 Soak the dried chillies and dried shrimps separately in warm water for 10 minutes, then drain well in a sieve.
2 Shred the Chinese leaves roughly, then place in a colander and mix well with the salt. Leave to stand for 1 hour, then rinse well under cold running water and leave to drain.
3 In a large bowl, mix the Chinese leaves with the remaining ingredients. Cover with a clean cloth and leave to "cure" for 3–4 days, in a cool, dark place.
4 Pack the pickle into airtight glass jars. Can be kept refrigerated for up to 4 weeks.

GORENG BAWANG

Crisp-fried onions (Malaysia / Indonesia)

Most Southeast Asian soups, salads or fried rice call for a sprinkling of crisp-fried onions. To make them at home, I suggest you use Asian red onions or shallots. They become crisp far quicker than ordinary onions and do not need to be floured before frying. If you do not want to make your own, you can buy them at Asian supermarkets.

INGREDIENTS

125ml (4fl oz) vegetable oil
500g (1lb) Asian red onions (see page 21), or shallots, finely sliced

PREPARATION

1 Heat the oil in a wok. Add the onions in 2 batches and stir-fry for 6–8 minutes per batch, or until golden brown. Remove from the wok with a slotted spoon and transfer to kitchen paper to drain.
2 Transfer the cold, crisp onions to an airtight container. Store in a cool place for up to 4 weeks.

BALACHAUNG

Chilli and dried shrimp relish (Burma)

This relish can be eaten with raw or steamed vegetables as an accompaniment to rice. I also use it in Burmese Chicken Curry with limes (see page 87 for recipe). Balachaung is available in most Asian supermarkets; it is usually chilli-hot and garlicky. Makes about 300g (10oz).

INGREDIENTS

250g (8oz) dried shrimps (see page 31)
3 tbsp groundnut oil or vegetable oil
2 onions, very finely chopped
8 cloves garlic, finely sliced
2 tsp sesame oil
3–8 large fresh red chillies, deseeded and chopped
2 tsp finely chopped fresh ginger root
½ tsp ground turmeric
1 tbsp fish sauce (nam pla), (see page 28)
½ tsp salt, plus extra to taste
1 tsp sugar, optional
juice of 2 limes or lemons

PREPARATION

1 Put the dried shrimps in a bowl and cover with warm water. Leave to stand for 10 minutes, then drain in a sieve. Chop them finely, or grind using a pestle and mortar, or process in a food processor.
2 Heat the oil in a wok, add the onions and garlic and fry, stirring continuously, for 5–8 minutes. Remove from the wok with a slotted spoon and transfer to a bowl.
3 Add the sesame oil, chillies, ginger, turmeric, fish sauce, salt and sugar, if using, to the wok. Stir-fry, for 3 minutes. Add the ground shrimps and stir-fry for 4 minutes.
4 If the mixture becomes too dry, add about 4 tablespoons of water and stir-fry for 2–3 minutes. Return the onions and garlic to the wok, stir once and add more salt, if necessary.
5 Stir-fry for 1–2 minutes, then add the lime juice and stir for a few seconds more. Remove the wok from the heat and leave the Balachaung until cold. Transfer the relish to an airtight glass jar. Can be kept refrigerated for up to 4 weeks.

SERUNDENG

Roasted grated coconut (Indonesia)

Several Asian countries use roasted coconut as a garnish. In Indonesia, however, it is something more: Serundeng contains ingredients that make the grated coconut tastier, more savoury and aromatic. It is often mixed with fried peanuts or small pieces of fried or grilled steak and served as a buffet dish.

INGREDIENTS

250g (8oz) freshly grated coconut (see steps below),
or 250g (8oz) desiccated coconut soaked in
125ml (4 fl oz) cold water for 5 minutes
5 fresh kaffir lime leaves (see page 26)
For the paste
5 shallots, chopped
3 cloves garlic, chopped
2 tsp ground coriander
1 tsp ground cumin
1–2 small dried red chillies
1 tsp dried shrimp paste (see page 31), optional
2 tbsp tamarind water (see page 101)
3 tbsp vegetable oil
1 tsp salt, plus extra to taste

PREPARATION

1 Put the paste ingredients into a blender and blend until as smooth as possible. Transfer the paste mixture to a wok and simmer, stirring frequently, for 3 minutes.

2 Add the freshly grated coconut or soaked desiccated coconut and the lime leaves. Cook over a medium heat, stirring continuously, until the coconut is golden bown. Add more salt, to taste, and remove the pan from the heat.

3 Use the Serundeng immediately, or transfer to an airtight container and store in a cool place for up to 2 weeks.

GRATING FRESH COCONUT

1 Wrap the coconut in a plastic bag, then tap it sharply around the middle with the back of a heavy knife until it breaks in half. Cut the meat into sections and prise away from the shell.

2 Pare off the brown skin from the coconut meat using a small vegetable knife or a peeler. If making coconut milk (see page 141), the brown skin does not need to be removed.

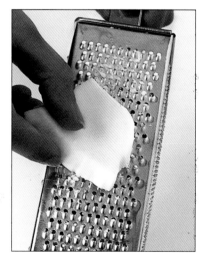

3 Grate the coconut on the fine side of a hand grater. Use immediately or, if necessary, transfer to an airtight container and keep refrigerated for up to 24 hours.

INDIA

Rich, almost earthy, spice pastes, and the fragrance of food cooked in ghee or coconut milk, mark the endless variety of Indian dishes. This is a warm and welcoming cuisine, which turns the simplest meal into an occasion, yet lends an informal atmosphere to the grandest dinner.

NAVRATAN PULLAO
Mixed vegetable pilaff.
(See page 126 for recipe.)

PATRANI MACHCHI
Baked fish wrapped
in banana leaves.
(See page 75
for recipe.)

MANGAI ACHAR
Mango pickle, centre (see page 130 for recipe) with sliced raw onion, cucumber and poppadoms.

VINDALOO
Pork cooked in chilli-hot and sour sauce. (See page 101 for recipe.)

DESSERTS

Every country has its own way of concluding a meal. In most parts of Southeast Asia, dessert is simply fresh seasonal fruit; its sweetness and acidity cleanse the palate and aid digestion. Dishes such as sticky rice cakes and rice porridge, or spiced fruit salads and custards, are considered snacks to be eaten at any time. India and China, on the other hand, have created all sorts of magnificent desserts, most so elaborate that only a wealthy family has the resources to make them. I believe that desserts should be simple and should use local ingredients to their best advantage; that has led me to this selection.

KULFI

Ice cream (India)

This is adapted from a recipe by Camellia Panjabi. It is the best recipe I have found for this Indian dessert, and the easiest to make. In India, kulfi is usually made by professional sweetmakers and served at grand occasions. It is formed in cone-shaped moulds and decorated with chopped nuts and edible silver leaf.

INGREDIENTS

2 x 410g (14oz) cans evaporated milk
4 tbsp sugar
3 green cardamom pods
about 12 strands of saffron
3 tbsp double cream

PREPARATION

1 Put the evaporated milk, sugar and cardamom pods into a heavy-based pan. Cook over a low heat for 10 minutes, stirring and scraping the sides and bottom of the pan continuously.
2 Remove the pan from the heat and discard the cardamom pods. Add the saffron strands, mix well and leave to cool. Stir in the double cream.
3 Spoon the kulfi into individual moulds, or alternatively, pour the mixture into ice-cube trays or a shallow freezer-proof baking dish. Transfer the kulfi to the freezer and freeze for a minimum of 4–5 hours, or until solid.
4 To serve, dip each mould quickly into hot water, to loosen the ice cream, then invert on to a serving plate and press out the kulfi.
5 Alternatively, press the kulfi out of the ice-cube trays or, if using a baking dish, cut the kulfi into 4cm (1½in) squares. Pile up several squares on each plate and serve immediately.

BUBUR KETAN HITAM

Black glutinous rice porridge (Indonesia)

I have eaten this porridge since I was a little girl. It is delicious served hot or cold for breakfast, or as a dessert after any meal. I was not at all surprised to learn, during a recent trip to Bali, that this has become a popular breakfast dish in big hotels with visitors from all over the world.

INGREDIENTS

2 litres (3 pints) coconut milk (see page 141)
125g (4oz) black glutinous rice (see page 24), soaked in cold water overnight, drained
½ tsp salt, plus extra to taste
1 cinnamon stick
2 tbsp grated palm sugar (see page 30)
2 tbsp caster sugar

PREPARATION

1 Reserve 250ml (8fl oz) of the coconut milk and pour the remainder into a large pan. Add the drained black rice, salt and cinnamon stick. Bring to the boil, then reduce the heat and simmer slowly for 10 minutes.
2 Add the palm sugar and caster sugar to the pan and simmer, stirring frequently, for about 1 hour, or until the porridge is thick. Remove from the heat.
3 Discard the cinnamon stick and pour the rice into a serving bowl. Leave the porridge to cool slightly. Serve warm or transfer to the refrigerator when cold and chill until required.
4 To serve, put the reserved coconut milk and a large pinch of salt into a small pan. Heat gently for 1–2 minutes and serve with the rice porridge. Alternatively, serve the rice with single cream or pouring double cream.

RUJAK

Hot, spicy fruit salad (Indonesia)

Like Gado-gado (see page 52 for recipe), this is another classic Indonesian dish that has made its way to Malaysia. There it is known as "rojak" and ingenious chefs serve meat dishes with rojak sauce. But this original Indonesian version is still a favourite, especially with women, who eat it as a snack at almost any time of the day. Eat it like a fruit salad, or serve instead of a vegetable salad with satay or any other grilled meat.
See page 73 for illustration.

INGREDIENTS

1 pomelo, segmented
1 firm medium mango, peeled, flesh removed from either side of the central stone, halved and sliced
1 green apple, quartered and cored, cut into chunks
2 firm pears, peeled, quartered and cored, cut into chunks
1 small pineapple, peeled, quartered and cored, cut into chunks
½ cucumber, halved lengthways, deseeded and sliced
For the sauce
1–3 fresh red bird's eye chillies
1 slice dried shrimp paste, grilled (see page 31), optional
175g (6oz) palm sugar (see page 30), chopped
½ tsp salt
2 tbsp tamarind water (see page 101), or lemon juice

PREPARATION

1 For the sauce, crush the chillies and shrimp paste, if using, in a pestle and mortar.
2 Add the palm sugar and salt, and pound until everything is blended together. Add the tamarind water or lemon juice and stir well with a spoon.
3 Transfer the sauce to a serving bowl, add all the prepared fruit and cucumber, and mix well. Serve immediately or chill lightly, if desired.

VATALAPAN

Spiced coconut custard (Sri Lanka)

My Sri Lankan friend, Thana Srikantha, gave me this recipe. She uses kitul treacle, which is only available in Sri Lankan food stores, but palm sugar will also work well.

INGREDIENTS

4 eggs
200ml (7fl oz) kitul treacle or melted palm sugar
(see page 30) or brown sugar syrup (see page 156)
100ml (3½fl oz) water
200ml (7fl oz) thick coconut milk (see page 141)
1¼ tsp mixed spice (see page 156)

HAHNG YAHN DAUH FUH

Almond float (China)

This recipe, similar to Gulaman (see page 138 for recipe), is an almond jelly served on a fruit sauce.
See page 97 for illustration.

INGREDIENTS

For the jelly
450ml (¾ pint) water
4 tsp powdered gelatine
450ml (¾ pint) full fat milk
3 tbsp caster sugar
1 tsp almond essence
For the fruit sauce
450ml (¾ pint) fresh orange juice
100g (3½oz) sugar
425–500g (14oz–1lb) fresh fruit, such as cubed pears, peaches and melon and whole blueberries and redcurrants

PREPARATION

1 For the jelly, pour 125ml (4fl oz) of the water into a small pan. Sprinkle the gelatine over it and leave to stand. Put the remaining water, the milk and sugar in another pan. Bring almost to the boil, stirring frequently, then remove from the heat.
2 Warm the soaked gelatine over a low heat until completely dissolved. Stir into the milk and add the almond essence. Stir for 1–2 minutes, then pour into a container about 20cm (8in) square. Leave until cold, then refrigerate.
3 For the sauce, put the orange juice and sugar in a pan. Bring to the boil and boil for 4–5 minutes, until syrupy. Add the fruit and simmer for 2 minutes. Transfer the sauce to a bowl and leave until cold.
4 Remove the jelly from the refrigerator and cut into diamond shapes or triangles. Arrange on top of the sauce and serve cold or lightly chilled.

PREPARATION

1 Put the eggs and treacle in a large bowl and beat thoroughly until quite pale in colour. Add the water, coconut milk and mixed spice. Continue beating until all the ingredients are well mixed.
2 Pour the mixture into a 1.25 litre (2 pint) pudding basin. Put a circle of greaseproof paper across the top of the basin, then tie a piece of muslin over it.
3 Stand the basin in a large pan. Pour enough hot water around the basin to come halfway up the sides. Cover the pan and steam for 25 minutes.
4 Remove the basin from the pan and take off the muslin and greaseproof paper. Turn the custard out on to a serving plate and serve hot or cold.

GULAMAN
Fresh fruit jelly (Philippines)

*Fruit jellies are typical of Southeast Asia. They are
"set" with agar-agar, made from a type of seaweed, which
can gell without being chilled. The Filipino version
is usually made creamy with evaporated milk, but here
I suggest coconut cream and eggs. Though mango is
a favourite fruit, almost any fruit in season can be used,
and the strawberries make this a delicious summer
dessert for temperate climates.*

INGREDIENTS
For the jelly
1.25 litres (2 pints) cold water
15g (½oz) agar-agar strands (see page 31), soaked
in cold water for 1 hour, then drained
500g (1lb) fresh strawberries
2 tbsp caster sugar
2 eggs, beaten
120ml (4floz) coconut cream (see page 141)
pinch of salt
To decorate
fresh fruit, such as raspberries, redcurrants
and blueberries

PREPARATION
1 For the jelly, put the water and drained agar-agar
strands into a pan. Bring to the boil, then simmer,
stirring occasionally, until the agar-agar has
dissolved. Remove the pan from the heat.
2 Strain the liquid through a sieve into a
measuring jug, then pour half of it into a bowl.
3 Reserve a few of the strawberries for
decoration and put the remainder into a blender
with the sugar. Blend the mixture for a few
seconds, then pass the resulting pulp through a
fine sieve into a bowl.
4 Pour the strawberry juice into one quantity
of the agar-agar mixture, stirring vigorously with
a wooden spoon.
5 Pour the strawberry jelly mixture into a
flat-based container, such as a baking tin, about
23cm (9in) square. Leave to set in a cool place,
or refrigerate for about 30 minutes.
6 Pour the remaining agar-agar mixture into a pan
and add the beaten eggs, the coconut cream and
salt. Heat very gently for about 5 minutes, stirring
continuously, until the mixture thickens enough to
coat the back of the spoon. Do not over-heat the
mixture or the eggs will curdle.
7 Pour the coconut jelly mixture into a second
flat-based container, preferably the same size as
the one used for the strawberry jelly. Leave to
stand in a cool place or refrigerate until set.

Egg

Caster sugar

Strawberries

Agar-agar

8 To serve, cut the jelly into equal-sized diamond
shapes, about 6cm (2½in) long. Arrange the jelly
in a decorative pattern on a large serving platter
or individual plates. Decorate with the reserved
strawberries and the other fresh fruit.

Raspberries

Redcurrants

Salt

Blueberries

Coconut cream

PISANG GORENG

Fried bananas (Indonesia / Malaysia)

These are very easy to make. In the tropics we have many varieties of banana that are suitable for frying, each with its own distinctive flavour. Ordinary bananas are perfectly good, but even better are ripe yellow plantains, which fry with a firmer and nicer texture. Serves 4–6.

INGREDIENTS

90g (3oz) rice flour (see page 31)
30g (1oz) plain flour
pinch of salt
30g (1oz) melted butter
175ml (6fl oz) coconut milk (see steps opposite)
3 yellow plantains (see page 20), or 4 fairly ripe bananas
groundnut oil or clarified butter for frying

PREPARATION

1 Sift the rice flour, plain flour and salt into a bowl. Mix the melted butter with the coconut milk and gradually stir into the dry ingredients until the mixture forms a smooth batter.
2 Cut the plantains lengthways down the middle, then cut each half across into 3 pieces. For bananas, cut each in half and then across into 2 pieces.
3 Heat some oil in a frying pan or a deep-fat fryer. Dip several pieces of banana in the batter and coat well. Add to the oil and shallow or deep-fry for 3–4 minutes per batch, or until golden brown.
4 Remove from the pan with a slotted spoon and drain on kitchen paper. Keep warm while frying the remaining batches and serve hot or cold.

KOLAK LABU KUNING

Pumpkin in coconut syrup (Malaysia)

You can find this dish in most Southeast Asian countries, with various names. The pumpkin can be replaced with sweet potatoes or bananas. Serve by itself or as an accompaniment to sweet glutinous rice (see below) instead of the mango. Serves 4–6.

INGREDIENTS

500g (1lb) peeled pumpkin, cut into 1cm (½in) cubes
600ml (1 pint) boiling water
90g (3oz) grated palm sugar (see page 30), or demerara sugar
600ml (1 pint) thick coconut milk (see steps opposite)
pinch of salt

PREPARATION

1 Put the pumpkin in a large pan with the boiling water. Return to the boil and boil for 5 minutes. Drain and set aside.
2 Put the sugar into another pan and melt over a medium heat. When the sugar is liquid and bubbling, pour in the coconut milk, a little at a time, stirring continuously. Add the salt and simmer for 2 minutes.
3 Add the pumpkin and cook over a low heat, stirring occasionally, for 5–8 minutes. Remove from the heat and serve hot or cold.

MAMUANG KUO NIEO

Mango with sweet glutinous rice (Thailand)

Although this is considered a classic Thai dessert, it is equally popular in Malaysia, Indonesia and the Philippines. Mango is the favourite fruit, with durian a close second, followed by jackfruit. Pumpkin in Coconut Syrup (see above) also goes well with this rice. Serves 6–8.

INGREDIENTS

500g (1lb) white glutinous rice (see page 24), soaked in cold water for 1 hour and drained
600ml (1 pint) coconut milk (see steps opposite)
pinch of salt
3 tbsp caster sugar
4 small or 2 large ripe mangoes, peeled, flesh removed from either side of the central stone and sliced or cubed

PREPARATION

1 Put the rice, coconut milk, salt and sugar in a pan. Stir and bring to the boil. Stir again and simmer, uncovered, until all the liquid is absorbed by the rice. Remove the pan from the heat, cover, and leave to stand for 5 minutes.
2 Transfer the rice to a bamboo steamer (see page 149) lined with muslin, or the top of a double saucepan. Cover and steam for 15–20 minutes.
3 Line 6 or 8 ramekins or individual pudding moulds with clingfilm and press the rice into them. Alternatively, press the rice on to a clingfilm-lined tray to make a cake about 1cm (½in) thick, then cut into diamond-shaped pieces.
4 Place one unmoulded rice cake, or a few diamond shapes, in the centre of each dessert plate. Arrange the slices or cubes of mango around the rice, to decorate, and serve immediately.

MAKING COCONUT MILK & CREAM

1 Put 175g (6oz) desiccated coconut or freshly grated coconut (see page 133) into a blender and pour in 600ml (1 pint) warm water. Blend the two together for about 4 seconds, until evenly mixed.

2 Pour the mixture into a sieve over a bowl and squeeze it to extract the milk. This produces **thick milk**. For **thin milk**, return the coconut to the blender and add 600ml (1 pint) warm water. Repeat the blending and squeezing.

3 To make **cream** or **very thick milk**, refrigerate the first extraction for 1–2 hours. The **cream** or **very thick milk** will rise to the surface and **thin milk** will be left underneath. For **standard milk**, mix the first and second extractions together.

Mamuang Kuo Nieo

MENU PLANNER

When planning a meal, it is unusual to think, "I want a soup from Burma and some Thai fish…" Like any art, cooking starts from the resources that are available. But for most people the recipes in this book will be more or less exotic, and some of the ingredients will need to be bought from shops you do not visit every day. So the chances are that you will be driven by a sense of adventure or curiosity, or perhaps a desire to recreate the flavour of a dish sampled during a holiday in Asia or at a rather good local restaurant. These menus are intended as an introduction to the rich and diverse cuisines of Asia. The meals are more or less Western-style in plan, divided into courses (which is not how meals are actually served in many Asian countries). The selection of dishes, too, is not necessarily typical of the traditions from which the recipes originated. I have simply tried to make each menu reflect the food that people in Delhi, Jakarta or Beijing now like to eat for lunch or dinner. There are no suggestions for desserts, except for the vegetarian menus, because most Asians prefer to end a meal with fresh seasonal fruit.

CHINA

LUNCH
Daan Far Tong (see page 60)
Egg drop soup

•

Sze Chuan Jar Gai (see page 90)
Fried chicken Szechuan-style

Steamed rice

DINNER
Hojan Hsin Taiji (see page 79)
Stir-fried scallops in oyster sauce

Hak Tjin Tjan Nah Hiu (see page 93)
Stir-fried duck with black pepper

Huhng Siu Ngauh (see page 104)
Red-cooked beef with broccoli

Lo Han Chai (see page 115)
Buddha's delight

Steamed rice

LUNCH
Shuen Guen (see page 64)
Spring rolls

•

Hai Jo Mah Ji Mee (see page 124)
Yifu noodles with crabmeat sauce

Huhng Siu Ngauh

INDIA

LUNCH
Rasam (see page 60)
Vegetarian soup

•

Jingha Kari (see page 83)
Prawn curry

Brinjal Pullao (see page 125)
Spicy pilaff with aubergines

LUNCH
Samosa (see page 65)
Pastries with vegetable filling

•

Vindaloo (see page 101)
Pork cooked in chilli-hot and sour sauce

Plain boiled basmati rice

SUPPER
Navratan Pullao (see page 126)
Mixed vegetable pilaff

Rogan Josh (see page 48)
Lamb in rich chilli sauce with yogurt
with *Mangai Achar (see page 130)*
Mango pickle

SUPPER
Jingha Kari (see page 83)
Prawn curry

Dhansak (see page 89)
Chicken cooked with lentils and vegetables

Plain boiled basmati rice

Rogan Josh

INDONESIA/MALAYSIA

LUNCH
Pergedel Jagung (see page 64)
Sweetcorn fritters

•

Oseng Oseng Ayam Dengan Sayuran (see page 86)
Stir-fried chicken with vegetables

Nasi Goreng (see page 127)
Fried rice

LUNCH
Laksa Lemak (see page 61)
Hot noodle soup with coconut milk

•

Rujak (see page 137)
Hot, spicy fruit salad

DINNER PARTY
Gado-gado (see page 52)
Cooked vegetable salad with peanut sauce

Rempah-rempah (see page 70)
Prawn and beansprout fritters

Ikan Masak Molek (see page 36)
Fish curry

Bandakka Curry (see page 115)
Okra curry

Nasi Kuning (see page 126)
Savoury yellow rice

Gado-gado

THAILAND

LUNCH
Kai Tom Ka (see page 61)
Chicken and galangal soup

•

Yam Woon Sen (see page 119)
Spicy salad of cellophane vermicelli,
prawns and pork

LUNCH
Hoy Lai Phad Nam Prik Phao (see page 85)
Braised clams with basil

•

Moo Wan (see page 98)
Sweet pork with marigold

Plain boiled Thai fragrant rice

DINNER
Kung Thord (see page 63)
Marinated and fried prawns

•

Kai Tom Ka (see page 61)
Chicken and galangal soup

•

Massaman (see page 103)
Beef curry

Yam Makhua Phao (see page 113)
Sweet and sour aubergines

Khao Pad Khai Horapha (see page 124)
Fried rice with chicken and basil

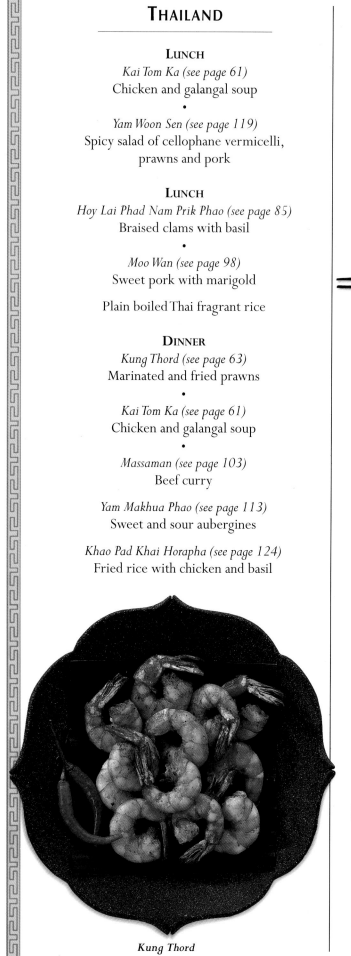

Kung Thord

JAPAN

LUNCH
Udon Suki (see page 120)
Hot pot with udon noodles

•

Japanese green tea

LUNCH
Bara-zushi (see page 50)
Sushi rice with julienne of omelette

•

Japanese green tea

DINNER
Satsumajiru (see page 57)
Miso soup with mixed vegetables

•

Suzuki Sashimi (see page 78)
Raw sea bass with vegetables
and dipping sauce

•

Fish Teriyaki (see page 77)
Glazed grilled fish

•

Shira Ae (see page 118)
Mixed vegetable salad with sesame dressing

Plain boiled Japanese rice

•

Fresh fruit

•

Japanese green tea

Bara-zushi

BUFFET (FOR 10–12)

MENU 1

Muc Don Thit (see page 38), Vietnam
Stuffed squid

Kajitchim (see page 112), Korea
Steamed stuffed aubergines

Pad Som Sin Moo (see page 99), Laos
Pork in coconut milk with pickled onions

Chapchae (see page 122), Korea
Warm rice noodles with vegetables

Steamed glutinous rice

Namjeem (see page 129), Laos / Thailand
Sweet chilli sauce

MENU 2

Mohinga (see page 56), Burma
Fish soup with rice noodles

Plea Tray (see page 76), Cambodia
Fish salad

Kyet Thar Hin (see page 87), Burma
Chicken curry with limes

Adobong Baboy (see page 100), Philippines
Red stew of pork

Gado-gado (see page 52), Indonesia
Cooked vegetable salad with peanut sauce

Steamed white rice

Muc Don Thit

VEGETARIAN

MENU 1

Gado-gado (see page 52), Indonesia
Cooked vegetable salad with peanut sauce

Pergedel Jagung (see page 64), Indonesia
Sweetcorn fritters

•

Navratan Pullao (see page 126), India
Mixed vegetable pilaff

Kajitchim (see page 112), Korea
Steamed stuffed aubergines

•

Pisang Goreng (see page 140), Indonesia / Malaysia
Fried bananas

MENU 2

Chai Siu Ngo (see page 118), China
Vegetarian goose

•

Shira Ae (see page 118), Japan
Mixed vegetable salad with sesame dressing

Chapchae (see page 122), Korea
Warm rice noodles with vegetables

Phool Gobi Aur Aloo Ki Bhaji (see page 113), India
Cauliflower with potatoes

•

Mamuang Kuo Nieo (see page 140), Thailand
Mango with sweet glutinous rice

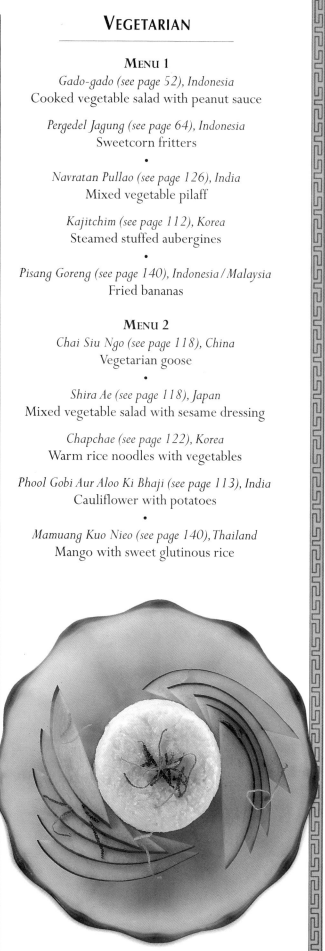

Mamuang Kuo Nieo

TECHNIQUES

Watching an experienced cook at work gives me great pleasure. Much as I love, and use, kitchen gadgets, for me the real joy of cooking comes from utilizing simple, elegant utensils, and from performing tasks made familiar through years of practice. This is especially true in Asian kitchens, where high technology assists but has still not quite replaced clay cooking pots, the charcoal fire, and utensils made of bamboo and coconut shell.

EQUIPMENT

M any of the recipes in this book can be cooked to perfection without the need for special kitchen equipment, but the items described here will make many tasks easier to complete. As this in turn will increase your enjoyment of the preparation and cooking of food, the finished dishes will taste better still. Of all the items of equipment shown here, perhaps the most useful and versatile is the wok.

PESTLE & MORTAR
Made of marble, stone or wood, this is invaluable for grinding small quantities of spices that would be lost in a food processor. Add a little coarse salt to make grinding easier, or some chopped shallot, garlic and ginger to make a paste.

CHINESE CLEAVER
This lethal-looking tool is a useful kitchen aid. It chops and slices efficiently, the blunt edge is useful for cracking open coconuts, and the broad blade flattens fillets of steak or fish.

CHOPPING BOARD
A wooden chopping board is more hygienic than a plastic one, and knives stay sharp longer when used on a wooden surface. Clean after every use, particularly after chopping meat, scrubbing it well under hot running water.

DUCK HOOK
This is almost essential for Peking Duck (see page 46 for recipe). It consists of three hooks, loosely shackled together, two of which fit under the wings of the scalded and glazed duck. The duck is then hung for 12 hours or so, until the skin is dry and taut.

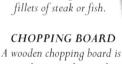

Cook's knife

Paring knife

KNIVES
Grip and balance are important, and of course knives must be sharp. You need a large knife for cutting up meat and one or two small ones for vegetables; other special knives are useful but not essential.

RICE COOKER

If you eat rice more than once a week, I suggest you invest in one of these. It is not too expensive, lasts a long time, and ensures perfectly cooked rice every time, provided you add the correct amount of water. It keeps cooked rice hot, but the rice quickly loses its texture and is best eaten soon after cooking. Leftover cooked rice should be kept refrigerated and eaten within 24 hours.

Rice cooker

Sukiyaki pot

SUKIYAKI POT

In Japan, this pot is strictly for making sukiyaki, but it can be used on the hob like any other pan and then brought to the table to stand on a heatproof mat or hotplate. For cooking at the table, it requires a powerful electric ring.

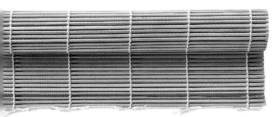

ROLLING MAT

This is ideal for rolling rice for sushi. It is also useful for pressing excess liquid from blanched Chinese leaves. Always use a bamboo mat; plastic is not as good.

WOK

A wonderfully versatile pan — and not only for Oriental cooking. A wok is ideal for stir-frying and deep-frying; a large one, with a domed lid, is also useful for steaming. It can be made of carbon steel, stainless steel or aluminium. The latter are often enamelled, and I find these best because they do not corrode and are easier to clean. Some woks have one handle, others have two — this is a matter of personal choice.

BAMBOO STEAMER

Most people recognize this as the container in which dim sum are served in Chinese restaurants. Steamers are sold in many kitchen shops but are cheapest in Chinese supermarkets. They are excellent for steaming fish and vegetables, inside a lidded wok or saucepan. After use, scrub the steamer under hot water and leave to dry.

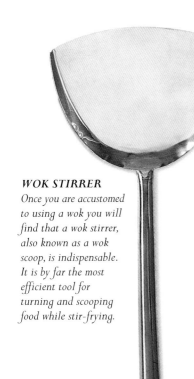

WOK STIRRER

Once you are accustomed to using a wok you will find that a wok stirrer, also known as a wok scoop, is indispensable. It is by far the most efficient tool for turning and scooping food while stir-frying.

PREPARING FISH & SEAFOOD

Most of the fish recipes in this book use fish fillets or steaks. However, in some recipes the fish is cut into thin slices or julienne strips for stuffing and rolling, or using raw in salads. If you use whole fish that require scaling, it is easiest to ask the fishmonger to descale them. Seafood must be cleaned thoroughly before cooking.

SLICING THIN STRIPS

For best results, *use a skinned fillet about 4cm (1½in) thick in the centre. Cut the fillet vertically into thin slices, using a sharp knife. The slices can then be cut into julienne strips, if required.*

DIAGONAL SLICING & ROLLING

1 Take a skinned fillet and trim off any ragged edges. Lay the fillet sideways in front of you and cut it on the slant, horizontally (from head to tail), into four slices of equal thickness.

2 For rolling and stuffing, the slices must be flattened. Using the flat of a knife blade, press down on the fish, then drag it across the width of the slice to make it wider and thinner.

PREPARING SQUID

1 Pull the head of the squid away from the body or "pouch" to remove the contents, making sure you discard the transparent backbone or "pen". Rinse the pouch under cold running water.

2 Separate the crown of tentacles from the head of the squid, cutting it off just before the eyes. Rinse the tentacles under cold running water and discard the head and the intestines.

3 Open up the centre of the crown and press out the mouth or "beak" with your fingers. Discard the beak and reserve the tentacles as one piece, or cut into sections.

4 Remove the thin black skin covering the pouch by rubbing it with your fingers, or by scraping it off with a small knife. Rinse the pouch under cold running water and pat dry with kitchen paper.

5 Lay the pouch flat and, using a sharp knife, cut it into rings about 1cm (½in) wide. Alternatively, cut the pouch in half, lengthways, then cut into diamond shapes or bite-sized pieces.

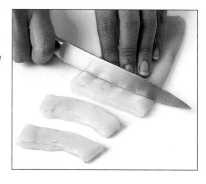

PREPARING COOKED CRAB

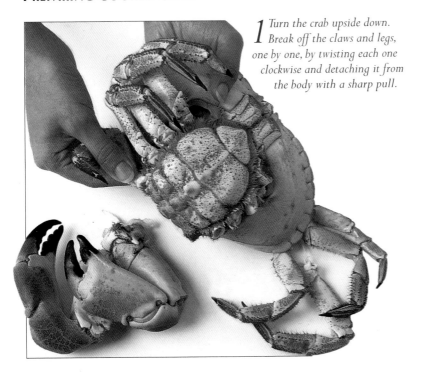

1 Turn the crab upside down. Break off the claws and legs, one by one, by twisting each one clockwise and detaching it from the body with a sharp pull.

2 Crack the shell of each claw with a mallet or the back of a heavy knife. Extract the flesh and discard the central cartilage. Crack open the legs and pick out the meat with a crab pick or skewer.

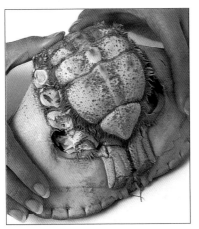

3 Slide a small knife into the join between the body and shell near the tail. Prise it apart, then with both thumbs push the body away from the shell.

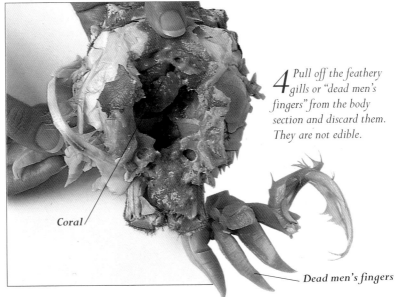

Coral

4 Pull off the feathery gills or "dead men's fingers" from the body section and discard them. They are not edible.

Dead men's fingers

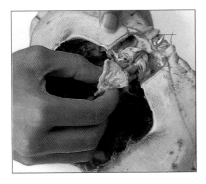

5 Locate the small, round stomach sac or "head sac" situated just behind the eyes in the main shell, then pull it out with your fingers and discard it. It is not edible.

6 Use a teaspoon to scrape out all the soft brown meat inside the main shell. In female crabs, you will also find some edible bright red roe or "coral". Spoon this into a separate bowl.

7 Cut the body section open and poke out all the white meat with a crab pick or skewer. To serve the meat in the shell, neatly break the shell along the line running around the underside.

PREPARING MEAT

For curries and stews, meat is usually cut into 1.5–2cm (½–¾ in) cubes. When stir-frying, meat or poultry should be thinly sliced or cut into julienne strips, but these must be big enough to be conveniently picked up with a pair of chopsticks, or a spoon or fork. A chicken or duck that is to be cooked on the bone is usually jointed into 8 or 10 pieces, see steps opposite. If the bones are removed before cooking they can be made into stock. The whole carcass of a duck or chicken that has been cooked and the meat removed is also good for making stock – for example, Deep-fried Crispy-skin Chicken (see page 86 for recipe) or Peking Duck (see page 46 for recipe). For a very flavoursome stock use a combination of chicken, beef and pork bones.

THINLY SLICING MEAT

Freeze the meat for 30 minutes to make it firm. Using a sharp knife, cut it into very thin slices across the grain. For julienne, cut the slices into thin strips.

BONING CHICKEN THIGHS & DRUMSTICKS

1 Using a small knife, scrape the meat from the thigh bone down to the joint. Bend the joint backwards, then cut through it and remove the thigh bone.

2 Scrape the meat from the drumstick, pulling the meat and skin downwards. Pull the bone away, cutting through the cartilage at the bottom if necessary.

SCALDING A DUCK

1 Place the duck in a colander over a large pan in the sink. Take a kettle full of boiling water and pour half over the duck. Turn the duck over and pour the remaining water over the other side.

2 Remove the colander and duck from the pan and place in the sink. Ladle half the hot water from the pan over the duck. Turn the duck over and ladle the remaining water over the other side.

HOOKING A DUCK

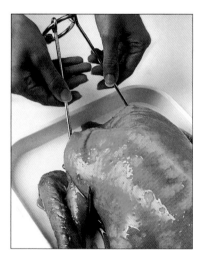

Lay the glazed duck on a tray. Place the two longer arms of the duck hook under the wings of the duck and make sure they are secure. The duck is now ready for hanging.

JOINTING POULTRY

1 Pull one leg away from the body. Cut through the skin to reveal the joint, then cut through it to remove the leg. Repeat with the other leg.

2 Place the legs skin side down. Cut through the joint to separate the drumsticks from the thighs. Cut off and discard the ends of the drumsticks.

3 Pull one wing away from the body until the joint is visible. Cut through it, leaving some breast meat attached to the wing. Repeat with the other wing.

4 With a large, sharp knife, cut through the rib cage beneath the breast meat, until about halfway along. Bend back the underside of the rib cage and cut it off.

5 Turn the breast on to its side and cut through the shoulder bone joints on either side to detach the breast section from the rest of the rib cage.

6 Turn the breast upside down. Using a large, heavy knife, and a mallet if necessary, chop through the breast bone to cut it in two down the centre.

7 Jointing a chicken or duck into 8 pieces is suitable for most curries and long-cooked stews. If you require 10 portions, cut the two breast pieces across in half. The carcass bones and the wing tips can be used for stock.

Wings   *Breasts*   *Thighs*   *Drumsticks*

PREPARING VEGETABLES

The preparation of vegetables should really be a matter of individual taste and preference. However, most of the recipes in this book specify that vegetables be cut into a particular size and shape – usually short sticks or julienne strips. In Asian cooking, nothing is cut too large because a knife and fork are not used at the table. Individual pieces of food are picked up with a spoon or fork, with chopsticks or with fingers, so they must be the right size to be conveyed to the mouth gracefully. In dishes containing mixed vegetables – some curries and stir-fries, for example – I suggest that all the different vegetables are cut into similar-sized pieces. For the Chinese, Japanese and Korean recipes, vegetables are usually cut into matchstick-sized julienne strips.

CUTTING SHORT STICKS & JULIENNE STRIPS

1 For short sticks, peel and trim the vegetable, then cut across into 4–5cm (1½–2in) sections. Cut each section in half, then cut again into 3–4 sticks.

2 For julienne strips, cut the sections lengthways into thin slices. Stack a few slices together and cut lengthways again, into very thin matchsticks.

MAKING CARROT FLOWERS

Peel and trim *the carrot. Using a sharp knife, cut 3 or 4 V-shaped channels lengthways to form "petals". Slice the carrot across into rounds.*

ROLLING CHINESE LEAVES

1 Place the blanched Chinese leaf flat. Shave off the thickest part of the stem at an angle, so that the whole leaf is, as near as possible, of uniform thickness.

2 Lay 2 leaves side by side, overlapping slightly, across the rolling mat. Roll them up tightly, without rolling the mat inside, to form a solid cylinder.

3 Repeat the shaving and rolling procedure until all the Chinese leaves are used, then cut each roll across into 4 equal-sized sections.

MAKING SPRING ONION BRUSHES & CHILLI FLOWERS

1 Trim the spring onion into 6–7cm (2½–3in) lengths. Make repeated cuts lengthways at both ends, leaving at least 1cm (½in) intact in the middle.

2 Using a medium-sized red chilli, slit it in half from near the stem end to the tip. Cut these strips in half, and in half again to give eight "petals".

3 Place the prepared spring onions and chillies in iced water and refrigerate for 2–3 hours, or until curled into shape.

CUTTING GINGER ROOT

MAKING GINGER JUICE

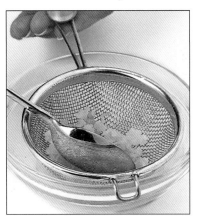

1 Cut off the required amount of ginger root, and peel. Cut it into very thin slices, then stack up the slices and cut again into very thin slivers or needles.

2 To finely chop the ginger, cut the slivers crossways into tiny dice. Add these to sauces or blend with other ingredients to make a curry paste.

Mix 1 tablespoon of finely chopped ginger with an equal amount of warm water. Mash with a spoon, then strain through a fine sieve or a piece of muslin.

REHYDRATING DRIED MUSHROOMS

ROASTING SEEDS & NUTS

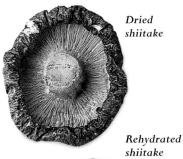

Dried shiitake

Rehydrated shiitake

Cover dried shiitake with boiling water. Place a plate over the bowl and leave for 15–20 minutes. Remove the stems. Soak wood ears for 15 minutes, then trim.

Heat sesame seeds in a dry frying pan over a low heat, stirring constantly, until pale brown. Allow 5 minutes for pine nuts; 6–8 for peanuts; 8–10 for cashew nuts.

GENERAL TECHNIQUES

COOKING RICE

Long-grain & Short-grain Rice

The easiest way to cook rice is in an electric rice cooker (see page 149 for illustration), but just as good results can be achieved in an ordinary saucepan or a steamer.

1 Measure the rice into a heavy-based pan: 1 cup (about 250g/8oz) is sufficient for 2–4 people. Rinse the rice once or twice in cold water, and pour off all the water. Using the same cup, measure an equal amount of water and add it to the rice. If you like rice fairly moist, add a little more water. Do not add salt.

2 Bring to the boil over a moderate heat, stir once with a wooden spoon, then simmer, uncovered, until all the water has been absorbed – about 10 minutes.

3 To "finish" the rice, cover the pan tightly. If the lid is not tight-fitting, put a layer of foil or a tea-towel between it and the pan. Turn the heat right down to minimum and let the rice cook, undisturbed, for 10–12 minutes more.

4 Leave the lid on, but place the pan on a cold, wet cloth to rest for 5 minutes. (This will prevent the bottom layer of rice sticking to the pan.) The rice is then ready to serve.

5 Alternatively, to "finish" the rice, put it in a steamer and steam over boiling water for 10 minutes. (If you do not have an ordinary stainless steel steamer, wrap the rice in muslin and steam it in a Chinese bamboo steamer, inside a large pan or wok with a domed lid.) Serve immediately.

Jasmine Rice   *Glutinous Rice*

Glutinous Rice

Soak the glutinous rice for at least 30 minutes (2–3 hours is preferable) in cold water, then drain well in a sieve. Put the rice in an ordinary steamer or bamboo steamer, as step 5 above, and steam for 10–15 minutes.

MAKING SPICE MIXES & OTHER FLAVOURINGS

Garam Masala

This is a traditional spice mixture from India and, like all spice mixtures, the ingredients and proportions vary according to personal taste. You can buy garam masala ready-made or make your own. The usual basic ingredients are 1–2 parts cloves, some cinnamon, 2 parts each black peppercorns and cumin seeds, 3–4 parts each coriander seeds and cardamom seeds, and a little grated nutmeg. Slightly crush the spices, then grind them using a pestle and mortar or an electric spice mill. The cumin and coriander can be lightly roasted before grinding, if preferred.

Mixed Spice

As with garam masala, the type of spices and proportions can vary, and a lot of commercial blends contain too many ingredients. I prefer to use equal quantities of freshly ground cinnamon, cardamom seeds, cloves and nutmeg.

Brown Sugar Syrup

This is a reasonable substitute for kitul treacle (see page 31). Dissolve 125g (4oz) coconut palm sugar or demerara sugar in 250ml (½ pint) water, and simmer for 5 minutes.

Bonito Stock (Dashi)

Bonito stock can be bought ready-made in an instant form, although it is best to make your own. It is used as a stock or soup in Japan.

1 Put a length, about 50cm (18in), of kelp (kombu) into a pan with 1 litre (2 pints) water, and bring almost to the boil.

2 Remove the kelp, return the water to the boil, then add 125ml (4 fl oz) cold water and 60g (2oz) bonito flakes (katsuobushi).

3 Bring to the boil again, then remove from the heat, skim and strain to clarify.

INDEX

Figures in **bold** type refer to pages with illustrations

A

Acar Kuning, 131
Adobong Baboy, 100
agar agar, **31**, 138
Ajad, **129**
Alimango Tausi, 84
Almond float, **97**, 137
Aloo Baigan Korma, **116-17**
Aloo Gosht, **108**
anchovies, dried, **30**
Aromatic lamb stew, 107
asafoetida, **30**
Asian red onions, **21**, 132
aubergines, **20**, 116
　Aubergine pickle, 131
　pea aubergine, **20**, 42
　Spicy pilaff with
　　aubergines, 125
　Steamed stuffed
　　aubergines, 112
　Sweet and sour
　　aubergines, 113
Ayam Goreng Jawa, 92

B

Baak Ging Ap, **46-7**
Baked fish wrapped in banana
　leaves, 75, **134**
Balachaung, 132
bamboo shoots, **21**
　Bamboo shoots with
　　prawns and pork in
　　a spicy sauce, 114
　Beef with bamboo
　　shoots, 106
bamboo steamer, **149**
bananas:
　Baked fish wrapped in
　　banana leaves, 75, **134**
　banana flower, **20**, 56
　banana leaves, 15, **20**, 74
　Fried bananas, 140
Bandakka Curry, 36,**37**, 115
Bara-zushi, **50-1**
Basic chilli sauce, 128
Basic fish curry, 79
basil, **26**
　Braised clams with basil, 85
　Fried rice with chicken
　　and basil, 124
basmati rice, **24**
Batakh Vindaloo, 95
bean curd: see tofu
beancurd sheet (skin), **25**, 118
beans: see specific types
beansprouts:
　Prawn and beansprout
　　fritters, **34**, 70
Bebek Betutu, 93

beef: 48, 86, 95, 108
　Beef and vegetable hotpot
　　(Sukiyaki), 106
　Beef curry, 103
　Beef with bamboo shoots, 106
　Noodle soup with beef and
　　lemongrass, **58-9**
　Red-cooked beef with
　　broccoli, **104-105**
　Skewered beef, **44**, 67
black bean sauce, **28**
　Fish in black bean sauce, 77
Black glutinous rice
　porridge, 136
bonito flakes, **30**
bonito stock, **30**, 50, 156
Boxao Mang, 106
Braised clams with basil, 85
Braised mixed vegetables with
　yogurt, **116-17**
Brinjal Pullao, 125
brown sugar syrup, 156
Bubur Ketan Hitam, 136
Buddha's delight, **97**, 115
buffet menus, 145
Bun Bo Hue, **58-9**
Burma, 11
　Balachaung, 132
　Kyet Thar Hin, **87**, 132
　Mohinga, 56
　Nga Wehin, 79

C

cabbage:
　Pickled cabbage, 17, 132
　Stir-fried cabbage with
　　eggs, 113
Cambodia, 12
　Plea Tray, **76**
　Sech Tea Ang-krueng, 95
candle nuts, **22**
carrot flowers, making, **154**
cashew nuts, **22**
　Chicken in cashew and
　　coconut sauce, 92
cassia bark, **27**
Cauliflower with potatoes, 113
cellophane noodles, **25**
　Spicy salad of cellophane
　　vermicelli, prawns and
　　pork, **110**, 119
　see also Noodles & Rice
Cha Dum, 100
Chai Siu Ngo, 118
Chao Tom, **45**, 66
Chapchae, **122-23**
Char Kwee Teow, 121
Char Siu, 98
Char Siu Paaih Gwat, **96**, 102
chicken: 86-92
　boning thighs and
　　drumsticks, **152**
　Chicken and galangal
　　soup, 61

Fried rice with chicken and
　basil, 124
Green curry of chicken,
　42-3
jointing, **153**
Savoury rice with fried
　chicken, 125
Skewered chicken, **44**, 67
see also Poultry
chillies, 26, **27**
　Basic chilli sauce, 128
　Chilli and dried shrimp
　　relish, 132
　chilli bean sauce, **28**
　　Deep-fried sole with
　　　chilli bean sauce and
　　　asparagus, 75
　chilli sauce, **28**
　chilli flowers, making, **155**
　chilli oil, **29**
　Pan-fried fillet of cod
　　coated in chillies, 78
　Sweet chilli sauce, **129**
China, 16, **96-7**
　Baak Ging Ap, **46-7**
　Chai Siu Ngo, 118
　Char Siu, 98
　Char Siu Paaih Gwat, **96**, 102
　Daan Far Tong, **60**
　Hahng Yahn Dauh Fuh, 137
　Hai Jo Mah Ji Mee, 124
　Hak Tjin Tjan Nah Hiu, 93
　Hojan Hsin Taiji, 79, **96**
　Huhng Siu Ngauh, **104-105**
　Jui Jin Jeun Ho Hai, 84
　Lachap Longlei Guin, 75
　Lo Han Chai, **97**, 115
　menus, 142
　Shuen Guen, **34**, 64
　Sze Chuan Jar Gai, **90-1**
　Tsoi Pe Tsa Ji Gai, 86
Chinese chives, **26**
Chinese cleaver, **148**
Chinese leaves, rolling, **154**
Chinese red vinegar, **29**
clams:
　Braised clams with basil, 85
coconut, **23**
　Chicken in cashew and
　　coconut sauce, 92
　coconut cream, **23**, 138
　　making, **141**
　coconut milk, 10, **23**
　　making, **141**
　desiccated coconut, 23
　Duck pieces in rich coconut
　　sauce, **94**
　grating fresh coconut, **133**
　Hot noodle soup with
　　coconut milk, 61
　Lamb curry with coconut
　　milk, 107
　Marinated fish baked with
　　coconut, 74
　Mixed seafood in coconut
　　milk, 80

Pork in coconut milk with
　pickled onions, **99**
Prawns in rich coconut
　sauce, **82**, 83
Roasted grated coconut, 133
Spiced coconut custard, 137
Venison cooked in rich
　coconut sauce, 109
Cooked vegetable salad with
　peanut sauce, **52**
cooking rice, 156
coriander, **26**
crab, 80
　Deep-fried soft-shell crab, 84
　preparing crab, **151**
　Stuffed crab with yellow
　　bean sauce, 84
　Yifu noodles with crabmeat
　　sauce, 124
Crisp-fried onions, 21, **31**, 132
Cucumber relish, **129**
curry:
　Basic fish curry, 79
　Beef curry, 103
　Chicken curry with
　　limes, **87**
　Duck curry, 95
　Fish curry, **36**
　Fried squid curry, 85
　Green curry of chicken,
　　42-3
　Lamb curry with coconut
　　milk, 107
　Meat curry, 108
　Okra curry, 36, **37**, 115
　Prawn curry, 83
　Red curry of chicken, 88
curry leaves, **26**

D

Daan Far Tong, **60**
daikon: see mooli
Dalcha, 109
dashi, **30**, 57, 156
Deep-fried crispy-skin
　chicken, 86
Deep-fried soft-shell crab, 84
Deep-fried sole with chilli
　bean sauce and asparagus, 75
Desserts, 136-41
deveining prawns, **82**
Dhallo Badun, 85
Dhansak, 89
dried shrimp paste, 15, **31**
dried shrimps, **31**
　Chilli and dried shrimp
　　relish, 132
duck: 86, 93-5
　duck hook, **148**
　hooking and scalding, **152**
　jointing, **153**
　Peking duck with pancakes
　　and hoisin sauce, **46-7**
Dui Ga Nhoi Thit, 89

E F

eggs:
Stir-fried cabbage with
eggs, 113
Egg drop soup, **60**
equipment, **148-49**
fenugreek, **26**
fish, 74-9
fillets: slicing and rolling, **150**
Fish curry, **36-7**
fish sauce, **28**
Fish soup with rice noodles, 56
Minced fish on skewers, 66
Steamed stuffed fish, **40-1**
see also Fish & Seafood
Fish & Seafood, 74-85
five-spice, **27**
Fresh fruit jelly, **138-39**
Fried bananas, 140
Fried chicken Szechuan-style,
90-1
Fried noodles with mixed
meat, 121
Fried rice, **127**
Fried rice with chicken and
basil, 124
Fried squid curry, 85
fruit, nuts & seeds, **22-3**

G

Gado-gado, **52-53**, 137
Gaeng Keo Wan Kai, **42-3**
Gaeng Ped Kai, 88
galangal, **27**
Chicken and galangal soup, 61
garam masala, making, 156
ghee, **29**, 10, 48
ginger, **27**
(pink) pickled ginger, **31**, 77
ginger juice, making, **155**
ginger root, cutting, **155**
ginkgo nuts, 17, **22**
Glazed grilled fish, 77
glutinous rice, **24**
cooking, 156
golden needles, **27**, 38
Goreng Bawang, 132
Gradook Moo Nueng Tao
Jeaw, 103
Green curry of chicken, **42-3**
Green mango and squid salad,
111, 119
Gulaman, 137, **138-39**
Gule Kambing, 107

H

Hahng Yahn Dauh Fuh, **97**, 137
Hai Jo Mah Ji Mee, 124
Hak Tjin Tjan Nah Hiu, 93
herbs & spices, **26-7**
hoisin sauce, **28**
Hojan Hsin Taiji, 79, **96**
Homok Talay, **80-1**
Hot noodle soup with coconut
milk, 61

Hot pot with udon noodles, 120
Hot spicy fruit salad, **73**, 137
Hoy Lai Phad Nam Prik Phao,
85, **111**
Huhng Siu Ngauh, **104-105**

I

Ice cream (Kulfi), 136
Ikan Masak Lada, 78
Ikan Masak Molek, **36-7**
Ikan Masak Tauco, 77
India, 10, **134-35**
Aloo Baigan Korma, **116-17**
Aloo Gosht, **108**
Batakh Vindaloo, 95
Brinjal Pullao, 125
Dalcha, 109
Dhansak, 89
Jingha Kari, 83
Kulfi, 136
Mangai Achar, 130, **135**
menus, 143
Murgh Salar Jung, 92
Navratan Pullao, 126, **134**
Patrani Machchi, 75, **134**
Phool Gobi Aur Aloo Ki
Bhaji, 113
Rasam, 60
Rogan Josh, **48-9**
Samosa, **65**
Vindaloo, 101, **135**
Indonesia, 15
Acar Kuning, 131
Ayam Goreng Jawa, 92
Bebek Betutu, 93
Bubur Ketan Hitam, 136
Gado-gado, **52-53**
Goreng Bawang, 132
Gule Kambing, 107
Kalio Bebek, **94**
Nasi Goreng, **127**
Nasi Kebuli, 125
Nasi Kuning, 73, 126
Orak-arik, 113
Oseng Oseng Ayam Dengan
Sayuran, **73**, 86
Pepes Ikan, 74
Pergedel Jagung, **34**, 64
Pisang Goreng, 140
Rujak, **73**, 137
Sambal Goreng Udang, **82**, 83
Sambal Kacang, 130
Sambal Ulek, 128
Sate Pusut, **45**, 66
Serundeng, 133
Indonesia & Malaysia, **72-3**
menus, 143
Ingredients, **18-31**

J

jaggery (palm sugar), **30**
Japan, 17, 24
Bara-zushi, **50-1**
Fish Teriyaki, 77
menus, 144
Satsumajiru, **57**
Shira Ae, 118

Sukiyaki, 106
Sushi, 35, **71**
Suzuki Sashimi, 78
Tempura, **68-69**
Udon Suki, 120
Yakitori, **44**, 67
Japanese rice, **24**
jasmine rice, **24**
Javanese fried chicken, 92
Jingha Kari, 83
jointing poultry, **153**
Jui Jin Jeun Ho Hai, 84

K L

kaffir limes, **22**
kaffir lime leaves, **26**
Kai Tom Ka, 61
Kajitchim, 112
Kalio Bebek, **94**
Kambing Korma, 107
Khao Pad Khai Horapha, 124
Khoua Sin Fahn, 109
Kimchee, 17, 132
kitul treacle, **30**, 137, 156
Kolak Labu Kuning, 140
Korea, 17
Chapchae, **122-23**
Kajitchim, 112
Kimchee, 132
Oson, **40-1**
Twaejigogi Saektchim, 102
Kulfi, 136
Kung Thord, **63**
Kyet Thar Hin, **87**
Lachap Longlei Guin, 75
Laksa Lemak, 61, **72**
lamb: 86, 95
Aromatic lamb stew, 107
Lamb cooked with
lentils, 109
Lamb curry with coconut
milk, 107
Lamb in rich chilli sauce with
yogurt, **48-9**
Meat curry with potatoes, **108**
Laos, 12, 13
Khoua Sin Fahn, 109
Namjeem, **129**
Nuoc Cham, 128
Pad Som Sin Moo, **99**
lemongrass, **27**, **45**
Noodle soup with beef and
lemongrass, **58-9**
lentils, 10, **31**
Chicken cooked with lentils
and vegetables, 89
Lamb cooked with lentils, 109
Lo Han Chai, **97**, 115

M

macadamia nuts, **23**
Malaysia, 115, 137
Acar Kuning, 131
Goreng Bawang, 132
Ikan Masak Lada, 78
Ikan Masak Molek, **36-7**
Ikan Masak Tauco, 77

Kambing Korma, 107
Kolak Labu Kuning, 140
Laksa Lemak, 61, **72**
Nasi Kuning, **73**, 126
Pisang Goreng, 140
Rempah-rempah, **34**, 70
Sambal Kacang, 130
Satay Daging, **44**, 67
Mamuang Kuo Nieo,
140, **141**
mandarin pancakes, **25**
Mangai Achar, 130
mangoes, **23**
Green mango and squid
salad, **111**, 119
Mango pickle, 130
Mango with sweet glutinous
rice, 140, **141**
marigolds, **22**
Sweet pork with
marigold, 98
Marinated and fried prawns, **63**
Marinated fish baked with
coconut, 74
Massaman, 103
Meat: 10, 98-111
Meat curry with
potatoes, **108**
menu planning, 142-45
Minced fish on skewers, **45**, 66
mirin, 17, **29**
miso (red, white, yellow), **30**
Miso soup with mixed
vegetables, 17, **57**
Mixed seafood in coconut milk,
80-1
Mixed seafood with vegetables
deep-fried in batter, **68-9**
mixed spice, making, 156
Mixed vegetable pickle, 131
Mixed vegetable pilaff, 126, **134**
Mixed vegetable salad with
sesame dressing, 118
Mohinga, 56
mooli, **20**, 77
Moo Wan, 98
Muc Don Thit, **38-9**
mung beans, **31**
Murgh Salar Jung, 92
mushrooms: *see specific types*

N

Namjeem, **129**
nam pla, **28**
Nasi Goreng, **127**
Nasi Kebuli, 125
Nasi Kuning, **73**, 126
Navratan Pullao, 83, 126, **134**
Nga Wehin, 79
nigella (black cumin), **27**
noodles, **24-5**
cellophane noodles,
vermicelli, **25**, 38
Fish soup with rice
noodles, 56
Hot noodle soup with
coconut milk, 61, **72**
Hot pot with udon
noodles, 120

Noodle soup with beef and
lemongrass, 58
rice noodles, **25**
Rice stick noodles with pork
and prawns, 121
udon noodles, **24**
yifu noodles, **24**
Yifu noodles with
crabmeat sauce, 124
see also Noodles & Rice
Noodles & Rice, 120-26
Nuoc Cham, **45**, 128
nuts, **22**
roasting, **155**

O

okra, **21**
Okra curry, 115
onions:
Asian red, **21**
crisp-fried, **31**, 132
Orak-arik, 92, 113
Oseng Oseng Ayam Dengan
Sayuran, **73**, 86
Oson, 40-1
oyster sauce, **28**
Stir-fried scallops in oyster
sauce, 79

P Q

Pad Som Sin Moo, **99**
palm sugar, **30**, 137
pancakes, mandarin, **25**
Pancit Guisado, 121
Pan-fried fillet of cod coated in
chillies, 78
Pastries with vegetable filling, 65
Patrani Machchi, 75, **134**
Patties, **35**, 62
Peanut sauce, **44**, 66, 67, 130
Chicken and pork in peanut
sauce, 88
Cooked vegetable salad with
peanut sauce, **52-3**
peeling and deveining
prawns, **82**
Peking duck with pancakes and
hoisin sauce, **46-7**
Pepes Ikan, 74
Pergedel Jagung, **34**, 64
Philippines, 16
Adobong Baboy, 100
Alimango Tausi, 84
Gulaman, **138-39**
Pancit Guisado, 121
Pipian, 88
Phool Gobi Aur Aloo Ki
Bhaji, 113
pickled chillies, **31**
pink pickled ginger, **31**
Pipian, 88
Pisang Goreng, 140
plantains, **20**, 140
Plea Tray, **76**
pork: 38, 45, 86, 95
Bamboo shoots, prawns and
pork in a spicy sauce, 114

Chicken and pork in peanut
sauce, 88
Pork cooked in chilli-hot and
sour sauce, 101, **135**
Pork in coconut milk with
pickled onions, **99**
Pork loaf, 100
Pork Satay, **45**, 67
Pork spare ribs in barbecue
sauce, **96**, 102
Red stew of pork, 100
Rice stick noodles with pork
and prawns, 121
Roast strips of pork, 98
Spicy salad of cellophane
vermicelli, prawns and
pork, **110**, 119
Steamed and grilled spare
ribs with yellow bean
sauce, 103
Steamed wonton with
prawns and pork, 70
Stuffed pork with
vegetables, 102
Sweet pork with marigold,
98
potatoes, 42, 116
Cauliflower with potatoes, 113
Meat curry with potatoes, 108
Poultry, 86-97
jointing, **153**
prawns: 34, 45
Bamboo shoots, prawns and
pork in a spicy sauce, **114**
Marinated and fried
prawns, 63
peeling and deveining
prawns, **82**
Prawn and beansprout
fritters, **34**, 70
prawn crackers, **31**
Prawn curry, 83
Prawns in rich coconut
sauce, **82**, 83
Rice stick noodles with pork
and prawns, 121
Skewered prawnballs and
prawns, **45**, 66
Spicy salad of cellophane
vermicelli, prawns and
pork, **110**, 119
Steamed wonton with
prawns and pork, 70
Pumpkin in coconut syrup, 140
quince, **22**

R

Rasam, 60
Raw sea bass with vegetables
and dipping sauce, 78
Rebong Char, **114**
Red-cooked beef with broccoli,
104-105
Red curry of chicken, 88
Red stew of pork, 100
rehydrating dried mushrooms,
155
Rempah-rempah, **34**, 70
ribbon rice noodles, **25**

rice, 13, **24**, 35, 50, 124-26
Black glutinous rice porridge,
136
cooking, 156
electric rice cooker, **149**
Mango with sweet glutinous
rice, 140, **141**
rice flour, **31**
rice noodles, vermicelli, **25**
rice powder, **31**
Rice rolls (Sushi), **35**, **71**
Rice stick noodles with pork
and prawns, 121
rice vinegar, **29**
rice wine, 17, **29**
Sushi rice with julienne of
omelette, **50-1**
Warm rice noodles with
vegetables, **122-23**
see also Noodles & Rice
rice, noodles & wrappers, **24-5**
Roasted and grilled duck with
spices, 95
Roasted grated coconut, 133
roasting seeds and nuts, **155**
Roast strips of pork, 98
Rogan Josh, **48-9**
rolling mat, **71**, 149
Rujak, **73**, 137

S

sake, **29**
salads:
Cooked vegetable salad with
peanut sauce, **52-3**
Fish salad, 76
see also Vegetables & Salads
sambal goreng, 15
Sambal Goreng Udang, **82**, 83
Sambal Kacang, 130
Sambal Ulek, 128
Samosa, **65**
sashimi, 17, 78
Satay, **44-5**, 66-7
Satsumajiru, **57**
sauces: see specific types
Sauces & Accompaniments,
128-35
Savoury rice with fried
chicken, 125
Savoury yellow rice, **73**, 126
scalding a duck, **152**
scallops: 80
Stir-fried scallops in oyster
sauce, 79, **96**
seafood:
Mixed seafood in coconut
milk, **80-1**
Mixed seafood with vegetables
deep-fried in batter, **68-9**
see also specific types
Sech Tea Ang-krueng, 95
seeds, **23**
roasting, **155**
Serundeng, 133
sesame seeds, **23**
sesame oil, **29**
seven-spice (shichimi), **27**
Shaohsing wine, **29**

shiitake mushrooms, **21**
rehydrating, **155**
Shira Ae, 118
shirataki, 24
Shuen Guen, **34**, 64
shrimps, dried, **31**
Chilli and dried shrimp
relish, 132
dried shrimp paste, 15, **31**
silken tofu, 24
Singapore, 6, 14
Char Kwee Teow, 121
Pork Satay, **45**, 67
Rebong Char, **114**
Sambal Kacang, 130
Siu Mai, 70
Siu Mai, 70
Skewered beef, **44**, 67
Skewered chicken, **44**, 67
Skewered pork, **45**, 67
Skewered prawnballs and
prawns, **45**, 66
slicing fish fillets, **150**
Small filled pies, **35**, 62
Snacks & Appetizers, **34-5**,
62-73
Soups, 56-61
soya beans, 28
soy sauce, 15, 17, **28**, 104
Spiced coconut custard, 137
Spicy pilaff with
aubergines, 125
Spicy salad of cellophane
vermicelli, prawns and
pork, **110**, 119
spring onion brush, making, **155**
Spring rolls, **34**, 64
wrappers, **25**, 65
squid:
cleaning and preparing, **150**
Fried squid curry, 85
Green mango and squid
salad, **111**, 119
Stuffed squid, **38-9**
Sri Lanka, 11
Bandakka Curry, 36, **37**, 115
Dhallo Badun, 85
Patties, 11, **35**, 62
Vambotu Pahi, 131
Vatalapan, 137
star anise, **27**
Steamed and grilled spare ribs
with yellow bean sauce, 103
Steamed stuffed aubergines, 112
Steamed stuffed fish, **40-1**
Steamed wonton with prawns
and pork, 70
steamer, **149**
Stir-fried cabbage with
eggs, 113
Stir-fried chicken with
vegetables, **73**, 86
Stir-fried duck with black
pepper, 93
Stir-fried scallops in oyster
sauce, 79, **96**
storecupboard, **28-31**
straw mushrooms, **21**
Stuffed boned chicken legs, 89
Stuffed crab with yellow bean
sauce, 84

Stuffed pork with
 vegetables, 102
Stuffed squid, 38-9
Sukiyaki, 24, 106
 sukiyaki pot, **149**
Sushi, **35**, **71**
 Sushi rice with julienne of
 omelette, **50-1**
Suzuki Sashimi, 78
Sweet and sour
 aubergines, 113
Sweet chilli sauce, **129**
Sweetcorn fritters, 34, 64
Sweet pork with marigold, 98
Sze Chuan Jar Gai, **90-1**

T

tamari soy sauce, 28
tamarind, **30**
 making tamarind water, **101**
Techniques, 146-56
Tempura, 68-9
Teriyaki, Fish, 77
Thai basil, **26**
Thailand, 10, 12, **110-11**
 Ajad, **129**
 Gaeng Keo Wan Kai, 42-3
 Gaeng Ped Kai, 88
 Gradook Moo Nueng Tao
 Jeaw, 103
 Homok Talay, 80-1

Hoy Lai Phad Nam Prik
 Phao, 85, **111**
Kai Tom Ka, 61
Khao Pad Khai Horapha,
 124
Kung Thord, **63**
Mamuang Kuo Nieo, 140
Massaman, 103
 menus, 144
Moo Wan, 98
Namjeem, **129**
Yam Makhua Phao, 113
Yam Pla Muek Mamuang,
 111, 119
Yam Woon Sen, **110**, 119
tofu, **24**
Vegetarian goose, 118
Traditional long-cooked
 Balinese duck, 93
Tsoi Pe Tsa Ji Gai, 86
turmeric, **26**
Twaejigogi Saektchim, 102

U V

udon noodles, **24**
 Hot pot with udon
 noodles, 120
Udon Suki, 120
Vambotu Pahi, 131
Vatalapan, 137
vegetables, **20-1**

Beef and vegetable hot
 pot, 106
Chicken cooked with lentils
 and vegetables, 89
Mixed vegetable pickle,
 131
Mixed vegetable pilaff,
 126, **134**
Mixed seafood and
 vegetables deep-fried in
 batter, **68-9**
preparing vegetables, **154**
Stir-fried chicken with
 vegetables, 86
Stuffed pork with
 vegetables, 102
Warm rice noodles with
 vegetables, 122-23
 see also specific types
Vegetables & Salads, 15,
 112-119
vegetarian dishes, 60, 64, 65,
 118, **122-23**, 126, 127
 menus, 145
 see also Vegetables & Salads
Venison cooked in rich
 coconut sauce, 109
Vietnam, 12, 13
 Boxao Mang, 106
 Bun Bo Hue, **58-9**
 Cha Dum, 100
 Chao Tom, **45**, 66
 Dui Ga Nhoi Thit, 89

Muc Don Thit, **38-39**
Nuoc Cham, 128
Vindaloo, 95, 101
vinegar, 17, **29**

W Y

Warm rice noodles with
 vegetables, **122-23**
wasabi paste, **31**
water chestnuts, 21
water spinach, 21
wonton, 70
 wrappers, **25**
wok, **149**
wood ears, **21**
 rehydrating, **155**
Yakitori, 44, 67
Yam Makhua Phao, 113
Yam Pla Muek Mamuang,
 111, 119
Yam Woon Sen, **110**, 119
yard-long beans, 21
yellow bean sauce, **28**
 Steamed and grilled spare
 ribs with yellow bean
 sauce, 103
 Stuffed crab with yellow
 bean sauce, 84
Yifu (Yi) noodles, **24**
 Yifu noodles with crabmeat
 sauce, 124

ACKNOWLEDGMENTS

AUTHOR'S APPRECIATION
Like my other books, this book
involved a lot of travel and research.
Many people helped me in all sorts of
ways; I want particularly to mention
the Regent Four Seasons group of
hotels. I do not have space to name
everyone, but I remember them with
deep gratitude and send them my
sincere thanks.

For this book, I must first thank
Rosie Kindersley, who proposed my
name to Daphne Razazan, Editorial
Director at Dorling Kindersley. I am
grateful to Daphne and to Managing
Editor, Susannah Marriott.

I learned much about India, not only
from my travels, but also from Joyce
P. Westrip, author of *Moghul Cooking*.
On Sri Lanka, I was helped by Thana
Srikantha and her mother, Mrs.
Siwasambu, and on Burma by Kate
Riley, who gave me recipes from her
Burmese mother and aunt. Soun
Vannithone and his wife Keo helped
with Laotian recipes. On Japan I am
greatly indebted to my friend Hiroko
Sugiyama in Seattle, and to Professor
Richard Hosking of Hiroshima, on
the Philippines to Professor Doreen
Fernandez, and on Korea to David
Wilkinson, formerly of the Seoul

Hilton International. My teachers for
Vietnamese cooking were Lan Anh
Phung and her mother Mme. Kim,
who for many years had a restaurant
in Paris. Also in Paris I thank Rosine
Ek for her Cambodian recipes,
translated for me into English by my
friend Suzy Benghiat. In Indonesia I
was able to call on William Wongso,
Anak Agung Gede Rai and Ni Wayan
Murni. Special thanks, too, to Chef
Tam Kwok Fung of the China House
Restaurant at the Oriental Hotel,
Bangkok, who taught me how to make
several Chinese dishes and devised a
Chinese New Year menu so that I
could watch him cook the food and
then taste it. Most of the Chinese
recipes in this book, however, are
from Chef Simon Yung of the Oriental
Restaurant at the Dorchester, Park
Lane, London. My good friend Deh-ta
Hsiung gave me his recipe for Buddha's
Delight on page 115, and checked the
names of the Chinese dishes.

I have had the pleasure of working
with a great team at Dorling Kindersley:
Nicola Graimes, Kate Scott, Tracey
Clarke and Toni Kay; as well as
designer Sue Storey, home economist
Oona van den Berg, and photographers
Clive Streeter and Patrick McLeavey.

Finally, I must say thank you to Sallie
Morris for supplying Cherry Valley
ducklings for photography, and to Roz
Denny for Tilda rice; to my agent
John McLaughlin; and, as ever, to my
husband Roger.

Dorling Kindersley would like to
thank Carole Ash for initial design
work; Alexa Stace for initial editorial
work; Hannah Atwell for design
assistance; Sarah Ponder for the
artworks; Camellia Panjabi, author of
50 Great Curries of India, published by
Kyle Cathie, for her kulfi recipe on
page 136; Roger Owen for the index;
Patrick McLeavey for photography on
pages 4; 10b, r; 12b, r; 13r; 15b; 17b;
63b; 65–6; 70–1; 74; 76b; 77–9; 82t;
83–5; 88; 92–3; 95; 100–1; 103;
106; 109; 112; 114b; 118–19; 124–6;
128; 130–33; 140; 141t; 142l; 143t;
145t; 150–55; Ian O'Leary for
photography on pages 39b, 82b,
123b; Amy Hearn and Charlotte Krag
for photographic assistance; home
economists Sunil Vijayakar and Kara
Hobday for additional food styling;
Rahat Ára Siddique for hand modelling;
make-up artist Sue Sian; and Yohan
Plaza for supplying a sukiyaki pot.
Photography credits key: t= top,
c = centre, b= bottom, l= left, r= right